VETERAN-CY
MARQUE ALBUM NO 3

RENSCH AND PARIS CYCLES

ALVIN SMITH,
NEVILLE IRELAND AND FRANK HERNANDEZ

Figure 1: Harry Rensch – from an Accles and Pollock advertisement of the late 1940s.

Front Cover:- Design modified from early 1946-7 PARIS seat tube transfer by David Lovegrove. Original courtesy Peter Underwood.

Back Cover:- Original design by David Lovegrove.

© John Pinkerton Memorial Publishing Fund 2012
Design and layout by Alvin Smith & Brian Hayward
Printed by Quorum Print Ltd, Cheltenham, England
ISBN 978-0-9566337-7-4
Version 2. Reprinted with minor additions Sept. 2012

Contents

Foreword

From my involvement in the 'classic' lightweight movement commencing in the early 1980s, I have been amazed at the growth of the interest both here in the UK and, latterly, worldwide. It has matured into a serious subject and gone from a small minority interest within the Veteran - Cycle Club since its inception to now, arguably, dominating the activities. Collectors, restorers and enthusiasts trawl the cycle jumbles and internet auction sites for a constant source of parts and projects.

The quest for information about bespoke cycle frame builders has been the 'holy-grail' for most of us enthusiasts for many decades now, and this thirst for knowledge about many of the craftsmen came about just at a time when many had either already passed away, or were too old and frail to impart the detail for which we craved. Regrettably, this has resulted in much conjecture and hearsay about many.

Just occasionally, however, there were some younger skilled craftsmen left who had either developed their skills, under the watchful eye of more senior gifted frame builders, or learnt as apprentices to the famous names around this period. Men such as Tom Board, Ron Cooper, Bill Grey etc who 'filled in' the gaps in the history of the post-war boom of lightweight frame builders to us 'youngsters' who were perhaps, just boys at the time and never really took much notice of the history passing us by, without realising it.

In recent years a few diligent cycle historians have emerged who realised that if they didn't capture this knowledge now, it would be too late and those that could contribute first-hand information to assist in the research of selected marques would also be lost. So it is the likes of the author of this book who has risen to that challenge by writing the history of his chosen area of lightweight interest – Harry Rensch, who produced Rensch and PARIS marques.

Alvin has spent some years diligently researching his subject, despite there being very little documentation on the man, or business he built up. Despite this, Alvin has produced an excellent in-depth study and should become great historical reference point for any lightweight enthusiast wishing to know more of this remarkable man and his business development.

All-in-all, I think this book is a terrific example of how a well researched document on a lightweight frame builder should be written...with future historical study in mind. Some hypothesis has had to be made with virtually no documentary evidence extant, but nonetheless without such examples of books of this kind, in years to come there will be nothing for future enthusiasts to learn from. This represents another sizeable piece of the post-war lightweight cycle jig-saw dropped into place. I only wish more marque enthusiasts like Alvin would rise to the challenge – given the time!

Derek Athey, (fellow member of the Veteran-Cycle Club)

Acknowledgements

I have indicated in the author statement for this history and on the frontispiece the debt that I owe to my predecessors in the role of Marque Enthusiast, Neville Ireland the immediate past ME, who died suddenly in 2005, and Frank Hernandez who was the first. Both of them spent a great deal of time and effort on garnering a mass of published evidence and first hand accounts from a wide range of previous owners and riders of Rensch and Paris bicycles. I have collated their notes and continued this practice and have identified by footnotes to the text the origin of the information provided, whether it be by publication, notes in my predecessors files, correspondence or telephone conversations that I have had.

I need to make a number of personal acknowledgements at this point. The first is to the help and encouragement I have had with this text and over the years from Hilary Stone who sold me my first PARIS – an elegant late period racing tandem, a tip off for my first Rensch and who has just recently kept me informed as first a Dame and then a rare Champion du Monde appeared. The second is to Derek Athey who over a similar length of time has patiently advised me whenever I needed information on the cycling greats and who graciously agreed to write the Foreword to this book. Finally, the help and enthusiastic assistance of Mick Butler who has been a regular and unstinting source of information and photographs from his collection to both Neville Ireland and myself.

I have listed most but perhaps not all of my contacts below, some alas, are no longer with us. I am very grateful for your time and interest in this subject, and if per chance you do not appear to be mentioned, my sincere apologies.

Lastly a caveat – the text is as accurate as I can make it, but any errors are down to me – please advise me when you see anything that needs correction and it shall be done! Minor corrections to the text and changes to reflect new additions to the Register made in August 2012.

Alvin Smith, August 2012

Listed alphabetically by surname:-

Derek Athey;
Colin Barrett;
George Bickerstaffe;
Tom Board;
Michael Beazley;
Michael (Mick) Butler;
Mervyn Cook;
Robert (Bob) Drake;
Marc Edwardson;
Peter Hammond;
Peter Holland;
Ken Janes;
Harold Jones;
William (Bill) Hurlow;
David Lovegrove;
Scotford Lawrence;
John Lee;
Peter Lowry:
Neville March:
Ken Mais;
Stuart Norquay;
Dave Orford;

Felix Ormerod;
David Palk;
Neil Palmer;
John Rowbottom;
John Scott;
Paul Spivey;
Dennis Talbot;
Colin Skipp:
Hilary Stone;
Tony Stringer;
Peter Underwood;
Alexander Von Tutschek;
Robin Walker;
John Wilde;
Donald Workman;
Phil Wray;
Monty and Grant Young;

Not to mention a host of other Rensch and Paris owners from the Veteran-Cycle Club whose infectious enthusiasm has driven me onwards!

Introduction

Harry Rensch had vision. He knew he could build a bicycle that was the equal of any made on the Continent – so went ahead and did it. For four years prior to the Second World War he built RENSCH bicycles in Stoke Newington, North London and then after the war he built them as the PARIS CYCLES marque for a further eight years. Several reasons for this name change have been advanced over the years. Though knowledge of the actual reason died with Harry Rensch; many believe it was to avoid the public revulsion of all things Germanic during the Second World War. This aspect is examined in detail later in the story. Other cycle marques inevitably picked up some of the innovations that Harry Rensch introduced and one top line lightweight manufacturer, Condor Cycles which itself was created by a young man who grew up admiring Harry Rensch, is still making two of his most iconic designs, sixty and more years later.

Rensch was not however surrounded by friends who would record the details of his venture and this story has therefore had to be pieced together long after the key events. When the first start was made it was found that very few people had any first hand knowledge of the period when Rensch was forming his firm and no one could be found who was familiar with the whole of his life, whilst as time has gone on so many other people who had had an input to the firm's history and who might have been able to help complete the picture have themselves died without the opportunity to contribute.

It has been a great disappointment to me that the question of where or from whom did the inspiration come for some of those innovations -the bronze welding (fillet brazing), embellishment of the frame by bilamination[1] and the strong colour ways that characterise Rensch and PARIS products cannot be fully answered, though I have advanced some suppositions. I have argued that Rensch was the originator, but recognise that seldom do individuals work alone – they exist within their peer groups and generally are not in some artistic or technical vacuum. Rensch's contribution to frame design and decorative styling should for example be seen as being influenced by many other cycle makers.

Rensch was his own man, yes, but as mentioned he was certainly also influenced by changes occurring in related industries and by colleagues such as Jim Collier (Hobbs), Maurice Selbach, Bill Rann (Holdsworth) and Jack Denny (Hetchins) to trigger his efforts, and was one of that handful

---

1 Bilamination is described more fully later but the term describes the use of sleeves made from sheet metal added to joints and resembling lugs or sometimes just extending lugs. They are commonly attractively shaped.

of celebrated cycle designer/builders working in London in the mid 1930s. Equally, Rensch's classic designs such as his post war bilaminations and frame detailing must be high amongst other influences as part of the stimulus for the later intricate lug cutting that reached a climax with men such as Les Ephgrave and WB (Bill) Hurlow, both of whom worked with Rensch's firms, as well as Jack Denny, and HR Morris, master frame builders who brought their own magic to post war bicycle design.

Within the Veteran Cycle Club there is a system of Marque Enthusiasts for selected marques or cycle interest. Since 1993 there have been three Marque Enthusiasts for RENSCH and PARIS bicycles and this history records the findings of the first two men by naming them here as joint authors. As might be expected with research inputs over a fifteen year period not all points made in this history are equally or readily referable to an exact source but as far as is possible the origin of most important assertions has been provided in the footnotes. A normal caveat made by authors is that despite all the help that has been received the authors accept responsibility for any errors; in this case the responsibility is solely that of the first named author, who would nevertheless be delighted to be corrected where readers can produce evidence for his errors. Unravelling this history is an ongoing task and any changes to these findings will be published in the Veteran-Cycle Club's journals.

Alvin Smith,
February 2012

Chapter 1: Rensch – The Personal Story

H.RENSCH Cycles was set up in 1935 or thereabouts by Harry Rensch[1]. Harry, known to many in the cycling world as 'Spanner' Rensch, soon became well known for his colourful well-built bicycles, which were seen as up-to-the-minute creations in the "Continental" mode, then increasingly fashionable.

Rensch's early life is however almost uncharted territory. As behoves a man so successful, many lurid and exotic tales have been spun about his origins. He has been reportedly (and variously) a German from Alsace Lorraine, an Austrian, a Swiss watchmaker and/or a refugee from Hitler's Germany. He is known to have favoured a flashy crimson hued Ford Pilot V8 in the late 1930's – a time when most cars and nearly all bikes were black – this was a suitably flamboyant vehicle for Rensch, who according to his old friends[2], developed a liking for hand painted silk ties which in the post war years were sourced for him by travelling friends in the Merchant Navy!

However, the truth of Rensch's background is now out and is rather more prosaic. As a result of Neville Ireland's research[3] it is now known that Harry Rensch was born Henry Horace Rensch on 27 March 1913 to Flora Rensch(nee Kornzig) and Henry Horace Rensch (senior) furniture dealer and latterly a railway porter, of 118 Beckton Road, Canning Town. Mr Rensch senior apparently never applied for British citizenship, a failing that perhaps never worried him unduly. It was to cause his son some inconvenience a little later, but even then that also brought some benefits, as will be explained in due course.

Harry Rensch met his wife-to-be sometime in the late 1930s. Ethel Ellen May Jennings may have been involved in the cycling trade before she met Rensch.[4] The Rensch's were married on 19 October 1940 by which time Rensch gave his batchelor address as 133 Stoke Newington Church Street. His employment at that time in the war was recorded in his Marriage Certificate as Oxy-acetylene welder (Munitions) and Ethel Rensch was at that time recorded as a Wholesale Tobacco telephonist. Their first borne daughter Christine Frances sadly died in March 1944, just two years of age. Sometime later, on 10 September 1944, their second daughter Jill was born, the home address now being 35 Lordship Road N16. This house had been the address given in their marriage documents for Rensch's parents and thus was probably the home of the whole Rensch family at this time. This family home was only a few hundred yards away from 133 Stoke Newington Church Street, Harry's old pied á terre and an address which we shall see in use by the firm in later years

1　H Stone 1993 *Cycling* Plus Vol 13 February 1993 and notes on the ME's file.
2　AJE Smith 2007 K Janes Remembers. Boneshaker 175 Winter pp36-43
3　Unpublished data of N Ireland, ME Collection
4　Research on the Hackney Rates books by F Ormerod

At present we know very little indeed about Rensch's technical education– how he learnt his cycle making skills. There are tales that he learnt his frame building from working on motorcycle frame repairs[1], but one old friend could not believe this – he remembered Rensch's antipathy towards motorcycles. We do know that he spent some time with the cycle company *Hobbs of Barbican* just before he opened his first bicycle shop and that at sometime he attended an advanced welding training course[2]. The first Rensch shop was at 245 Balls Pond Road, Islington, London N1 at or about 1935. Rensch would have been just 23 years old; it was a bold step and he must have felt he had something to offer - as indeed he did - to open a shop selling his own products at such an age.

Rensch himself did describe his inspiration and the start of his enterprise in an advertisement[3] for Accles & Pollock tubing. This appears to be the only first hand account of how his firm was able to introduce bronze welding to the cycle industry started –but also leaves many questions unanswered, though these are discussed later!

The text of this advertisement has Rensch saying :- " It was in 1935 that I first saw a bronze welded frame (in France). Whether it was practical in action I didn't know, but when I queried the fact, they showed me tests which proved that it was the coming thing. We saw the possibilities, came back, and in 1936 produced the first bronze welded lightweight machine in this country. From then on, we cut out brazed machines." Of course the text for this 1950 article was itself written fifteen years after this introduction of lugless frame construction but perhaps we may still take this statement as a true account.

Rensch's new bicycles appear to have sold well and by 1937[4] he had had to move to larger premises just down the road at 132 Balls Pond Road. Perhaps too this change was to accommodate more of the skilled frame builders that he was taking on as increasing demand required.

People who can remember Harry Rensch personally are now few and far between. Monty Young, the young man who would later co-found Condor Cycles, grew up in nearby Dalston in the 1930's. Young remembers[5], as a young lad, being lured by Rensch's exciting shop in Balls Pond Road. There he watched frame making in the cellars of the shop. Monty also remembers Rensch somewhat later, probably between 1945 and 1949, by which time the firm had re-opened, now re-named as **PARIS**, at 133 Stoke Newington Church Street, the premises which had once been Rensch's home address.

Harold Jones[6] who visited this shop in the early post war years remembers

1   Bill Bush in conversation with Mick Butler
2   WB Hurlow Telecon with AJE Smith 5 09 2005
3   CTC Gazette 1 October 1950
4   An advertisement in *The Bicycle* 4 April 1937 and *Cycling* 5 May 1937
5   Young M Telecon 16 September 2005
6   Conversion with H Jones 4.01.06

MR. RENSCH OF PARIS CYCLES, STOKE NEWINGTON, SAYS—

"We reckon to know a bit about tubes"

It was in France in 1935 that I first saw a bronze welded frame. Whether it was practical in action I didn't know, but when I queried the fact, they showed me tests which proved to me that it was the coming thing. We saw the possibilities, came back, and in 1936 produced the first bronze welded lightweight machine in this country. From then on, we cut out brazed frames. Always on the look-out for improvements is our motto to-day as it was then. That is why we use on our best machines what we believe to be the finest tube steel available to-day—KROMO (chrome molybdenum). We use it for frames, forks, handlebars, seat and chain stays, knowing that nothing can do the job better—and we reckon to know quite a bit about tubes, British and Continental.

Here is our latest Rensch Tandem which has KROMO *tube throughout.*

The sign of a good tube.

KROMO
CM
TUBING
THROUGHOUT

Made by
Accles & Pollock Ltd.

SPECIFICATION

A very rigid and lively machine at home both for fast touring and racing.

FRAME: A. & P. KROMO tubing throughout, specially taper butted at each end; gauges to suit design and purpose for which it is to be used. Frame can be had in the Lateral tube type with triple rear stays, giving an extra degree of rigidity. Lugs of our own design are cut to a superb design, filed and polished. This frame can be had to customer's individual requirements.

SIZE: 22½" x 21½" wheelbase, 59½" or to order. Curved seat tube with short bases. Angles 73° head, 71° seat tubes.
FORKS: Rensch Continental type with Continental style fork crown.
CHAINWHEEL set chromium plated.
FINISH: The famous RENSCH Continental finish in any colours. Chromium plating extra.
WHEELS: 26" x 1¼" Chrome Endrick Rims. D.B. Spokes. Chromium plated Tandem Hubs.

TYRES AND TUBES: DUNLOP Tandem Sprite. WING NUTS G.B.
HANDLEBARS: Alloy Continental type on chromium plated steel stem and clip.
MUDGUARDS: Bluemel White Noweight.
PEDALS: Tour de France rat-trap.
GEARS: Simplex 4-speed ¼" chain.
SADDLES: Brooks B.17.
BRAKES: Chromium plated Cantilever front and rear.
CHAIN: Coventry or Renolds. A ⒯ COMPANY

A cycle is as good as its frame

TBW7

Figure 2 Publicity for the firm, and a useful little history lesson.

that the shop was a welcoming place and that Rensch was a popular figure, being full of fun and kind to youngsters. Harold recalled that Rensch understood and was sympathetic to the lack of ready cash that many keen young cyclists experienced and how he would sometimes sell at reduced prices to them[1]. To Peter Hammond[2], however, the situation was somewhat different. Peter visited the shop in Stoke Newington Church Street at about the same time, and what he saw also made a very vivid impression; arguably something out of a Hieronymus Bosch painting. The premises were seen as a tall gloomy house wreathed at least internally with sulphurous smoke and it seemed as if on every one of the three or four floors there were many small rooms – rooms in which demonic sweating men were piercing, grinding, hammering, and gripping things with red-hot tongs before plunging them into steaming and sulphurous smelling water! A vision from the Bosch depiction of the 'happy hunting grounds'(Hell), perhaps? Peter was not sure! Should he be impressed or start running for his life! He decided to be impressed.

With the resumption of peace in 1945 and the start of PARIS Cycles, Rensch, the enthusiastic supporter of all things 'continental' cycling, would have had little time to himself. He threw all of his energies into this new venture and so began the glory days with his supported **PARIS** and later **Rensch** cycle racing teams which ran from 1947 to 1949. Ken Janes[3], then just a youngster, remembers how tiring he found it when he accompanied Rensch on one of his Saturday's business trips.

"I still remember just how physically exhausted I was after joining Harry on his jaunts one Saturday. He and I were up early at 6 am, first to fill up Harry's bright crimson Ford V8 Pilot, with Harry laughing and joking most of the time on the way to the West End. First stop Charing Cross Road for Solosi's news agency where the Italian owner supplied Harry with the continental cycling newspapers – *But et Sport* and *le Miroir de Sport,* etc, - which were always available in the PARIS Cycles shop. Then round the corner to Soho and Percy Street and Fonteyns –the Massed Start man's paradise- owned by an Italian who was also President of the London Italian Racing Club all of whom were of Italian stock and who reputedly made an excellent BLRC team! Then on to 40 Fulham High Street to see Italo Berigliano, another Italian friend, who was later famous for bringing Fausto Coppi over to race on the Isle of Man and at Herne Hill at the Meeting of Champions[4]. By the end of a bewildering day of visits to customers and old friends I was knackered!"

By 1949 however, the dream days were over and for reasons not yet

---

1   Later Rensch nephew and Harold Jones' great friend Clive Parker would be taken on as a part time worker and member of the PARIS Team. Supporting team members with part time employment was a common feature for PARIS
2   Conversation with P Hammond 15.02.06
3   K Janes telecon AJE Smith 2006
4   Thanks to J Coulson for correcting these Italian names in *Boneshaker* 176

Figure 3. This photograph is the only picture we have of the PARIS Cycles buildings. Centre stage it shows 131 Stoke Newington Church Street for sale in 1977. On the left of 131 the white stucco edge of 129 Stoke Newington Church Street can just be seen on the left edge of the photograph. It appears from this image that 133, the house which had been Rensch's batchelor home and then the first named address for Paris Cycles had been a building to the right of 131 (the dark faced brick building) but which has already been demolished by 1977 allowing the building behind in the next street to be seen in the distance. In 2009 only the original façades of 129 and 131 remained, all the old internal building structure behind the façades having been demolished and now replaced by a new build structure. In 2009 the owner of the 129-133 plots had already applied for permission to erect a new building on the site of the old 133 building but permission had so far been withheld.

understood there had been within the firm a substantial turnover of staff.[1] Ostensibly the firm should have been doing well, as this was the period of great interest in cycling after the war, and the BLRC – the club founded by road racing's avid supporters – was in the ascendency. **PARIS** bicycles themselves were in great demand amongst the racing fraternity as well as other discerning cyclists. Tandems had always been in the firm's catalogue but from

1   The "evidence" for this is indirect coming largely from the personal histories of PARIS staff
     pieced together from individual accounts of their life stories

1948 tandems seemed to be particularly doing well and there was also the development in 1949 of a four wheel sociable 'bike' – the **PARIS** *Social Cycle[1]*. This was a design for recreational cycling at the then new seaside Holiday Resorts, and all of this diversity had led to the expansion of the firm – now into yet another building (129) in the street.

Monty Young remembers that it was at that time in the post war period that Rensch became somewhat diverted from cycling and had developed a love for sea fishing, something in which he indulged frequently. His interest was expensive as he favoured tunny and game fish sport based at the then growing centre for offshore fishing from Southend- a coincidence that he should also have become involved in the new holiday camps? Several people, not just Young, recall how he built a steel hulled boat in the shop. However, like others before him, Rensch had not thought it through properly and then had to knock a wall out of the workshop in order to remove the finished hull! Hurlow remembers that the landlord was not amused and threatened Rensch with dire consequences if he did not repair the damage – which he eventually did. In addition to this penalty the boat was so heavy that it required special lifting tackle to get it away.

Sadly though, despite the meteoric rise of the first firm, **H Rensch,** in the 1930's and then the Phoenix–like resurgence of the newly named **PARIS** firm after the war, Rensch was not to grow old and enjoy the fruits of his labours. Something went wrong in Rensch's private life, whether it was simply his health or perhaps both this and his relationships. The official records reveal that despite the birth of their second child, their daughter Gill in 1944, Rensch's marriage to Ethel did not long survive the stress of the post war period and getting the new larger firm going. This was despite Ethel being an integral part of the firm, being in day to day charge of financial management in the firm.

By 1948 Rensch had become known to be touchy and difficult to deal with, and it appears that this may have been due to chronic illness from diabetes on top of the worries of being a major player in post-war cycling manufacturing; though of course he would not have been the only cycle maker to be harried by money worries and the taxman at this time. His poor health and a dalliance with his young secretary who accompanied him on most of his "fishing" trips may be in part the reason why at some point he ceased to attend to the firm's business and indeed to his family. Currently the reason why in 1948/9 there was a major upheaval in the firm with some erstwhile key employees choosing to leave is not known, but this also seems to have coincided with PARIS Cycles being registered as a commercial entity and it may have been coincidence that at the 1948 Cycle show that some models designs changed their styling, the details being discussed under the machines themselves.

1   *Cycling* 3.11.1950 Report on the Show

Rensch's marriage was clearly under considerable pressure in this key period and it was eventually dissolved sometime in late 1951, some say with the tacit agreement of Ethel, with the requirement that Rensch should surrender all his interests in PARIS Cycles. After Easter 1952 Rensch had gone and Ethel Rensch, who remarried on 20 December 1952 to William Ashman, took over the reins. Bill Hurlow[6] who was appointed by Mrs Rensch to manage the firm's affairs so as to close it down, recalled that he only briefly met Rensch at the time of the divorce, but did confirm that Rensch had suffered badly from diabetes, and thought that perhaps it was the debilitation from this disease as well as the complications caused by the poorly managed firm and the personal conflicts that induced the poor control of Rensch's temper and his lack of interest in the firm's problems at this time.

After Rensch left **PARIS** Cycles he was to be seen a few years later operating a fleet of the Social cycles – these two rider tricycles were the last machines he had designed. They were available for hire at a public pier at Southend. For some years he and his new lady remained living nearby the shop but after some years they moved away. Harry Rensch died on 11 June 1984 in St Margarets at Cliffe near Dover from diabetes related causes. He was described on his death certificate as a retired mechanical and electrical engineer whilst there are reports that he continued with sporting interests and amongst other things developed commercial air guns for use in amusement arcades. He was still relatively young by today's standards at 71.

Figure 4 on the next page sets out a time series for Harry Rensch's personal life and related cycle firm events.

Year	HH Rensch	EEM Jennings	Family	Activity	Cycle company	Cycle manufacture
1913	Born in Canning Town 23/3/1913					
1930	Chez Ephgrave at 70 Gunton St E5			HHR works with Hobbs		
1934						
1935	Lived 133 SNCS				HR at 245 Balls Pond Rd	HR visits France
1936					HR at 245 BPR	HR builds lugless TdF
1937		Also Lived in 133 SNCS		HHR directs HRensch	Move to 132 BPR in May	HR sells lugless TdF
1938					132 BPR all year	First catalogue, then 2nd
1939		Works in bike shop at 207 BPR?			Move to 362 Old Street in June	Third catalogue
1940	Wartime welding in dockyards	HHRensch marries EEM Jennings		HHR interned then employed in dockyards for duration of WW2	362 OS closed before July, OS bombed in October	Galibier strut frame exists as Rensch,
1941		Wartime telephonist and bringing up family				WW2 activities on
1942			CFR born			cycles not known
1943			CFR dies			
1944			JR born			
1945					133 SNCS from July	Paris Welding Co set up
1946					131 SNCS also used for the shop and later includes workshop.	Galibier brochure
1947				HHR directs PARIS		1st }
1948			Family home is 35 Lordship Rd			
1949					From 1949 129 SNCS added	2nd } Large page catalogues
1950						
1951	HHR leaves PARIS	EEMR takes over PARIS in March				3rd }
1952			EEMR marries Ashman		133 SNC now relinquished	WBH assists EEMR as manager
1953					PARIS Cycles closes	WBH leaves PARIS
1984	HHR died 11/6/1984					

Figure 4 A time series for Harry Rensch's personal life and related cycle firm events.

Chapter 2: The First Rensch Firm : H RENSCH

Harry Rensch's first commercial venture[1] began in the mid 1930's. Rensch's new frames appeared late in 1935 or early 1936 with the simplified but distinctive Gothic font transfers **H Rensch** on the down-tubes.

Figure 5 The ornate Gothic style font used by Rensch on the down tube.

They soon acquired an enthusiastic following and the early advertising in 1938 made much of the attractiveness of his colour finishes and 'Continental' styling. As described earlier the range started with lugged frames but soon included the bronze welded or lugless frames, introduced shortly after the firm became established.

Continental styling was a key driver in the mid 1930's British cycle world with envious eyes being cast over the exciting light alloys and multi-gears being used in massed start racing in France and Italy. Numerous lightweight makers in the London area were at the same time making much of such imported styles with strong competition from the likes of specialist makers *FH Grubb, Granby* or *Selbach* and then such major competitors as *Claud Butler, Hobbs, Hetchins, Holdsworth, Maclean* and not a few others.

H Rensch advertisements before World War II always stressed the continental design features of the bikes. The expression covered technical aspects of the bicycle not just colour ways and fittings –though these too were important. In the first 1938 catalogue frames were offered as lugged or lugless. The lugless frames were made by "low temperature bronze welding", as this was the phrase which then described what is today known as lugless or fillet brazed construction. This phrasing was used by Rensch to explain the new process of brazing up the frame without any lugs using the newly introduced silicon bronze (SIF bronze) techniques. Whether many of his customers understood from the catalogue's wording what it meant is another matter. The description of the system given in the Accles & Pollock advertisement together with the account of how he changed from building lugged frames to specialising in bronze welded frames may not have been common knowledge or was at least not spelt out in so many words until the late 1940s when the A&P advertisement came out.

1   Summary history of Rensch, ME's notes by Frank Hernandez 1999

This bronze "welding" technique was not entirely novel within the engineering world, although Rensch's manufacture of lugless brazed frames using it was certainly uncommon in the British cycle industry at that time and appears to have just predated Claud Butler's first lugless design, the Mass-Start Model of 1938/9.[1]

Before it was applied to bicycle frame production it had been developed for use with the newly available lightweight alloy steel tubing originally devised for aeroplane construction, indeed the improvement in high tensile alloys probably precipitated the development of the technique. The British firm then known as Suffolk Iron Foundry (SIF) invented its system for low temperature bronze welding, with specific brazing rods and fluxes, around 1925[2]. Thus was Sifbronze born, though it was not until Reynolds started to market their High Manganese (HM) steels in 1932 and then the more heat critical manganese molybdenum alloys of 531 steel in 1935 that the combination of the need for this technique to preserve the strength of the metal after frame construction and its signal advantages in lightweight custom made bicycle frames was realised by its pioneers in the cycle trade such as Rensch.

The way that Rensch learnt of the technique is not known apart from his own statement in the A&P advertisement but two simple conjectures are given here. The first is the strong Continental influence that Rensch always seems to have favoured: he did record that he had first seen the technique in France. Interestingly WB Hurlow[3] has said that by 1936 Bill Rann, then working for Holdsworth was, at that time, using a French bronze "Bronzigene" system to make lugless frames for Holdsworth. It is more likely this work was restricted to the construction of the Holdsworth tricycle attachment.[4] The account by Hurlow of Holdsworth using bronze welding was made some fifty years later and may not be correct. In near contemporary (post war) advertisements Holdsworth themselves stated that only the later, post war, Holdsworth La Quelda models were bronze welded. In the pre-war (WWII) period Holdsworth claimed in their publicity material of that time that their La Quelda model, itself introduced in 1937 was "steel welded."[5] The firm stated that steel welding was possible solely due to their continued use for this model of High Manganese steel (Reynolds HM steel). This then may be technical confirmation that bronze welding was not in use at that time by Holdsworth. It was only when, immediately after WWII the availability

1   A note in the Advance 1939 Claud Butler catalogue for this model refers to CB's delaying the adoption of this technique until it was proven to be sound. A meritorious approach but can it be coincidental that in 1938 Les Ephgrave had moved to CB's? Perhaps it is reasonable to assume the development of proving the soundness of fillet brazing for lightweight cycles had been down to Rensch?
2   SIFbronze literature see www.sifbronze.co.uk
3   WB Hurlow to AJE Smith telephone call 5.09.2005
4   Hilary Stone in conversation with AJES 2012
5   Welded frames outstanding in new Holdsworth range, *The Bicycle* 28 January 1939

of Reynolds steels were restricted to 531 manganese-molybdenum alloys that Holdsworth's lugless models had to be made using bronze welding techniques, because in the absence immediately after the war of the older HM steels the only other material for which welding might have been acceptable would have been low strength and therefore heavy mild steel tubing - which would have been unacceptable for lightweight high quality frames.

The second way that Rensch might have heard about bronze welding was through local British trade sources. It seems possible that Reynolds sales agents could also have helped to introduce SIF bronze to its regular users of 531 steel but no evidence for this has yet emerged. Equally, the use of the hand held gas torch for brazing was after all well known and then as now SIF had an active trade information and training force. Indeed as already noted Rensch did train at some period at the training school at De Havilland's at Hatfield and later sent his prodigy, a young Les Ephgrave, to the school.

Rensch, if not the first to use the technique of welded or lugless frames for production lightweight bikes, must have been amongst the first English makers to combine the advantages of welding with the use of the new lightweight alloy steels which required the Sifbronze technique, though bigger marques such as Royal Enfield had used an American electric welding methodology from about 1934 onwards.[1].

It is known that Rensch had worked at Hobbs of Barbican sometime in the 1930's and Jim Collier, who went on to build for Gillott, was also at Hobbs pre-war. It is not perhaps surprising that Gillott themselves went on to offer lugless and bilaminate lugless bronze welded frames, although in their case it was a post war production.

A may-be winning sales line that Rensch used was that "welded frames" were "as used in the Tour de France", you can be sure this would have attracted the attention of the increasing numbers of young men who were avid followers of continental road racing. The shop's catalogues also mention that continental newspapers could be bought in the shop and certain riders who competed in France are known to have brought back rare bicycles such as the CNC which could be bought there on occasion, ironically a product of Fletcher, an expatriate Englishman, in Paris.

Another of the features of Rensch welded frames was the use of the proprietary Bayliss Wiley Patent Oil Bath bottom bracket, which is shown in Figure 6. The use of the unit[2] in new bikes may have been a first by Rensch and whilst its use was not restricted to Rensch it is a commonly used, though not an absolute, diagnostic feature of the Rensch pre-war frames. Its use was not just a stylistic fad: with lugless construction the expensive threaded bottom bracket lug from proprietary sources did not need to be bought, with

---

1   Reviewed in *Cycling*'s 1934 Show number section on Royal Enfield's proposed new range.
2   Introduced in 1932, *Cycling* 15.01.1932

just a lighter housing being provided at the frame bottom. Rensch also had a real flare for frame colours and finishes and the bikes were beautifully presented. This was seen by Rensch as another feature of his marque to be presented to the buying public of H Rensch bicycles as being of 'continental" style. The expression "glass hard finishes" that was used for the top models – *Galibier, Pyrenees* and *San Reno* was however one that was shared at least later by Gillott whilst *"polychromatic"* paint finishes though a very early use of this technique were also advertised by other makers[1]. It seem quite likely that at this pre-war stage the finishing would not have been in-house (as it certainly was after the war) but was carried out locally by others.

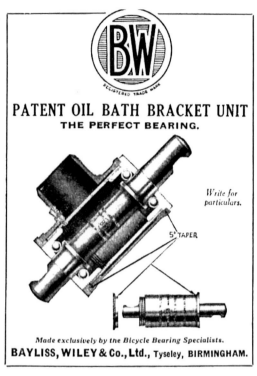

PATENT OIL BATH BRACKET UNIT
THE PERFECT BEARING.

Write for particulars.

5° TAPER

Made exclusively by the Bicycle Bearing Specialists.
BAYLISS, WILEY & Co., Ltd., Tyseley, BIRMINGHAM.

Figure 6 Bayliss Wiley unit used by Rensch in welded frames. Originally the system was marketed in 1932 as a repair method for bottom brackets that had stripped their threads.

Certainly in the later 1930's H Rensch as a firm quickly established a market niche and, in order to expand had, as already been noted, by May 1937 to move to larger premises at 132, Balls Pond Road. There was a further expansion, or at least another move, in 1939. The evidence for this is that, after the first known catalogue (which is dated 1938) from 132 Balls Pond Road, a new full catalogue of entirely a different format was issued in or for 1939 showing a change of address to 362, Old Street, EC1 in the City of London.

WB (Bill) Hurlow reported that talk in the PARIS Cycle days was that H (Harry) Parr had once been partner with Rensch. Parr seems to have had no 'hands on' experience with bicycles, as his interests were in the enamelling and lacquering 'shop' which was latterly (1952/3 period) run separately and this could indicate that have had been a division in ownership which reflected a

---

1   Words and phrases in italics are as used in the first known catalogue, dated 1938

split between two prior partners.

One further strand of "evidence" for a new broom affecting the outfit in 1939 - in the absence of any true information - may perhaps be gleaned from the catalogues. The earliest known catalogue is for 1938 models and has its eight frames or models numbered 1 to 8, with the first five models being of brazed construction. In a later single page edition of a 1938[1] catalogue these eight models had been re-numbered 1 to 5 with alphabetic sub codes egg 1a,1b, etc, to cover the original eight. Then, in a new, full and completely revised catalogue, of 1939, any numbering of the catalogue models has gone and a number of new cheaper models listed. Is this change for 1939, of what was clearly an early well thought out but perhaps by now obsolete production model policy, an indication of a new management coming in during 1939? Ken Janes was dismissive of interpreting this change as anything other than simply a modernisation of the **Rensch** range of cycles. He pointed out that the use of numbers for the models was probably initially due to the fact that each model would have had its own jig (identified doubtless by a number) on which frames for that model were built – and that by 1939 Rensch had probably decided to personalise his model range a bit more with special names in just the way that his competitors such as Claud Butler and Holdsworth, not to mention the major manufacturers such as Raleigh, Rudge, Royal Enfield were already doing.

The well known models of Rensch and the post war PARIS marque are described in more detail later on but in this section it is appropriate to illustrate on the following page the early *Tour de France* and the beautifully lugged *Continental Road Racers*. Strangely none of the other new top end models described in the 1939 catalogue appear to have survived.

There is considerable uncertainty about the dating of frames around the end of the Rensch period and the beginning of the Paris period i.e. at the beginning of WWII. However, frame 1081 ordered in 1939 and delivered in 1940 as a PARIS has bilaminations on its head tube. The term 'bilamination" for this technique was of course only coined for Claud Butler's use and that was later in 1947[2]. This frame and other Rensch models such as the *Galibier* *mainstrut* model which appeared in the wartime period appear to provide evidence that Rensch had already introduced this technique prior to WWII.

---

1   This brochure is stated to cover "1938 models" ie not for those for the following year, and is thought to be later as the costs of the machines had risen from those quoted in the first "1938" catalogue.
2   Vincent M on www.classiclightweights.co.uk dated 30 January 2012.

Figure 7 Rensch Tour de France from the 1938 catalogue

Figure 8 Rensch Continental Road Racing model from the 1938 catalogue.

Chapter 3: The Later Firms: PARIS Cycles

The **PARIS** marque appears to have been already well known in the immediate post WWII period judging by the fact that by 1947 it was already running its own racing team. Similarly it seems that its status as the successor to **H Rensch** cycles and the fact that it was run by Harry Rensch was also common knowledge. It is intriguing to wonder whether this assumption of its origin being public knowledge is in fact due to our own improved information of cycle history, and whether in point of fact, apart from North Londoners, the majority of British cyclists in the 1940s might have known very little about the firm. No public announcement in the cycling press[1] has so far been found to explain how they might have heard about it, though perhaps one day a historian may turn up some announcement. Perhaps revelations about the new marque were all just by just word of mouth – one of many chaotic changes as the imminent war closed down civilian life in 1939.

What we do know is that the period just entering WWII was for many a complex and a worrying situation. Rensch would have seen an influx of German Jews into his part of London and in the industry it would have been inescapable just how many skilled and even part skilled men as well as cycle industry specialists such as welders were being seduced from small cycle shops by higher paying armaments industry jobs[2].

Whether keeping his shop open had been an option we do not know, but perhaps this was just hopelessly uneconomic, and it appears that later in October 1940 Old Street was bombed[3]. May be until that damage occurred Mrs Rensch managed somehow to continue the bicycle trading or perhaps one or two employees from the pre war firm remained available to make frames, possibly only in the evenings and using up the scraps of pre-war material stocks left to them. Certainly Janes[4] has said that certain young cyclists did carry out some work after the start of the war. This casual continuation seems to be true as, independent of this statement by Janes, we know that one PARIS bicycle, a *Tour de France* numbered 1081, which had been ordered late summer 1939 was built up in early 1940 after the owner, E Kinsey, had complained about non delivery. The machine was finally supplied by Easter of 1940.[5]

Accounts by Hilary Stone of the firm's history refer to the fact that early

---

1 See however the later section of this report where advertisements placed in the cycling press are annotated
2 Hewitt C op cit Chap2 Ref 8
3 Ormerod F Personal communication November 2011
4 Smith AJE op cit Chap1 Ref 2
5 This *Tour de France* (TdF) still retains most of its original finish. It has rather crude, presumably prototypical Eifel Tower shaped bilaminations which may therefore be the first known instance of this design of bilamination and was definitely supplied as a PARIS. Kinsey stated that it has always had the Eifel Tower (PARIS Cycles) head badge together with the TdF and PARIS type stencils on the top and down tubes that were to become so well known in later years

in WWII there was a ground swell of anti-German feelings particularly as a result of the London Blitz and it might well have been at this time, rather than later, that Rensch changed the name of the firm to **PARIS**. There is, however, no registration date for the PARIS company in Company House. The earliest published evidence so far unearthed is the use by Rensch of the name "Paris Welding Company" when he started to rent the premises at 129-131 Stoke Newington Church Street in 1945.

Nevertheless there has been other evidence to support the thought that the PARIS firm was founded sometime early during World War Two. This evidence was a second hand bicycle advertisement[1] in 1943 to sell a **PARIS** bike. This was – and still is - the first known published reference to the "new" trade name for bicycles made by Rensch. The advertisement is taken as evidence that by this time the marque was reasonably well known – at least to the seller and his expected buyers perhaps mostly within the London area.

Over the years there have been several theories about the reason for the choice of **PARIS** as the name for the new firm[2]. One general reason for the name change that is sometimes put forward is that Paris, the French capital, was synonymous with attractive bicycle design and redolent of the romance of massed start racing. A new firm, as for example the new 1939 entity, might also have been influenced by new commercial partners (we suspect Rensch must have taken on financial support at this point) Clearly the reason already mentioned, that the name **H Rensch** would have become extremely unpopular in the area of London in which Rensch lived as this was where many Jewish families had established themselves and due to the assumption (incorrect as it happens) that the firm and its maker had an association with nationalistic German interests could have been a key factor. A continuation of this thought was that there was a risk that retaining the RENSCH name and attempts at its future promotion might have led to commercial losses, an important factor perhaps more for the new backers that Rensch had only just picked up in 1939. Another influence upon the name change and which might have been felt early in the commencement of hostilities was strong public sympathy with the Free French movement in England after the collapse of France in 1940[3].

The address of the firm has been examined by means of reference to the surviving official **PARIS** advertisements in *Cycling* magazine, and to official records kept by the local authorities, now Hackney and Islington[4]. Examination of every copy of *Cycling* from 1941 to 1953 shows that advertisements by the firm were only placed in *Cycling* after the end of WWII - and these appear to

1   *Cycling* for 6 January 1943 and discussed in Appendix Appendix A4, page 187.
2   Telecon Derek Athey September 1995
3   Derek Athey Telecon Smith/Athey 2006
4   Smith AJE. Mike Beazley recollections *The Boneshaker* 177 December 2008.

be the first official documentary evidence of the new name of the firm. The advertisements show the shop to be back in North London, and in 1946 at 133 Stoke Newington Church Street. This address was the home address used by Rensch prior to his marriage. The move of the company away from the immediate pre-war shop in Old Street was probably due to bombing in that area of London, although it could also have been because Rensch was himself involved in full time war work and as Mrs Rensch is known to have had another war time job, she would not have been able to operate the shop.

Monty Young[1], who remained in contact with Harry Rensch and the firm in this period, recalls as a teenager being taken perhaps in 1947 in Rensch's car to race meetings in which there was a **PARIS** team of independent riders racing under British League of Racing Cyclist (BLRC) rules. Rensch was well known for his love of continental mass start road racing and it is no surprise therefore to find that at this time he was a keen BLRC supporter. This organisation which had became a national movement after Percy Stallard's epoch making 1942 Llangollen to Wolverhampton Race was readily adopted in the London area where supporters of road racing in England like Rensch and many riders in the local clubs identified with the heady mixture and ethic of road racing, and rebellion from what was seen as a hidebound convention of time trialling and petty bureaucracy.

There is a marked similarity between the emblem developed for BLRC as shown shown in Fig. 9 and the racing cyclist or coureur illustration already in use by Rensch for his RENSCH bicycle transfers.

Figure 9 The rider in the BLRC symbol

Whether Rensch may have donated, or just allowed, BLRC to use the emblem of a thrusting hill climbing coureur is not known As noted this image was already associated with **H RENSCH** bicycles, and would become even better known as the **PARIS** Cycles seat tube transfer, which was identical to the **H RENSCH** transfer except for the use of the name **PARIS** in the transfer instead of **H RENSCH.**

Figures 10 Transfer designs for RENSCH and PARIS Cycles

1   Monty Young is the owner of Condor Cycles.

The great similarity of the riders in the transfers and in the BLRC symbol can be clearly seen in these illustrations – the transfers taken from actual machines, the symbol extracted from the BLRC emblem.

If this use of an existing **H RENSCH** emblem by BLRC was intentional and agreed with Rensch, then it must be seen as an astute marketing ploy. Doubtless his competitors in the commercial cycle world did not particularly appreciate it! It was perhaps typical of the man?

All in all, considering the acquisition of his new wife in 1940, who may have helped bring more money into the business and certainly brought a new broom, the pressures of antipathy towards Germanic sounding names starting in 1940, and the need to move the business from Shoreditch, a tentative conclusion can be drawn that the marque **PARIS** was probably born in 1939/40 and formalised after the wedding in 1940 – though there was never any registration of the new firm at this time. In all probability very few bicycles were made during the war with the new firm only effectively reconstituted sometime in 1945.

Figure 11 The racing cyclist taken from the BLRC emblem

One of the features claimed in PARIS catalogues was the superlative finish on the bicycles and owners relished the beautiful use of fading from one colour to another. This method of fading does appear to have been a definite Rensch first – although it was only used in the post war **PARIS** days. It was thought until recently from comments made by Norman Taylor[1] that Rensch, who had been on a tour of continental workshops in 1939, had brought back some of the continental ideas on frame enamelling that then later flowered on the post-war bicycles. However, a more plausible explanation of this perhaps unexpected excellence in frame finishing may have been given by Ken Janes[2] - who claimed he had it straight from Harry Rensch himself in 1947- was that these finishing techniques were initially described to Rensch by a Jewish refugee who had been an industrial chemist in Germany's paint industry. Janes' letter states :- 'Six weeks after the start of WWII, there were thousands of aliens , non-naturalised foreigners, living in this country, lists of these being kept at local police stations. As Harry's father had never sought naturalisation, this made Harry Rensch an alien. Thousands were incarcerated

1   Norman was one of the revered three brothers who together made the Jack Taylor bicycles and
     who raced together in pre war road races where they first met Harry Rensch.
2   Letter on ME's file dated 5 April 2007 from K Janes

for short periods, some on the Isle of Wight. During the six weeks Harry was there he met an industrial paint chemist of German origin. This was an important meeting. It lead to Harry's development of polychromatic finishes (meaning the combination of several distinct colours fading not mixing into each other) of the cycle frames, a feature for which he and the PARIS marque later became famous.'

Demand for the bikes – certainly the diamond frame *Tour de France* and *Professional Road Racer* was considerable. The possible commercial success of the **PARIS** *Galibier* model may also have been an issue[1] In *The Bicycle's* review of the 1948 London Show[2] the article said "*Centre piece of attraction has been the Galibier frame with its stepped seat tube. Now in regular use among mass start enthusiasts---*". The demand for volume sales soon led to development of batch production of the bikes and to yet greater expansion of the facilities. At one time there was said to be over twenty men[3] working for the concern at any one time. These premises remained the firm's centre and it traded from variations of this address – advertisements sometimes quoting 129 sometimes 133 and sometimes 129/133 Stoke Newington Church Street - until the firm was closed sometime in 1952. It is noteworthy however, that at least in the early post war years the enamelling department was in yet another old premises at 245 Balls Pond Road[4].

In fact the firm's advertisements, which are described in a later chapter, reveal that 129 became part of the firm's address for the 1948 season and this may have been required as a show room area. In 1948 several iconic features of PARIS design such as the Eifel Tower transfer now seen on most seat tubes first appeared and it must have been about this time that the second of the now well known large page catalogues was issued, the margins of which show the New Welded Tour de France model. There may have been something bigger going on at this time that we currently do not understand, or it may be that incidental change just came, but during 1948/9 a number of older staff members left the company and this would surely suggest there were changes in management as well. Other changes at this time which are dealt with later are the introduction of the rectangular head badge and the appearance of the *Paris Sport* variation

It is sad that the meteoric rise of the firm appears to have outstripped the ability of any of the key players to have recorded their success and indeed it may have been so fast that they had little or no time to enjoy it either. Certainly it is the case that we now have to turn our attention to its end – virtually before it had time to mature.

1   The V-CC register suggests that the number of *Galibiers* made was very considerable.
2   *The Bicycle* 24 November 1948 pp31-35
3   S. Beale conversation with N Ireland 2003
4   Monty Young's recollections

The collapse of the firm has been said to be due to cash difficulties and many other firms in the cycle trade were badly affected at that time, but the end was probably made inevitable by Rensch's marriage breaking up and the probable need to realise assets to pay off creditors and possibly erstwhile partners. This impending matrimonial and commercial dilemma may have been a key reason for the floating on 13 June 1951 of the PARIS CYCLE Company Ltd [1]. Prior to this registration there are no known formal business registrations[2] of either H Rensch or PARIS cycle entities so that we can presume that these earlier arrangements were loose business associations entered into with mutual trust by the various individuals.

Rensch appears to have left both his home and wife during 1951. He certainly quit the firm in late 1951. This departure was apparently part of the divorce agreement. At this time the firm was in considerable financial problems and it was only a little after this that Mrs Rensch asked WB (Bill) Hurlow to manage the frame building side of the business, which he started to do in the spring of 1952. At this time Hurlow had left *Holdsworth Cycles* and had become an independent frame builder who was still building frames on request for *Holdsworth Cycles*. He joined **PARIS** after Easter 1952.

Hurlow commented that at that time, in Rensch's absence, there was no clear direction within the firm, and he surmised that this situation had gone on for some time already, so that when Rensch had finally left there had simply been no natural manager available to replace him. In efforts to sell the bikes, it appears that many frames had been sent out to a number of agents and shops on a sale-and-return basis without proper security or record of where or how many had gone. This assertion is supported by the advertising pattern seen in *Cycling*, the detailed account of which can be found in Appendix A4. The difficulty the firm had in building their complex bilaminated bicycles is perhaps not surprising as many aspects of the work such as lug or bilaminate cutting had been outsourced to a ring of artisans many of them riders or ex riders, the whole situation resembling a loose knit cottage industry,[3] with the leader gone the system fell apart.

In trying to understand the situation Hurlow notes that Rensch, who he only briefly met once or twice during this period, was suffering from diabetes, a disease less well understood then than now. Rensch appeared to be both truculent and disturbed about his relations with those still running what had been his firm. Attitudes made more understandable in one suffering from what was then a particularly debilitating disease.

Hurlow also noted, with a degree of righteous outrage, that at the time he joined the firm the batch construction practice in **PARIS**, allied with piece

1   Companies House 1951, copy obtained by F Hernandez 1994
2   At least none have been found by previous researchers including Companies House.
3   Noted in the ME files after discussions with several early employees.

work payments for individuals, had meant that many frames passed through several hands, and, with the lack of good supervision at that time, all sorts of poor workmanship were getting through. He compared this situation with the strict quality control with which he had had to work in his times in *FH Grubb* and *WF Holdsworth*. In both of these workshops each frame had had one designated builder - whose name was on all the paperwork, if not actually on the frame itself. In these cases the responsibility of the frame builder would extend to carrying out any repair work on that frame if it was returned in the warranty period.

It seems possible that some of the problems often reported on *Galibier* machines – perhaps particularly the apparent Achilles heel of the design - the joint of the lower bottom bracket tube to the main strut - might well be down to the sort of poor quality control described above.

However, back to 1952 - Hurlow was tasked by Mrs Rensch with liquidating all the PARIS assets[1] and to do this he set out to organise the remaining staff to finish any uncompleted orders and bikes that had been begun to form stock in hand. Amongst other actions Hurlow was proud to own up to was that he personally cut up the jigs for the *Galibier* model after the sale of the last completed frames. Hurlow had no love for this model, which he always considered to be a poor design. Whether or not he and perhaps others also thought, or had found out, that its costly build was a partial cause of the firm's failure we shall probably never know.

Evidence from the advertisements suggests that in early 1952 PARIS may have been concentrating on selling tandems[2] –their ads simply did not refer to solo machines. Within months, possibly just before Hurlow joined at Easter, their tandem builder had also left, this makes it seem as though by this time the firm was at rock bottom with no experienced solo or tandem frame builders on the strength and possibly only Tom Board, then just beginning his career, around. Mike Beazley whose experiences with the firm are discussed later in Chapter 16 recalls Tom and few others with an isolated management team of a man and two women who led a different life from him in offices at the front of the building. Altogether not a picture of a busy or organised outfit.

At this time in the firm's fortunes Harry Parr and the finishing shop that he managed (and in which he probably had his own financial interest) really helped to keep the whole firm afloat. Hurlow recalled that in the last days of the old firm there was some vital income via Harry Parr which came from making advertising signs for India Tyres. The metal signs and their support frames were made in the firm's main workshop and the sign painting was by Parr's enamelling side of the business – through which the job had come in. Hurlow remembered that later, when the enamelling business had to go independent - due to losing so much money to the main bicycle side of the business - they refused to help finish the last batches of bicycle frames. Hurlow then had to go cap in hand to Bromerart, another North London enameller, in order to get the last few frames enamelled and lacquered.

Hurlow ended his time with the firm as a manager for Mrs Rensch by eventually taking over the goodwill and the remaining tools. He worked out of the old **PARIS** workshops for a period, before the original firm was finally closed. He did try to continue the **PARIS** name, advertising the "the re-organised **PARIS CYCLE CO. LTD"** for a short time from premises at 2 Wilton Mews[1]. This last gasp venture was not to be a success. The **PARIS CYCLE CO LTD** (Company Number 496466) was formally dissolved in 1955[2]. Hurlow had already begun working for *Condor Cycles* where, reportedly in 1953[3], he helped to establish the *Condor* reputation for excellence with the No. 1 to 3 and *Superbe* models before he moved on in 1958 becoming an independent frame builder, providing *Mal Rees* with a wonderful design used for the *Rameles* and perhaps other models, and where some would say his craft reached its zenith.

Remembering these last days with some nostalgia, Monty Young recalls[4] how at PARIS Rensch had used massive flat steel plates, doubtless acquired by Rensch from war time dockyard uses, on which the frames were built. Young remembers with sadness how, later in the 1950's when his firm *Condor Cycles* had its workshops in 211 Balls Pond Road, he watched as those same steel plates, which were too heavy to remove, were simply bulldozed into the ground - a little bit more history interred under London's streets.

The reorganised

PARIS CYCLE CO. LTD.

are now at

2 Wilton Mews, Wilton Way, Hackney : : London, E.8.

BILL HURLOW presents a new range of INDIVIDUALLY built machines to your own SPECIFICATION. Continental design and finish to the highest standard of BRITISH workmanship.

Figure 12 Advertisement placed by Bill Hurlow in 1953

PARIS as a make has had a number later re-incarnations – the designs were just too good to let go! The first was not a truly legal entity and the venture was restricted just to the production of a small number of diamond pattern

1   *Cycling* 16 April 1953
2   Records in Companies House- copy obtained by F Hernandez 1994
3   *The Condor Years*, by Peter Whitfield, published by Condor Cycles
4   Young M Chap 1 Ref 8 op cit

frames. Two ex **PARIS** frame builders set themselves up near Croydon or Mitcham between 1952 and 1955 and made their frames as either *Tour de France* or *Champion du Monde* copies[1]. This venture was either unsuccessful or at any rate did not last long enough to establish a perpetuating entity; no frames appear to have survived or else they have now been assimilated into the wider family of several-times-refinished PARIS frames!

Strangely the name Paris Sport was also used on a few frames made by John Robertson of Edinburgh in the 1950's, but this venture owned nothing to the Rensch inheritance, was quite unrelated and Robertson then built under the name of Robertson or Milano[2]. Yet another firm Paris Sport Cycle was set up in New Jersey USA in the 1970's[3]. The main frame builder for this marque in the late 1970's was Francisco Cuevas, though its owner Mike Fraysse originally employed Pepe Limongi. Certainly Cuevas frames carry his name on the chain stay, and as a master builder from Barcelona where he began in 1928 and then Argentina before reaching the US in 1969, he built his frames free without a jig. However recent research published in the V-CC journal *News and Views*[4] reveals that some at least of the later Paris Sport bicycles met with from the 1980s were imported French machines sold by Mike Fraysse's shop that had found their way to the United Kingdom. The story is told in full in the section dealing with the **PARIS** Sports model. Apart from these coincidental borrowings of the name the second real re-incarnation (or third if we include Hurlow's unsuccessful 1953 venture) was much more soundly based. This was started in 1981 and became a fully legal entity when Michael Kemp somehow acquired the legal rights to the **PARIS** name. There is no doubt that Kemp, who was a business man and keen club cyclist, provided the impetus and perhaps most of the initial financing and planning behind this venture. The new firm was set up as the Paris Lightweight Cycle Company Ltd in Potters Bar on 30 September 1981. Between 1983 and 1987[5] frames were built solely by Tom Board with Condor Cycles being the agents. M Young, T Board and S Mobley were also partners in the new firm, whose Secretary was D Kitemark.

Some diamond frame, what would now be termed retro style, models were made and marketed. by Paris Lightweight Cycles.[6] These were the *Tour de France* which was available in either lugged (£180) or bilaminated (£225-250) styles . But of course there was an improved *Galibier* style frame at £285 –the real reason behind the firm as Kemp had fallen head over heels in love with this classic design as a young impecunious enthusiast and wanted to bring his love to the world's attention once more.

1   This venture was reported to F Hernandez sometime in the 1990s the source not now known
2   Telephone conversation Robertson/Ireland 2003
3   Kolin MJ & de la Rosa DM The Custom Bicycle, Rodale Press 1979
4   On Your Marques N&V 339 and 340 Oct 2010 to January 2011
5   Correspondence from Companies House to N Ireland 2003
6   *Cycling* 6 March 1982

Board had worked for PARIS Cycles from 1949 to their closure[1], having started with them as an errand boy and then frame filer. Later, after further experience with Maclean and FW Evans, he had become a frame builder in his own right before joining Condors. He had worked for several years at the Condor work-shops making the highly thought of Condor house frames. Coincidentally for this history the Condor work-shops were located in 211 Balls Pond Road, just along from the original H RENSCH premises! Board's modifications to the design for the Paris Lightweight Cycles *Galibier* were said to strengthen the bottom bracket assembly by using T-45 steel instead of Reynolds 531 for the lower part of the "seat tube"- the tube connecting the bottom bracket to the main strut tube and subject to twisting action from the pedals. Additionally the adoption of modern microfusion castings was beneficial as was the use of Campagnolo drop-outs.

The figure below shows the original prototype prepared by Board for the *Paris Lightweight Cycles Galibier.* However, some customers wanted, not the new and better lugs on offer, but the older pattern bilaminations that had been so much a part of the original *Galibier's* appeal, so these too came back on some frames (see section on bilaminations).

Although this well publicised venture was initially well financed and enthusiastically driven, it was not a commercial success and closed in 1987. It may be surmised that the frames were too expensive and that once the small retro cycle sales niche had been satisfied there was insufficient attraction or technical

Figure 13: The preproduction Paris Lightweight Cycles Galibier built for the new managing director, Michael Kemp.

1   Bicycle October 1983 Tom Bogdanovitch on Tom Board p36-37

edge in the design to make it worthwhile for youngsters to buy into. At the time road bikes were in any case becoming less fashionable as the craze for BMX style bikes and mountain bikes was attracting the less serious but still fashion conscious riders. Additionally at this period time-triallists were largely keen on hyper lightweight, especially low –pro designs, and the richer ones were beginning to invest in aluminium, titanium and increasingly commonly carbon frames most of which were reaching the English market from the US.

Although *Paris Lightweight Cycles* had closed in 1987, Condors continued to offer the custom build of these bikes and there was to be small number of Tom Board re-creations of the *Galibier* that even included a real one-off - a *Galibier* tricycle - up to about 1993. By this time Board had severed his links with Condors so that any later replica or retro copies should really be called "Tom Board in the style of" machines. Monty Young meanwhile had retained the rights once owned by Kemp and never precluded building more Paris *Galibiers*.

So, no real surprise that Condor's revealed a new Paris *Galibier* model in October 2006 at the Cycle 2006 show at Excel in London. The exhibition frame set was beautifully made and kept very close indeed to the original, even being built in Reynolds 531, just then itself becoming a retro alloy, as frame builders moved to TIG and MIG welding techniques and the commercially available tubing following their needs. It had the later style of bilaminations at head and on the main strut, with correct paired small diameter top tubes carrying the rear

Figure 14 A new version of the Paris Galibier takes a bow in 2006

brake cable. Costs had risen however, the frameset now being offered at about £1250, the final cost depending on the tastes of the owner - with fading or box lining options to choice.

In the world of collectors there are of course the inevitable pressures to "replicate" where an article is desired but supply is limited. Thus there have been at least four if not more different unofficial copies of the *Galibier* that have circulated in the last 30 years or so. In general the poorer quality of the design and build of these unlicensed copies has been sufficient for the non–Rensch and non–*Paris Lightweights* origin of these machines to be readily detectable by someone familiar with the original machines, but one at least has been sufficiently good to be only detected when carrying out a detail check of minor styling points - this would certainly appear to be the case in a machine(s) made by Roy Cottingham.[1]

Condor in 2009 showed that Monty Young's admiration for Rensch's designs was still fresh when they re-introduced their version of the *Paris Tour de France* to the contemporary market.

Figure 15 The latest Paris Tour de France from Condor in 2009

1   Ken Janes, telephone conversation with AJES 3 April 2007

The table below lists the various productions of frames either original **H RENSCH/PARIS** specimens of the marque, or replicas and/or copies. Only a few of these variations can be said to be 'authorised' productions in the sense that there was at the time an entity to which the purchaser could identify as having legally admitted responsibility for a **H RENSCH/PARIS** item. The various productions are shown in the table below :-

Period	Authorised	Un authorised
1935-39	H Rensch	
1940-53	Paris Cycle Co	
1953-55	Paris Cycle Co Ltd	
1955-57?		'Paris' , Mitcham
1950's		Paris Sport, Scotland
Unknown		Jack Taylor Cycles
1970's		Paris Sport Cycles USA
1982-87	Paris Lightweight Cycle Company Ltd	
1987-1993?		Tom Board
1980-90's		Roy Cottingham
1990's		Rotrax builders
1995-2000		Northwest UK
2006-to date	Condor Cycles	

Chapter 4: Publicity by the Firms

Readers may be thinking "Its time to hear about some of those bikes now". Please bear with me, an examination of the firm's advertisements and then what they put in their catalogues is an important issue for this marque –this material is the only definitive information, partial though it is, that we have to understand what the firm was trying to do and did. Descriptions of the bikes follow in glorious detail in Chapters 6 to 15 of this book after the next two chapters; skip these two chapters if you must, but together with Appendix 4, they do give some of the thrill of the chase for finding out what happened as the months and as the years rolled by. Without any formal records by the firm they illustrate how the firm introduced itself and its products to the world. It is clear, though, that publicity was not a strong point for either the Rensch or PARIS managements. It would seem likely that Rensch probably had his own coterie of friends in the local racing community and depended upon them and their contacts for his main market

The first anyone ever heard or read about the new Rensch firm was a single liner in the new weekly magazine *The Bicycle* a week or so after it had started. After a short time though the advertisements did mention that Continental Design was a feature of the machines and shortly after that a new address was announced. This would have been when larger premises were needed for the additional staff taken on with the advent of bronze welding as the main means of frame construction in 1937. This was demonstrated by a phrase that coupled two ideas "continental style, frames welded or brazed"; Rensch was "covering all the bases" to use a modern expression.

Early in 1938 *The Bicycle* magazine carried a review of the firm's 1938 catalogue. The review whilst mentioning that some models were bronze welded did not attempt to explain the significance of a welded construction or draw the readers' attention to it other than repeating the catalogue's statement that the *Tour de France* was a "special welded model" –one wonders if the magazine's own staff writer himself understood?

Of course there may well have been earlier brochures or catalogues available from the shop which have not survived but which told potential owners about the new techniques, but it would not have escaped many readers of that period that just exactly at this time Holdsworth were advertising their La Quelda models which have already been mentioned as welded, though these appear to have been steel welded machines at this period.

As 1939 and the Second World War approached Rensch publicity improved with a major expense as the firm moved its premises yet again and introduced a new range of bicycles – of which more anon. The firm splashed out with a

THE WORLD'S BEST RACING CYCLES

H. RENSCH for HAND-BUILT, CONTINENTAL DESIGN LIGHTWEIGHTS, WELDED OR BRAZED
Send for our New List.
NEW ADDRESS :—362, OLD ST., LONDON, E.C.1 (Near Shoreditch Town Hall

Figure 16 The H RENSCH name in Germanic script seen in The Bicycle.

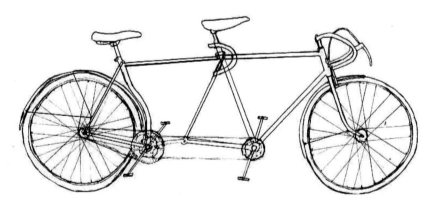

Figure 17 RENSCH 1939 Solo to tandem conversion attached to a solo machine. The image has had to be redrawn

box advertisement, their first ever use of art work in their advertising.

It was only too soon however that approaching war was undeniable and it began to close down cycling and other civilian activities. Just time though, for a final publicity effort with a letter to *The Bicycle* about a novel attachment devised to turn a solo into a tandem[1].

After the war all the advertisements were for the new firm, PARIS, though typically for a coy advertiser Rensch allowed the world to flow around him.

The first we hear of the new entity is in a secondhand bicycle advertisement in *Cycling* in 1943 - after which it would be 1945 before the first ever PARIS advertisement was placed and from then onwards *Cycling* saw the main thrust for such publicity as there was. Rensch did not bother in the advertisement to identify himself with the new firm now called PARIS cycles but he did address his old constituency by opening his typical one liner advertisement with the Greeting "Racing Cyclists --" Old habits die hard.

The advertisements placed by the firm are at this point influenced not by the firm but by events - though these may have been triggered intentionally by a devious Rensch effort at publicity? Of course, it seems much more likely that it was just serendipity. Whichever it was, IT was the shapely new PARIS *Galibier* strut frame model which *Cycling* showed in a street scene photograph taken by their reporter and which in 1946 caught people's eye and imaginations. We should remember that at this time England and English cyclists had been starved of innovation and spangley bright new things for six years or more. So that the new *Galibier* model must have really stood out and grabbed their

Figure 18 Perhaps the first signs of new life in cycling design late 1946?

This Bicycle is to wind by John Fairclough was sold by Gerry Moore in the 1990s attention in a way that only a fast supercar is likely to do in modern times. What Cycling actually showed (see Figure 74 on page 81) was the new bicycle parked against a kerb showing a PARIS transfer or stencil on the main strut and with a Rensch style diamond transfer on the upper seat tube. The caption in Cycling warned that the model was not available for sale in England and also stated that the weight 'was reported' as 12lb – both comments just heightening the anticipation even further. What an alluring dream the *Galibier* must have been!

It is interesting to contemplate the fact that to many clubmen in UK mentioning PARIS brought up – and still does for many - only the mental image of the *Galibier* design –although the firm made a so much wider range of models which were well known in the London area. Is this impression of the firm held just because it was the PARIS *Galibier* which was the first model that most people had first seen illustrated? In other words the firm's own publicity about its other models was so poor that few other than London racing men were aware of them?

One wonders whether it is reasonable to conclude from the first of these September 1946 advertisements that no advertising policy was yet in place - for example no name was given to their splendid new top model and there was no brochure on offer at this time. This fits in with comments recorded by one owner[1] who bought his bicycle from the shop in 1947/8 and who said that the shop only had their old 1939 (Rensch) catalogues available to show customers.

Then in spring 1947 a review article appeared in *Cycling* which must have been triggered by the firm sending them some publicity material which included another picture of the *Galibier*[2] and perhaps just mentioned the other diamond frame solos. Whilst this article was doubtless highly desirable publicity and infinitely better than none, (it certainly explained the design intentions of the new model) there was probably some grinding of teeth back at the ranch over virtual ignoring of the rest of the range of beautiful and well made bikes – models which had already and indeed would continue to contribute much more to the firm's coffers than did the elegant but specialist *Galibier*.

In 1947 interest in the scenic nature of the Yorkshire hills took a film crew north and in no time at all the joys of cycling came to be discussed. A young racing cyclist, Geoffrey Binns, approached the crew who had already started to talk about a cycling film with the local Clarion Cycling Club[3]. Binns wrote to the film crew about the Tour de France and how the local equivalent cycle races would make a good story. Soon scriptwriter Ted Willis[4] had created a storyline

---

1   Don Stephens owned frame 1382 at one time. Don Stephen's machine though is not currently on the register
2   It is clear from this picture which is reproduced in Appendix 4 that this was the drawing from which Figure 18 shown above was redrawn.
3   Binns G in Fellowship News 172/9 December 2007
4   Ted Willis, who later became Lord Willis after he had gone on to write the Dixon of Dock Green

with some road racing action added to bring about the film "A Boy, A Girl and A Bike" which was filmed during 1947 and 1948 in Yorkshire. It starred John McCullum, Honor Blackman and Patrick Holt with minor roles for Diana Dors, Meg Jenkins, Anthony Newley, Thora Hird and Maurice Denham. The film itself was released for showing in 1949. The film makers imported most of the cyclists' uniforms and racing appurtenances from France and took on 20 extras from the cycling world in May 1948. Some were local lads from the

Figure 19 Indirect promotion by The PARIS Team for the forthcoming film. Note the official notice says the bicycle was the "actual model" not the actual bike! The 1948 Team members are from the left 'Stoppa' Clarke, George Kessock, Karl Bloomfield and Clive Parker

Halifax RCC and Bradford RC as well from London.[1]

In the film a PARIS *Tour de France* bike had a starring role, and could be seen, fleetingly, as it was flung into an abyss that appeared to be Malham Cove. This nearly brought tears to the eyes of many cyclists in the audiences! Its

---

scripts
1   Binns quotes riders from both clubs being signed up as well as other 'names' from London's
     BLRC Section including Stoppa Clarke, Johnny Yearsley, Dave Bedwell, Aussie Johnson and
     even Jimmy Saville though the latter was said not to have been taken on.

destruction wasn't of course true. In Figure 19, a promotional photograph taken for the firm with the 1948 PARIS Team in support, the bicycle or at least a bicycle can be seen. In the film much was made of the PARIS being "new

Figure 20 A still from the film shows the head with bilaminations which are absolutely correct for a pre-1948 PARIS *Tour de France*, together with the very special brake cable tunnel.

Continental technology" and very different from British frame construction.

Several of these *Tour de France* machines were claimed to have been built in 1946/7 by Jack Jones for the film[1] and certainly Jones was on the strength of the firm at that time.

In recent years the film has attained a degree of cult following showing as it does those empty wild spaces of upland Yorkshire with an appearance of brooding stillness and poverty no longer seen there and for the social togetherness portrayed by the cast.[2]

Before we leave the subject of the firms' racing team, the firm's entry into cycle racing was also of course a publicity device, though whether Rensch saw it purely in that light is rather doubtful. It certainly would not have been a way of earning money directly! Rensch is known to have been an enthusiast for road racing and when the BLRC came along and in 1945 wanted the new London BLRC committee to organise a London and southern area race must

1   The fact that Jack Jones is said to have built these frames was reported by Michael Butler.
2   A cogent reason for the togetherness was of course the low income levels at that time and as two eminent cyclists Ken Russell and Mike Pears testified in Fellowship News 173, the film makers were a source of countless wheels and tubs claimed by the film extras as broken during the film-making. Stoppa Clarke told Neville Ireland that the PARIS Team was set up for tubs for several years!

have been delighted the way things were going. Stoppa Clarke was the route organiser for the Brighton to London stage in that first post war race in 1945 and as he was a key man in the North London cycling scene it may well have been down to Stoppa (who was Captain of the first team that Rensch decided to support) who helped create the small PARIS team in 1947 and later Rensch teams. A more detailed summary of the Independent riders inputs to and the Team's performances from 1947 to 1949/50 can be found in Chapter 18.

By 1948 the cycling industry was getting properly onto its feet after the war and competition between rival companies and the many small frame builders was becoming intense. The firm had by this time issued its main catalogues and was able to stress again the continental theme of its products not only by the nature of its frame making and colourful finishes but by the choice of models with the *Type Homme* and *Type Dame* being promoted at this time – and stands for the display of the firms products were taken at the London Shows of 1948 and 1949.

During autumn 1948 *Cycling* ran a number of articles on new features of frames and components that would appear in the 1948 Cycle Show at Earl's Court – the first post war London show. As *Cycling* crowed afterwards, Britons had had the spectacle of Paris and Geneva shows ever since the war – but it was the 1948 London Show which had really shown them how to do it! One wonders what our continental friends thought of that claim! However PARIS Cycles now had stand No 44 in the main hall, not a large stand, but there anyway.

Classic PARIS artwork first appeared at this time as well. The advertising box shown below with the famous image of the Eifel Tower[1]. The artwork for the Eifel Tower used in this advertisement is presumably the same work that has become recognised as the imposing and beautifully coloured transfer later seen on the seat tubes of many post war machines.

A little later we had the first appearance in *Cycling* of the

See a selection of the finest Continental Style Lightweights on our

STAND No. 164.

PARIS
CYCLES
RACING AND TOURING

Also the Cycle ridden by John McCullum in the film "*A Boy, a Girl and a Bike.*"

PARIS CYCLE Co.
131/3, Stoke Newington Church Street, London, N.16.

Figure 21 The first use of the Eifel Tower in the firm's published advertisements.

WORLD'S FINEST
RACING CYCLES

BEAUTIFULLY CUT OUT
FRAME LUGS AND THE
SMARTEST CONTINENTAL
FINISH IN THE COUNTRY

MODEL.   Frame Price £14-18-6.   PROMPT REPAIR AND ENAMELLING SERVICE
LIGHTWEIGHT RACING CYCLES   CATALOGUE

PARIS CYCLE CO., 129-133, STOKE NEWINGTON CHURCH STREET, LONDON, N.16

Figure 22 The first use of the Tour de France artwork in the firm's 1950 advertisements.

artwork that would later grace the top tube of many *Tour de France* bicycles
   In 1949 the firm was really becoming mainstream amongst the lightweight
frame makers as can be seen from Figure 23 where the small area in the 1949

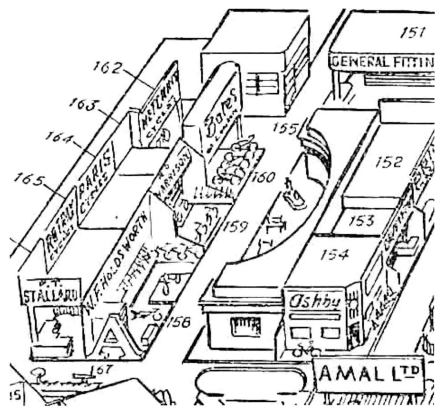

Figure 23:The PARIS Stand for the 1949 London Show was 164, and was amongst some
keen competition!

Show in which the firm (164) had their display can be seen.

The last major visual impact item of the firm's publicity returns to their earlier favoured methods of getting attention in that the publicity was indirect. The advertisement was placed by Accles & Pollock. As was often the case the majority of readers probably saw only the Rensch item and barely noted the A&P issues.

As it happens as the twilight period when Rensch was no longer with the firm approached the whole of the cycle trade was under economic pressure. The firm ceased to promote its solo cycles and concentrated on its tandems, leaving the agents that it had appointed to sell its products. The advertisements they placed are briefly described in Appendix A4.

MR. RENSCH OF PARIS CYCLES, STOKE NEWINGTON, SAYS—

"We reckon to know a bit about tubes"

It was in France in 1935 that I first saw a bronze welded frame. Whether it was practical in action I didn't know, but when I queried the fact, they showed me tests which proved to me that it was the coming thing. We saw the possibilities, came back, and in 1936 produced the first bronze welded lightweight machine in this country. From then on, we cut out brazed frames. Always on the look-out for improvements is our motto to-day as it was then. That is why we use on our best machines what we believe to be the finest tube steel available to-day—KROMO (chrome molybdenum). We use it for frames, forks, handlebars, seat and chain stays, knowing that nothing can do the job better—and we reckon to know quite a bit about tubes, British and Continental.

Here is our latest Rensch Tandem which has KROMO tube throughout.

The sign of a good tube.

KROMO TUBING THROUGHOUT

Made by Accles & Pollock Ltd.

SPECIFICATION

A very rigid and lively machine at home both for fast touring and racing.

FRAME: A. & P. KROMO tubing throughout, specially taper butted at each end; gauges to suit design and purpose for which it is to be used. Frame can be had in the Lateral tube type with triple rear stays, giving an extra degree of rigidity. Lugs of our own design are cut to a superb design, filed and polished. This frame can be had to customer's individual requirements.

SIZE: 22½" x 21½" wheelbase, 39½" or to order. Curved seat tube with short bases. Angles 73° head, 71° seat tubes. FORKS: Rensch Continental type with Continental style fork crown. CHAINWHEEL: set chromium plated. FINISH: The famous Rensch Continental finish in any colours. Chromium plating extra. WHEELS: 26" x 1¼" Chrome Endrick Rims. D.B. Spokes. Chromium plated Tandem Hubs.

TYRES AND TUBES: Dunlop Tandem Sprite. WING NUTS G.B. HANDLEBARS: Alloy Continental type on chromium plated steel stem and clip. MUDGUARDS: Bluemel White Noweight. PEDALS: Four de France rat-trap. GEARS: Simplex 4-speed ¼" chain. SADDLES: Brooks B.17. BRAKES: Chromium plated Cantilever front and rear. CHAIN: Coventry or Renolds. A ⓣ COMPANY

A cycle is as good as its frame

When replying to advertisements, please mention "THE C.T.C. GAZETTE," October, 1950   iii

Figure 24 A tandem illustrates the A&P tubing in 1950 though Rensch himself had moved on by this time.

Chapter 5: Catalogues of the Firms

H RENSCH catalogues

The following section is intended to describe the known firm's catalogues so that readers can appreciate what was offered to the public at what time. Some details of certain models are mentioned here to allow the range and scope of the production to be become apparent. However details of each model and in particular how these models changed over time would be too difficult to explain in this initial section. These details are given for each Rensch and PARIS model in subsequent chapters of this book[1].

The first known catalogue is the one that was referred to in *The Bicycle* of 18 January 1938, which according to *The Bicycle* article writer was "their new catalogue for 1938." No earlier catalogues are known to the V-CC but we live in hope that one may yet turn up!

This 1938 catalogue has no date on it any where so the only way it can be dated is from that description of it quoted above by *The Bicycle* as a catalogue for the firm at 132 Balls Pond Road for 1938. It could perhaps with some justification be regarded as a 1937 catalogue[2] that was perhaps delayed so that it could show the new address of the shop, this being 132 Balls Pond Road ie the second location of the shop. By this time, after may be three years of trading, the catalogue lists 8 solo models, all made with Reynolds 531 and the range also included three tandems.

The statements by Rensch that development of the firm's products with first of all the brazed up frames and then after early 1936 or 1937 the beginnings of welded frame models seems to be confirmed because in this first known catalogue the models numbered 1 to 5 were all brazed frames and, reflecting their status as later additions to the firm's offerings, the welded frames were numbered 6 to 8.

The top model by price at this time was the *Path Model*; this was listed as Model 5 with a lugged frame although now it could also be bought as a welded frame (Model 8). It is interesting to read in the catalogue entries for the welded *Tour de France* and the *Path* the expression that these frames use "*531 tubing of special diameter*", other models are quoted only as using 531 material. This may refer to the oversized 1⅛ inch diameter top tube suitable for lugless frames which Reynolds would have supplied, but could also imply that these models had heavier gauges than standard to suit the requirement for strength for massed start machines in the first case and track competition machines in the second.

---

1   Copies of the catalogues themselves can be seen and downloaded from the V-CC/NCM archive.
2   It was however a fairly common practice of cycle makers to issue their catalogues in the autumn and carrying next years date –and carrying illustrations of next years models.

There is a second version of a 1938 catalogue in the V-CC ME's archive but as it survives it is only a single page though double sided copy of an original brochure. The front of this single pager shows the diagonally shaped H Rensch shop transfer and is printed up "1938 MODELS" on one half it also shows a lugless *Tour de France* model, and this is the same illustration of this model used in the full first 1938 catalogue and chosen by *The Bicycle* to illustrate their Round the Trade article. The reverse side of the single pager then had some of the other models described and prices with short specifications. However these models differed from the first catalogue list and were now numbered in a new sequence. It listed as the top model by price not the previous holder the *Path* model but a diamond framed model called the *Galibier* (stated to be "An ideal machine for the massed start cyclist"). This machine when bought as Model 1a had a welded frame and if bought as Model 1b a brazed frame. This **H Rensch** diamond frame machine, that was stated to be built to "*Tour de France* design" and had all its main triangle tubes at 1⅛ in diameter (even for the brazed version?), should not be confused with the later post war *Galibier* which had a main strut frame and would be in any case the **PARIS** *Galibier*. The Rensch *Tour de France* had meanwhile become the Model 2a and was also, somewhat confusingly, offered as Model 3 if bought with wire-on rims instead of the sprints which were provided with Tour de France Model 2a. No tandems were listed in this partial catalogue. It is clear that by this time these model numbers could not be following any consecutive development of the models within the firm.

Then for 1939, but available only after the move to 362 Old Street in March[1], was a completely revised catalogue. This was a thicker but smaller format booklet of 42 pages each 4¼ by 5¼ inch. It showed a broadly similar range to the earlier Rensch catalogues but now there were no model numbers to help (or confuse?) the student of Renschiana, and of course at that size the illustrations could hardly be used to see details with any clarity. The 1939 range of some ten solo models still included the diamond frame *Galibier*, though this pre-war top of the range model now shared its top price spot with a new model –the brazed frame *Pyrenees*. Another new lugged model the *San Reno* was also offered. The *Path* model was available lugged or lugless to choice. Historians further grit their teeth when reading the catalogue as none of these potentially fabulous machines are illustrated at all! Three tandems were on offer.

Before we leave the pre war Rensch catalogues it is worthwhile noting that welded frame models were stated to be *"Welded together with our very special welding process and built throughout with Reynolds 531 double taper butted tubes, manufactured specially to Rensch specification. The seat tube, top tube and down tube are of 1⅛ inch*

---

1   *Cycling* 29 March. New address announced and new catalogue now said to be actually ready for collection.

diameter and of special gauges to suit weight of rider and the size of frame". This expression can be compared to the expression used by Gillott brochure writers[1] when describing their lugless bronze brazed technique which took the form *"using special gauge Reynolds butted 531 tubing. Top, Seat and Down tubes are 1¹/₈inch diameter".* The chances are that these two instances, the use by Rensch and the use by Gillott, both use phrases lifted direct from Reynolds sale literature.

Whereas 'welded' or bronze welded construction is known to have been practised by Rensch from 1936/7 onwards, it is not known whether such lugless frames were ever provided with bilaminations (decorative false lugs) before WWII. Now how excruciating is it that those top models *Galibier, Pyrenees* and *San Reno* were not illustrated –nor have any survived? True bilaminations are commonly found on the post war **PARIS** models, but at present all pre war models appear to be either lugged versions of the *Continental Road Racer* or lugless *Tour de France* models without such additional ornamentation.[2] The Rensch catalogues are silent upon this issue and before WWII it is understood that the technique was not in use and that the phrase "bilamination" was still to be coined.[3]

PARIS Cycle catalogues

After WWII all the catalogues are in the name of **PARIS Cycles** as this was now the formal name of the firm. There appear to have been either an A5 sized catalogue, or at least a collection of A5 single sheets, issued probably some time in 1946 or 1947; none of the surviving originals were dated. As far as we can tell this initial range did not include any **H RENSCH** models. However, there were **H RENSCH** models or framesets in the range by the period 1948-1953. These were the best diamond frame solo or tandem models to be sold by the firm and were presumably there in part to help retain the older and perhaps more staid but better financed customer[4].

Later these small single pagers were replaced for general circulation by at least three printings of a larger general catalogue. In addition to the early A5 sheets which covered three diamond frames models and the *Galibier* there was a dedicated *Galibier* strut frame model brochure. This was set out in black and white on a single A4 sheet which was printed on both sides and then folded to A5 size.

Unfortunately all of these catalogue substitutes were undated, but there are clues within their text or the prices quoted in them to allow them to be roughly dated.

1   Shown in a Gillot 1950 catalogue in Lightweight Cycle Catalogues Volume 1, JPMPF 2005
2   With the exception that frame #1081 which was ordered in late 1939 and delivered in 1940 does have prototype but definite bilaminations which must have been pre war in origin.
3   Bi-lamination is the name for this technique defined earlier as ornamental reinforcement of fillet brazed joints that was only coined by Claud Butler sometime in the 1940s. The technique was not available from Claud Butlers in 1939 but was already in use on their top models by 1949 as shown by their catalogues on the V-CC/NCM archive.
4   Harold Jones explains" Renschs were always more restrained in the use of colours when compared with the fades and bright contrasting colours of gaudy PARISs"

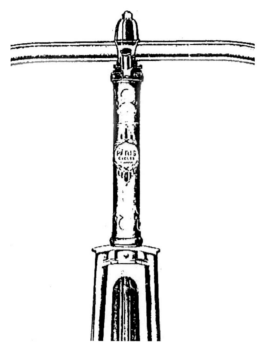

Figure 25 The new Galibier from
the rear page of the 1946/7
brochure.
The first ever view of the new PARIS
head badge and bilaminations?

Early small (A5) catalogue or pages

Only loose sheets from what may have been the initial **PARIS** catalogue
are now available– these are the single model sheets referred to above. This
collection covered only three diamond frame models and the illustrations were
of poor quality and small size - looking as if copied from the pre war art
work. There are several glaring errors in the pages of this version, perhaps
suggesting some hurry in their preparation or an amateur approach to them.
In the firm's address – and this would have been the first advertising from the
new Stoke Newington Church Street shop- the London area code is shown
as N6 where it should have been N16, whilst for the new *Galibier* model the
spelling for this prestige model is given incorrectly as Galabier[1]. In addition
to these errors there are two clues to its early date – the shop address is given
as 131 (only) Stoke Newington Church Street which was the building newly
taken on by Rensch for the firm – a single building number for the firm's
address is not used in any of the later documents – perhaps simply another
error but perhaps too indicating that at first only this newly acquired building
was in use for the firm? The second clue is the price of the *Galibier* –16gns

---

1   Probably just a misspelling, but possibly a phonetic spelling by someone who knew the word not
from the French mountain but, having returned from the war in North Africa, was familiar with the
djellaba or galabea worn by Arabs? The staff of PARIS has often been described at this time as
many returned ex-combatants.

in this early version whilst other, recognisably later 1947 or 1948, catalogues list the *Galibier* as £16.18.6d, and this price increase, as has been seen in the preceding section, was first quoted in a PARIS Cycles advertisement in *Cycling* in October 1947[1]. As it happens images of these small sheet advertisements have survived because they were used in–perhaps only produced for – a special *Cycling* magazine. This was known as the *Cycling Annual* and may have been a supplement only produced in the early post-war years.

It seems probable that **PARIS** rushed through somewhat dated 'copy' when asked for art work for this production. It is perhaps also noteworthy that from this point onwards the catalogues quote only the price for the frameset, and no longer quote a price for a complete bicycle, and consequently the frame fittings described in these later catalogues are just the frame fittings –seat pin, bottom bracket, lamp bracket on some models and the head set. At this point it is worth noting that the description of **Rensch** and **PARIS** enamelling options, always previously referred to as "famous Continental finishes" start to refer also to "glass hard enamel dried by the new Infra Red process, lines and colours added with painstaking care." New post-war equipment and/or new employees are suggested?

The later large folded (A3) catalogues

These were of an unusual size, 22 by 16 inches, though most copies now found have been folded to a nominal A4 from their approximately A3 size due to photocopying and book shelf storage needs. The original large size may have been so they could be used as wall chart displays as well being a talking point! When folded to A4 they gave 8 pages for mailing to the ordinary customer. They were attractively printed in multiple colours, red, black and white or green, black and white, not in full colour print. The first two versions give the firm's address as 131-133 Stoke Newington Church Street (SNCS). Copies of these versions in the ME's collection have been marked up in pencil to note that latterly the firm's address was 129-133 SNCS but whether the last version of the catalogue was indeed changed to this address is not known.

The earliest known version is said to have had green colour flashes and to have photographs of the successful 1947 BLRC team on the right hand edge of what was the front 'page' when folded. These photographs together with the price shown for the *Galibier* (£16 18s 6d) suggest the edition can be dated to be issued not before late 1947 or early 1948 as the BLRC team won the Brighton –Glasgow 6 day event in August 1947 and as noted earlier it was not before September that PARIS put an advertisement mentioning this success in *Cycling*. The second brochure was largely similar in technical content to the first. However, the strip of illustrations on the right edge of the front

---

1   Chapter 4 Ref 20 op cit

sheet now showed the bilaminations of what was referred to as the "New **PARIS** Welded *Tour de France*" model instead of the photos of the 1947 team members.

It is thought that this must have been the 1948 edition for the major **PARIS** promotion at the 1948 London Show, so could just have been brought out especially for that event, as this could be expected to show the new, presumably the definitive 1949 model of *Tour de France*. As noted earlier the difficulty of the public getting copies of this catalogue was the point of a specially worded advertisement in *Cycling* in December 1948. Copies

Figure 26 The first green and white A3 size catalogue

of this version of the catalogue printed in red rather than green have been reported but so far none have been shown to the V-CC Marque Enthusiast who holds only a photocopy of this middle period version. It remains possible that this version is in fact a reprint made for the 1949 London Show period, the original version made for the 1948 Show not having survived. The final known version was essentially unaltered[1].

It seems probable that this edition could have been produced in 1952 or slightly later as an original green catalogue which has prices for four styles of tandem, is identical to a photocopy which someone has independently dated as October 1952[2]. In all these large A3 catalogues the range of frames was six **PARIS** and three **RENSCH** models of solo bicycles and one each of the tandems until the second 1948 or 9 catalogue. Although some frames of both marques were bronze welded, brazed versions of some models were offered. The **PARIS** *Galibier* was the most expensive model at £16.18.6d. but the **RENSCH** diamond models tended to share top of the range status.

The catalogues refer only to welded and brazed frame construction, but one of the features that has made the **PARIS** marque so revered has been the beautifully filed and shaped false 'lugwork' or bilamination on many of the surviving frames. It seems clear that post war these decorative features were on offer from the outset on selected **PARIS** machines as it was first illustrated

1   A facsimile of this catalogue is available from the Veteran-Cycle Club.
2   Earlier versions of the catalogues show only two or three prices for tandem models.

in the 1946/7 *Galibier* brochure though not mentioned in the text. See further discussion of this aspect under the detailed history of the bilaminations in Chapter 17.

Mention should be made of an unusual and special **PARIS** cycle; though this one never appeared in the firm's catalogues, it did appear in *Cycling*. This machine was announced in the London Show in November 1950[1] and was the product, perhaps of some extramural marketing by Harry Rensch from his weekend activities. It was a side by side two seater, the *Social Cycle* , being a trike with a bench seat, tiller steering and single front wheel. It seems that this machine was inspired by Rensch's patronising of the Butlins (or was it Pontins) Holiday Camps, venues where an overall entertainment for the family was offered and private traffic free coastal promenades allowed the use of these leisure machines. It was this model that was effectively Rensch's grande finale in the cycle world. Mike Butler[2] has recalled the somewhat sad sight of Rensch, having left PARIS Cycles behind him, being seen managing a fleet of Social Cycles on the promenade at Southend a year or two after he had left **PARIS.**

One other model that neither the catalogues nor *Cycling* ever mentioned is the **Paris Sport**. Frank Hernandez feels that this model was a mainstream, PARIS product and recalls the model being around in the early 1950s[3]. A number of **Paris Sports** are listed in the V-CC register, and their frame numbers show they were made between 1949 to 1951. Whether there was someone in the firm who joined at the 1949 changeover of staff or there was a policy to introduce a sports bike model at this time is unknown at present – further discussion of this model and its un related Paris Sport cousins is to be found in Chapter 11.

Amongst a few accessories Rensch also made for sale a uniquely Continental (what else?) styled luggage rack that fitted beautifully

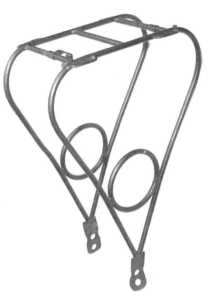

Figure 27 The curvaceous Continental accessory

1   *Cycling* 23 November 1950
2   M Butler Telephone conversation January 2006
3   F Hernandez conversation with AJES March 2006

with the shapely frame of his *Dame* multi-tube frame but was aimed also at other riders, it was priced at 18s6d.

Finally from the catalogues, the firm offered two sets of exercise rollers – the Home Trainer with 5 inch diameter rollers at 8gns and the Club Model with 8 inch rollers at 10gns. The Home trainer had first appeared in advertisements in July 1948.

"PARIS" HOME TRAINER

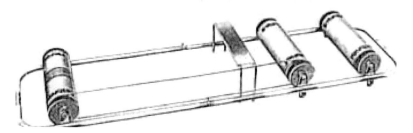

Figure 28 The PARIS rollers doubtless to a Stoppa Clarke design

Figure 29 A rare survivor seen in 2009.

An Introduction to the Bicycle Models

What's in a bike? Let us say -Hetchins-(for sake of argument!) - for some people at least it might mean curly chain stays, though for others just elaborate and intricate lug designs, for Bates perhaps Cantiflex tubes, for Granby may be the all brazed up frame or the taper tube frame-set, whilst for PARIS? - The main strut *Galibier* frame or may be some delicate bilaminations? Well, there is rather more to all of these marques than a single feature which may be on just one model or from one period – as owners of any of these marques can tell you. It may take some time in reading through this account to get to the essentials of the H Rensch and PARIS marque. It is such a shame that Harry Rensch never sat down and recorded what his design aims were either from the outset in the mid thirties, or when later he came out with his re-borne PARIS bicycles. Perforce we must rely on the remaining written words as no one now recalls talking to Rensch about his raison d'être. We can simply re-state some of the catalogues' words and phrases[1], always remembering the human vagaries of the copywriters who were themselves perhaps not completely familiar with what went on in the firm's workshop. Here are just a few :-

- The finest machines available for the Club cyclist -
- No innovations are ever adopted by us until they have been well and truly tried and tested -
- Welded cycles have been used with great success in many large countries for quite a few years -
- The cycles used in the Tour de France cycle race are welded -
- Welding is not experimental, but a sound engineering practice -

The account of the bicycles which follows is taken largely from the catalogues with occasional reference to surviving machines[2]. However a caveat must be made and that is that, in the absence of the works record books from both the Rensch and PARIS works, identification of some of the models can be difficult – many of the surviving machines have already been refinished several times and in nearly all cases have had alterations to the style of their finish or of their components.

---

1   Taken from the 1939 Rensch catalogue. The descriptive term 'welded' (or its modification 'bronze welding') was used in the firm's very first brochures. In terms of current usage (in 2012) it is thought that the most appropriate term to describe the process or technique used by H Rensch and PARIS bicycles would be 'lugless construction.'
2   It is intended to improve the accuracy of this record as more surviving bicycles are examined and recorded in sufficient detail.

Chapter 6: Rensch and PARIS Road Racing models

Rensch Continental Road Racing

The Rensch Continental Road Racing (CRR) was the first model made by Rensch and the first shown in the earliest known (first of 1938) catalogue. It was listed as Model No 1 in that catalogue. The illustration below, from that earliest catalogue, shows shapely cutaway lugs on the head tube, a front fork top with a short central dagger from the epaulette type crown and a long chamfered top eye on the seat stays. The frame can be seen to have the diamond shaped Rensch transfer set on cross-banding on the head and seat tubes.

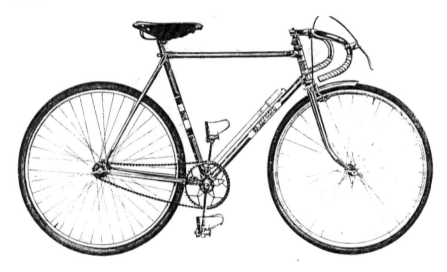

Figure 30 Illustration of CRR from the 1938 catalogue

The CRR had a brazed and lugged frame - "a combination of British and Continental design. It has most of the advantages of both types and is steady while sprinting, hill climbing and on the flat. A really superb machine for the British cyclist." The frame was described as having "special rigid chain stays, small section seat stays and lugs cut to a special Continental design".

The wheel base at 41inches was shorter than its sister machine the *Tour de France* (TdF)though the frame materials (Reynolds 531) and dimensions were otherwise the same. As the earliest information we have is 1938 when the TdF had already been introduced we have no idea whether, when the CRR and the Rensch marque were first marketed, there was such a strong emphasis on their

Figure 31a The CRR
head from the cata-
logues (Left)
b The CRR head in the
steel (right)

Continental attributes. Jack Salt writing in 1948[1] recalls how, as a member of the well defeated British team to the Worlds in 1934, the team bikes of the successful French team were avidly examined. The result was that wheel bases of team bikes went to 42 inches, frames got taller and angles steeper –the birth of Upright frames.

Steeper angles such as 74/72 were nevertheless offered by the firm and some machines were so built[2]. Competitors such as Granby were already advertising their Upright frame models with these steep angles in 1937[3]

As we have seen in the later A&P advertisements it was this model that set Rensch on the road to success when he first started. It seems to have been a successful frame that he could rely upon – initially to adorn with his always famous bright glassy colourful finishes and it appears that it was this model he would gradually experiment on before introducing welded frame construction as he and his builders developed their bronze welding skills.

The CRR was obviously aimed at the specialist market of clubmen - serious cyclists who valued continental influences. It was an all round useful design but its high quality materials of specially selected lightweight tubing meant it would be seen as a serious riders machine available for example with a choice of round or oval section front forks. It could be set up for Dunlop High Pressure wire-ons 26 or 27 inch, though sprints were optional as were BSA chain wheel and pedals.

In the second 1938 catalogue changes were truly being rung as already, within a few months, it had become listed as Model 2b (wired–ons) and Model 3b (sprints), just slightly cheaper, at £0. 5s less than the newly introduced

1   Cycling 26 May 1948
2   See secondhand bike specifications in Appendix 3
3   The Bicycle 19 October 1937

welded *Tour de France*. It had therefore been displaced from its original priority in the model sequence and additionally had been knocked from the catalogue top price position by the diamond framed *Galibier* as well as by the *TdF* model.

Figure 32a   A Continental Road Racing model and b its head

By 1939 the *CRR* in the catalogue had regained price equality with the TdF though it had now lost the Continental name and had become the *Professional Road Racing* model "It has been used with great success in many parts of the World during the 1938 season .... Makes it one of the World's best productions...... designed and built throughout on Continental lines". It was technically unaltered, although the catalogue now additionally claimed it as having " all lugs cut out to a unique Continental design by hand and filed with great care". So, professional it was, but still continental! The 1939 catalogue noted that it had "double taper butted tubes made especially to Rensch's own special specification in 531 alloy steel".

It was available with all the more expensive components listed for the other Rensch models already described.

The seat stays appear to have a wide say ½ inch diameter at the top with a 2 inch long cut sloping top, the front fork shoulder looking orthodox with a central dagger and curved returns on the shoulders, though solid or twin plate crowns were available to choice. Mudguards were optional.

There was somewhere in the Rensch and PARIS firmament a decision – which must surely have been made must be during WWII's moments - when Rensch formulated his new firm's name and strategy – when this oldest of models, though latterly with a new introductory first name, would become the base model for the new post - war marque.

Figure 33 The 1939 catalogue showing a lugged frame for the Professional (as the Continental would be known from now on), the illustration still shows RENSCH as the down tube transfer? The quality of this illustration is particularly poor because of the size of the original drawing..

PARIS Professional Road Racing

Post-war the PARIS *Professional* was initially promoted by the firm in one of the series of single model/single page A5 size brochures using similar wording to that of the *Professional* in the full 1939 catalogue except for two things. The first was the deletion of the reference to 1938 experience and the second was that the specification of the frame had to alter because the frame of this model was now lugless. Consequently the specification now borrowed– with slightly altered wording – that used for the *Tour de France*.

According to the catalogue the difference in wheelbase length of these two models had gone at this time[1], both shared a wheelbase of 42 inches and the same frame angles of 73° head and 71° seat. In the entry under frame size for the *Professional* was the rubric "Frame made to customers own design and requirements or in the now very widely used *Tour de France* design." The individual pamphlets issued at this time had a drawing of a bicycle showing the completely lugless welded and double butted frame whose enamel finish on the front forks and frame panels closely resembled but differed in detail from those of the *Tour de France*.

Despite the increased similarity between the *Professional* and the *Tour de France* , there had been a change in pricing of the pair as in *Cycling* of 13 Feb-

1 One wonders whether this was a real change –could it have just been the copywriters for the catalogue getting it wrong?

ruary 1946 the firm had advertised the *Professional* at £8.17s 6d compared to £12.12s 6d for the *Tour de France* . The apparently inexplicable price differential between the two models can probably be accounted for by the additional

Figure 34 PARIS *Professional* from a brochure/leaflet of about 1947 now clearly transferred as a PARIS.

detail work required on the bilaminations of the *Tour de France.*

The *Professional* model was used by the PARIS Team in the early post war BLRC massed start road races and this model can be seen in the hands of Stoppa Clarke in 1947 races.

Sometime in late 1947 or 1948 the firm introduced their well known large A3 sized folded catalogue. The *Professional* was now again described as having a 41 inch wheelbase and the price had risen to a perhaps more realistic £11.18s.6d. In the specification the front fork crown was described as 'Filed and neatly polished' but the drawing appeared to be the same as that used in the earlier single model advertising sheets which although not clear appears to show an epaulette with central dagger type of fork crown.

However, later versions of this folded catalogue appear to show that the front fork top is the twin plate crown type without the central dagger – there is however no alteration to the wording of the specification of the Professional to confirm this change. However there were also changes in later machines – described in the next section – which were certainly made but which were not mentioned at all in the catalogues or the technical press of the time.

1   All post war PARIS prices are for the frame only – as a small specialist producer of frames it was doubtless better marketing to avoid the high purchase tax that a buyer paid if a whole bicycle was purchased.

Figure 35 PARIS *Professional* from the 1948 folded catalogue, is this a central dagger type of fork crown?

Figure 36 PARIS Professional from a catalogue thought to be 1952 – note different fork crown and other differences between this drawing and the earlier drawing.

Reflections on this model and its features

There are a number of features of the frame set that were varied by the firm over the years through at least five distinctive time phases. First was the pre-war Rensch Continental period with the very early brazed up framesets with finely filed lugs. The second phase was the short lived pre-war Rensch Professional advertised in 1939. The third and all subsequent phases refer of course to the PARIS Professional . The third was the early post–war lugless model, followed by the later 1940's fourth phase and then the remaining fifth and final phase, which was not ever described or illustrated, but which is represented on the register with post 1950 machines.   All these lugless phases presumably share the use of the special Reynolds 531 tube set sold by TI Reynolds for lugless or bronze welded frames. This tube set included the familiar oversized, 1⅛ inch diameter top tube, to match the size of the double butted down tube and seat tubes, the latter with extra length for the seat pillar clip and finally the oversized but thin walled tubular bottom bracket housing for the Bayliss Wiley oil bath bottom bracket. This set of tubes might have been created for Harry Rensch as the Rensch catalogues refer to tube sets specially selected for his models, but certainly post-war the TI Reynolds lugless tube set was also commercially available to other frame builders, and of course a number of famous marques brought out lugless models and retained them in their ranges.

In the *Professional* there were four or five features that appear to have changed with the time phases. These are :-

- Front fork crown, either the epaulette with central dagger (ECD) type or the twin plate crown (TPC).
- The head badge or emblem, either the Eifel Tower badge (PET) or the Rensch or PARIS diamond transfer (RD or PD).
- The top eyes (seat stay tops) either chamfered (CH) or tapered and curved (TC).
- The chain stay type, either special rigid (SR) or Rensch elliptical[1] (RE)
- The front/rear drop outs, either Osgear type (OG)or Plain/Simplex (PS) [These are never visible in the catalogue drawings or mentioned in the specifications.]

---

1   The pre war catalogues refer to the *Special Rigid* chainstays fitted to the ***Professional*** and ***Path*** models whilst other models have no description of the chainstays or simply say "tube sets manufactured to Rensch's own specification". The elliptical chainstay thought to be the "*Rensch Chainstay*" was fitted on most post war **PARIS** ***Tour de France***, ***Galibier*** and some ***Professional*** models as well as on the post war ***Rensch Champion du Monde*** and ***Rensch Tour de France*** models as revealed by surviving machines. However, the catalogues themselves only refer to its use on the 1939 ***Pyrenees*** model and the post war ***Rensch Champion du Monde***.

It has to be admitted that these "phases" in the machine's history may in reality turn out to be random differences due to customers' or frame builders' preferences or just due to the timing of purchasing by the firm of stock items e.g. the badge type or drop out pattern. In the absence of build records we may never know whether or not the changes were thus incidental or really were intentional.

The table summarises the phases and their associated features :-

Feature	Phase 1	Phase 2	Phase 3	Phase 4	Phase 5
Fork crown	ECD	ECD	ECD?	TPC	ECD
Head badge	RD	RD	PD	PET	PET
Top eyes	CH	CH	TC	TC	CH
Chain stays	SR	SR	SR	RE	RE
Drop outs	OG	OG	OG	OG	PS

Note the initials for the features are explained in the bullet points listed above this table.

There is a final feature that many owners will associate with Harry Rensch's diamond frame PARIS machines – the large stencilled French script seen on the top surface of the top tube or sometimes on the down tube. Strictly speaking this stencilling seems to have been offered on both the *Tour de France* and the *Professional* in the mid 1940's and may have gone – out of fashion? – by 1949/50. Of course the stencilling for the *Professional* uses the French spelling for the *Professionale*.

A question of history must hang over the initial Rensch Continental – the brazed up lugged frame machine.   Was it this model that set Harry on the road to success when he first started? His newly established firm – set up in 1935 as far as we know- would need a successful frame that he could rely upon – initially to adorn with his latterly famous bright glassy hard colourful finishes. In later advertisements for Accles & Pollock[1] tubing Harry would say he first saw bronze welding in France in 1935. Convinced by its use in all the *Tour de France* competition bikes, he "came back, and in 1936 produced the first bronze welded lightweight machine in this country."   One can only presume that it must have been the *Continental* model that he would gradually transmogrify to a welded frame construction –but which would then be called the *Tour de France* model as he and his builders developed their bronze welding skills.

---

1   Advertisements placed between 1950 to 1952 by A&P for their Kromo tubesets which featured evidence from Rensch on the introduction of lugless frames

A number of things point that way. The catalogue wording shows that the PARIS diamond frame models were aimed at the specialist market of clubmen and probably those that Rensch knew best – the local North London clubmen and others who shared an interest in Continental cycle racing. These were serious minded racing cyclists who valued Continental designs in their machines. What better new development to offer customers than a reasonably close copy of such French machines?

One intriguing question has to be raised a this point. Harry Rensch is known to have worked with Hobbs of Barbican before he set up the Rensch shop. One of the Hobbs brothers is reported to have said of Rensch "Oh, we remember Harry- obsessed with anything Continental he was!" Now that can be taken two ways. The straight inference is that Rensch's love of European (continental) practice was being indicated, but there is the second less cosy inference, that Hobbs was referring to a thought that the new Rensch machines coming out from 1936 onwards may have resembled rather too closely for comfort the new Hobbs Continental models –a range of top quality models introduced in 1936 –and just possibly being developed when Harry was a member of the Hobbs firm?[1]

Figure 37 Was this 1936/7 Hobbs Continental
Superbe Harry Rensch's inspiration?

---

1   This issue is further discussed in Chapter 16.

Chapter 7: Rensch and PARIS Tour de France(s)

The *Tour de France* (TdF) model was and is for many cyclists the archetypal H Rensch or PARIS machine. Indeed in terms of surviving diamond frame machines, this model is about three quarters of all known machines[1]. Its name was doubtless chosen by Rensch because of the strong road racing associations with the French road race, and had by the mid 1930's already become synonymous with Continental style and racing practice, both of which Harry Rensch had fallen in love with and was at this time at such pains to promote.

Figure 38 Rensch *Tour de France* from 1938 catalogue

For many owners and riders this model was the clubman's dream. The model appears to have originated from the *Continental Road Racing* first seen in 1935 as a lugged frame, becoming lugless[2] by 1936/7 and post WWII as either a PARIS or Rensch model as a bilaminate frame. Towards the end of its days, it again became a lugged frame. It is as the bilaminate model that it is most commonly seen with its elegant tracery bilaminations and the unusual, arguably somewhat heavy looking, oversized 1⅛ diameter top tube the two features rendering it instantly recognisable. It had less obvious features too, a separate metal clip as the seat tube saddle pin clamp and the not quite so visible Bayliss Wiley Patent Oil Bath bottom bracket unit. As a PARIS model it was often available in bewilderingly beautiful, though for some observers,

1   R&P Register December 2011.
2   Lugless frames were referred to in the catalogues as welded or sometimes as bronze welded, these terms are used here interchangeably.

overly gaudy and bright, frame enamelling that made the marque famous. Although the early illustrations in the Rensch catalogues were only in black and white and were small it is possible to see in them that the finish included a contrasting head tube colour that extended someway along the top and down tubes as long tapering pennants ending on the down tube roughly where the white panel carrying the H RENSCH started. The seat tube carried contrast bands and within one of the bands was the Rensch diamond transfer –this was sometimes also used on the head tube as well, though a brass badge with a painted rider was also available. Incidentally these early pre-war illustrations of the H RENSCH *Tour de France* shows the bicycle as set up in its 'Sunday best' with Osgear, Durax Continental chain set and Gloria brake levers, though more readily available and lower cost English components were specified in the text!

The first known catalogue describes the model as "designed to meet the needs of the British cyclist who desires to ride in long distance or massed start races" – an aim probably calculated to make the old farts who ran the British cycling world of time trialling grind their teeth – Rensch started the way he intended to go! In this 1938 catalogue, in which Rensch had already adopted lugless frame building as his preferred method, the specification describes the *Tour de France* as "welded together under continental conditions in the Rensch workshops using 531 tubing "of special diameters as used by many leading cycle manufacturers on the continent." Its forks were "Rensch special oval continental type with rake to suit the head angle and with a crown genuine continental of pleasing design". The fork illustrated in the small drawing of the complete bicycle appears to have an orthodox crown with short central dagger from its shoulder. The frame shown in the catalogue illustrations was clearly lugless; the wheelbase was suitable for distance riding at 41½inches and the head and seat angles were 73°/71°. The wheels had 27inch Dunlop tubulars on Tabuchi rims on steel Constrictor hubs, with double butted spokes, tied and soldered. The transmission was Williams C1000 and Osgear as an option. Brake sets were Gloria or Bowden steel (alloy equivalents were also available as extras); the saddle was a Brooks B17 narrow or Flyer and the standard handlebars were Binda bends.

In the late 1930s the *Tour de France* design was fast becoming "Le Pur Sang" of racing bicycles. It had been born of continental racing stock and after several years it and its blood line were getting into their competition stride. The catalogues introduce it as "Our World Famous *Tour de France* model" and say "This model is the outcome of years of hard work both in racing and in engineering. It has been used in many parts of the world with great success. Built for the Massed Start and long distance racing, it is also very responsive for both hill climbing and sprinting. In the second catalogue, the smaller and more business like brochure of 1938, there were however changes- the frame specifications remained as before but new model numbers had been assigned. It seems clear that the TdF remained the mainstay of the firm's top class models, but a number of variations on this so successful theme had been introduced. As well as number changes there were two new framesets, one welded and one brazed, that both used frames of the *Tour de France* design – and which had been given priority by numbering them No 1a and No 1b to match their top of the range prices, together with slightly more expensive componentry.

This new No 1 model, which had the classic and well proven TdF diamond frame, was named, confusingly for later generations, the *Galibier*. This short lived diamond frame model has been described here as part of the *Tour de France* story, and should not be confused with the later and far more important *Galibier* model with a main strut frame. The *TdF*, with its welded frame and strongly identified with Massed Start competition work, now became Model 2a. It was available with wheels using Maplewood rims and 1 inch Dunlop tubulars. The brakes were Bowden steel and Osgear gears and a Brooks Flyer saddle were specified, the machine being without mudguards. The same welded frame was also available, perhaps as a top clubman's machine as Model 3, which now came with Dunlop high pressure wire-ons, Gloria brake set, Osgear and Bluemels Noweight Duplex mudguards.

Though the *Tour de France* was the first model mentioned in the Rensch 1939 catalogue it was the diamond frame *Galibier* model that was listed as the top model for the firm. This 1939 *Galibier* used the welded frame of the *TdF* though in its case a lugged frame was listed as an option. The welded frame version at least must have retained the classic 1⅛ inch top tube as this was required on a lugless constructed frame[1]. This 1939 top model's specification did however include the first ever mention of the option on a road frame[2] of the twin plate front fork crown – the standard road fork crown up to this point being "a very neat cut out crown.".

The welded *Tour de France* model was listed in 1939 as having a wheelbase of 42 inches instead of 41½ inches. The front forks for this model were still orthodox- "with superbly cut out continental crown, filed and polished neatly" but for the first time another feature was mentioned – the seat stays were now described as "small section seat stays, shaped and polished at the top ends, giving a very fast appearance." The illustrations in the catalogue of 1939 are too small to show the detail of the seat stay topeyes but it would be fascinating to know just what was being described here – could it be that this was the first appearance of the elegant long topeyes that taper from ⅜ inch down to almost ⅛ over lengths of 2 to 3 inches – a feature that graced the early post war Paris frames? It is interesting too

---

1   In fact Reynolds supplied a special set of 531 tubing for lugless frames, as shown by a catalogue page issued by Gillots in 1953 and published in Lightweight Cycle Catalogues Volume 1 JPMPF 2005

2   Until this time the twin plate crown had been offered only for the Path model.

that the "Rensch special reinforced rear brake bridge" is mentioned for the first time in the *TdF* section of the 1939 catalogue[1]. The use of an orthodox fork crown on the pre-war Rensch *TdF* seems to be borne out by early Rensch frames, cf frame *TdF* #145 which has a simple lugged fork crown and whose genuineness can be judged by the fact that the frame is stamped 145 on both fork and bottom bracket. Indeed how much should be read into the timing of changes by means of the catalogues could be questionable. For example, only in 1939's catalogue do we find the first mention of "special neat Rensch Continental chain stay protector" Yet this item was already present on TdF #145 - one of the earliest survivors and which is assumed to be 1936 or thereabouts.

It can be noted here that *TdF* frame #1081 – said by its first owner to have been ordered in late 1939 and delivered in spring 1940 as a PARIS *TdF* (the earliest known PARIS *TdF*) has orthodox front forks which though in principle like those of #145, yet has the central dagger of the long type known to PARIS cognoscenti as of the floorboards nail construction and its frame has tapering seat stay topeyes. It has to be said that all these features of #1081 are somewhat irregular and cruder than the smooth and curved later versions.

Figure 39a Early taper seat stays   b Mid 1940s taper seat stays

TdF #1081 was also built with the important and apparently "out of period" head tube bilaminations though these are simpler and indeed cruder than those used later in post war production.

1 This feature was never mentioned in any later post war literature from the firm, yet remained a highly characteristic PARIS feature useful for Rensch/PARIS differentiation.

Figure 40 a Head on #1081 b Head on mid 1940s TdF of late1939

In 1939 there was now a choice of wheels for the *TdF* - either sprints and tubulars or high pressure steel rims and mudguards, and choice of C1000 and Osgear or Durax and Simplex transmission. Handlebars with 1 inch alloy bars on an adjustable extension were now offered in Tour de Angleterre, Binda, Bailey or Pelissier shapes. The chain set now illustrated is the Williams C1200, its price at 16s being less than the Durax at 22/6d specified for its up market competitor the *Galibier* diamond frame, though more than the normal option the Williams C1000 at 10/9d[1]. Post war most Paris machines would be sold with the Williams C34, the industry standard for a decent quality chain set, until in the late 1940s it became possible again to import high quality continental accessories.

Before leaving the pre-war *TdF* and moving on to the post –war situation it is interesting to note that the intended flagship of the pre war Rensch *TdF* designs, the diamond frame *Galibier*, was by 1939 also offered with a four speed block and Durax Continental chain set using special ½ x 3/32 inch chain. Handlebar widths of 15,16 or 17 inches could be supplied.

Post war catalogues continued to give the *TdF* model its first place in the catalogue though now of course the firm's name had become PARIS. In the undated but probably 1945/6 A5 separate page advertisement pamphlet the text is generally identical to the 1939 Rensch material wording, although the wheelbase is now quoted as 42 inches with the fork crown being "a very neat crown filed and polished to give a smart appearance" and the seat stay tops

1   Brown Bros Catalogue dated 1938

"give a real super finish to the machine." For the first time the specification includes the Bayliss Wiley Patent Oil Bath special bottom bracket unit, though its presence in *TdF* #145 shows that this was already in use in the welded pre-war machines and the unit had been available on the market since the early 1930's[1]. The illustration of the *TdF* used in the pamphlets of 1945/6 was of poor quality being a negative reversal of a line drawing that was similar to that which had appeared in the 1939 catalogue. It differed from the 1938 illustration by showing a Williams C1200 chain set and a longer hand pump, whilst the front fork crown still appears to be an orthodox crown with a small central dagger. Figure 41 shows this illustration, taken from a post war pamphlet but turned in this case into an orthodox projection in which it is nevertheless possible to see that a lugless construction frame has been drawn.

Figure 41 The first post war TdF pamphlet illustration which in fact followed the 1939 catalogue drawings –with minor modifications

In the remainder of the post war catalogues the TdF continued its place of honour though slowly evolving during the period 1947 to 1952. The frame's wheel base now reverted to 41 inches, but longer 42 inch wheelbase frames could be ordered.

It did not stay long like that –and perhaps in the steel it never was –after all we have seen from *TdF* #1081 that by 1939/40 there were prototype bi-laminations on the front of the head tube and other putative changes. In the 1947/8 full A3 size catalogue which showed the 1947 Paris team members on the front cover it was now promoted as the PARIS *Tour de France* with welded frame and retained its oversize 1⅛ top tube. Figure 42 is taken from this first

1   Bayliss Wiley advertisement in Cycling during 1932.

obviously new post war catalogue and now the drawing shows that it also had the twin plate front fork crown, once the prerogative of the *Path* or the diamond frame *Galibier*, the other erstwhile top model.

Figure 42 1947/8 *TdF* from the early A3 catalogue.

This was indeed a new illustration, though perhaps it is difficult to see from the scale of this reproduction, and now showed the other key new feature. The head tube now carries the well known tracery of the Eifel Tower inspired bilaminations so familiar to PARIS afi-cionados as well as the PARIS style twin plate

Figure 43 PARIS TdF head redrawn from catalogue

Figure 44 Detail from an early TdF #3445

crown. The two Figures, 43 and 44, taken respectively from the Figure 42 sketch and an actual early frame, show these bilaminations and the fork top more clearly. It remains incredible, for later aficionados of the marque, that the catalogue has no mention at all of these now classic features, though the text does refer to the "special neat chain stay protector fitted only by "PARIS".

The long eared Osgear type of rear drop out was fitted, indeed the Osgear transmission was shown and the seat tube and lamp bracket are stated to be in alloy e.g. rather than chromed steel used on the *Professional Road Racing*. The shape of the stem strongly suggests the casting of a post war Strata alloy stem.

Later, for the second edition of the PARIS A3 catalogue, the front cover carries illustrations of the bilaminations for the "New PARIS Welded *Tour de France* model", and the *TdF* illustration does show "the new shape of lugs" (catalogue speak here). This model is now drawn with a generalised, possibly Simplex pull rod, derailleur At least in the catalogue the model has now lost the twin plate crown as the front forks now have "a very neat fork crown filed and polished to give smart appearance". The bilaminations are indeed different from those illustrated in the 1947/8 version.

Figure 45   A typical early post war TdF #3445 built in 1948.

Figure 46 Catalogue illustration of the New Welded TdF model.

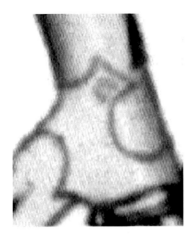

Figure 47a Head and fork of New Welded TdF   b head of TdF #5462

The New Welded TdF also now had bilaminations at the top of the seat tube and at the bottom bracket. The seat tube top bilams now allowed a seat tube clip to be provided as it would have been in a clamping lug whilst earlier TdFs had had a separate clamping clip on a vertical extension of the seat tube.

Later again, in the last known catalogue the PARIS *TdF* was listed as either a brazed frame or as welded with lugs(=bilaminations). This version of the catalogue was probably set out in late 1951. The same drawing was used for the welded

Figure 48 Front view of version as the second catalogue to
Head and fork of #5462 show the '*New PARIS Welded Tour de France* model'. The model seemed to be illustrated as the welded version judging by the drawn diameter of the top tube, and this was listed as *TdF* No 1, and it was just mentioned as brazed with lugs (listed as *TdF* No 2) with both models retailing at £14 18s 6d for the frame   Now, however, the specification text for the model states that it no longer has its once trade-mark larger diameter top tube, the diameter now being stated as

Figure 49a: Catalogue illustration b: New Welded TdF # 5462

the standard 1 inch diameter. The twin plate fork crown

had also gone – though Tom Board has stated[1] that at that time it would have been available if a customer had asked for it.

We have now run out of catalogues issued by the firm but we still have some eighteen months before the PARIS firm was closed. Evidence from the advertisements in *Cycling*, when the firm seems to have been channelling its sales through agents such as Georges Cycles of Colliers Wood, shows there was a model that had never been mentioned in any of the firm's publications, the *Tour de France Superbe*. This was listed at a hire purchase price of 7 shillings per week compared to 6s 6d weekly for a standard *TdF*. How this frame differed from the standard is not known but this weekly rate was the same as that asked for the current Rensch *Champion du Monde* –the top of the line diamond frame model. It is suspected that this "superior " TdF model may have had the seat tube top and the bottom bracket bilaminate as seen in many of the surviving New Welded *TdF* machines and as shown in Figure 50, leaving the standard machine with bilaminations only on the head tube.

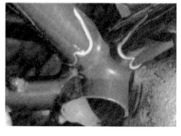

Figure 50 Bottom bracket bilaminations for later TdFs

Interestingly, on some surviving machines, there appear to have been several PARIS transfers that were never illustrated in the catalogues

Yet later in the firm's closing days it appears that the then manager WB(Bill)

Figure 51 Advertisement placed in Cycling shows the transfer design

Hurlow authorised the construction of PARIS frames using standard tube sets brazed and joined with proprietary lug sets. There are no illustrations or textual descriptions of these machines and strictly speaking therefore no real identification of them as *TdF* (unless their original transfers survive) – so that doubtless the few machines that have survived have inherited that title as the *TdF* was the archetypal diamond frame PARIS that was not either lugless nor a *Champion du Monde*. John Rowbottom's machine #7743 only appeared in

1   Tom Board in a conversation with Mick Butler, reported to AJES in 2007.

Figure 52 Another PARIS Cycles transfer –seen from the top paper cover Before application

2009 after Clive Copland - the son of its second owner (his father had bought it secondhand in the 1960s) - decided it should go to a good appreciative owner. Note the lugs on the head which appear to be Nervex Serie Legere design 145 though the rear dropouts still seem to be in-house PARIS in origin.

Neville Ireland, who needed a 25 inch seat tube machine ordered a TdF^1 direct from the firm in late 1951. He was bitterly disappointed when later in spring 1952 after having to pester the firm for it TdF #8028 was supplied to

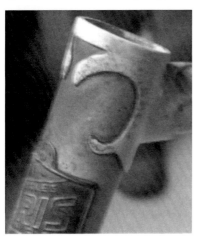
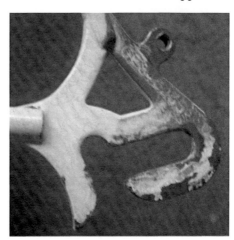

Figure 53a: Head of #7743   b: Rear dropout of 7743

him as a lugged frame with few of the expected TdF attributes that he had associated with the model. Was he dealt with as just a school boy client – may be he was seen as a "tuggo" by some contemporary monkey in the shop – or was he just a victim of the PARIS firm in its closing days? It was probably just

1   Ireland told M Butler that he had actually wanted a *Galibier* but Hurlow had refused point blank to build one for him. Personal correspondence.

the latter –one suspects the skills to make the *Galibier* and the lugless frames were scarce within the firm and doubtless it was cheaper for Hurlow to manage that way. Mind you these somewhat plainer lugs may well have appeared more subtle and modern to contemporary eyes? Figure 54 below shows the Nervex lug work on #8028

Figure 54: a Head of #8028   b #8028 head from the side

Rensch Tour de France

In the post–war A3 catalogues and perhaps aimed perhaps at older customers, was an H Rensch version of the *TdF* referred to here as (R-*TdF*). "An ideal machine for the "Continental Boys"" was the buy-line. In the first 1947/8 catalogue this Rensch version of the PARIS (*P-TdF*) was stated to be welded with an oversize top tube, and the front forks had a twin plate crown, but in the third and last catalogue the model had a brazed up frame with an industry standard 1 inch top tube and the front forks had the more orthodox lugged and "very neat"crown. Presumably the 1 inch top tube diameter was necessary when standard lug sets were bought by the firm using orthodox seat cluster lugs. Early frames were built in Reynolds 531 whilst the later final catalogue offered a choice between 531 and Accles& Pollock's Kromo. The catalogue illustration of the machine remained the same throughout the whole 1947-52 period with Osgear transmission and indeed the price remained constant at £15.15.0d. This price was intermediate between the prices of the PARIS TdF and the top of the range Rensch *Champion du Monde*.

Although this model and its details must have been very well known to contemporary bike purchasers the identity of this model at register level has until recently been confused with that of the Rensch *Champion du Monde*. At a personal level I now blame my own earlier conviction that the poor quality of several times copied catalogue illustrations could not reveal details of the build. This was not helped by the fact that none of the catalogues illustrated the *Champion du Monde* and that, as the text description of that model was placed close to the picture of the Rensch *TdF*, so the features shown in this illustration were erroneously considered to refer to the *CdM*. In fact closer

Figure 55 Rensch *Tour de France* from 1952 catalogue

Figure 56a: Rensch
TdF head redrawn from
catalogue

56 b: Bilams on #4576

examination reveals that they do show the R-*TdF* and the following should help to clear up these errors once and for all.

Until very recently machine #4576 had been taken as a Rensch *Champion du Monde*. However, as a result of taking the detail shape of the head lugs in the R-*TdF* illustration into account, as shown in Figures 56 a and b above, I now believe that the eight or so machines on the register with the same style of bilamination as # 4576 now have to be re-assigned as RENSCH *Tour de France* models.

Returning to the PARIS name, there have been two further productions of the PARIS TdF which the cycle enthusiast may meet. First there was the mid 1980s Paris Lightweight Cycle Co and then a later period, in the early 21st century when the Condor Cycle Company's version was built. Each of these firms has included this classic model in their line up. Paris Lightweight Cycles always had the TdF[1] and offered both lugless and lugged versions. The lugs used in Figure 57 were Prugnat Italia lugs.

Many buyers in the 1980s however wanted something more like Rensch had built and shown in Figure 58 is a very special Paris Lightweight Cycles frame with full bilaminations – a frame made by Tom Board specially for Mike Kemp, the MD of the company, this one rescued from the final sale of the assets, a time when it was finished in a subtle dark green and box lined - not quite so brightly finished as it is now.

Figure 57 A sales photograph of a lugged TdF from the PL archive

1   Cycling 6 March 1982 and The Bicycle August 1983

Figure 58 Mike Kemp's own Paris Lightweight Cycle Co TdF built with all its joints bilaminate and built about 1983.

In 2006 Condor Cycles who retained ownership of the Paris name reintroduced the Condor Paris *Galibier* and then in 2008 followed this by the reintroduction of the Condor Paris *TdF*. Following the then current interest in fixed wheel bikes this latest model is made as a top quality luxury single speed with selected components which hark back to its original period – leather Swallow model Brooks saddle and leather bar grips.

The bilamination pattern used in both these later *TdF* models differs slightly from the pattern of the Eifel Tower inspired tracery used in the Rensch period. The pattern used was first developed by Len Phipps, an independent bilamination maker and used by Board in the Paris Lightweight Cycles period – this later design has a more "gothic " feel than the original and has been described as resembling "Gothic Spires" rather than "Eifel Tower" the original inspiration for the 1940s/50s design. In terms of frame recognition the all bilaminate styles for PARIS have been named ET0 to ET4 to show their relational changes with the Paris Lightweight and Condor Paris machines both using ET4 style. The styles are illustrated on pages 151/2 in Appendix 1..

Figure 59 The prototype Condor Cycles Paris TdF built in traditional bilaminate lugless tubing 2008 and below the production version :-

Figure 60 The current Condor Paris *Tour de France* – hand made still.

Reflections on the *Tour de France* models and their features

As with the notes made on the *Continental/Professional* Road racer it is hoped these notes will help owners distinguish differences seen on their bike from the next *Tour de France* they examine and account for those differences as being due to evolution of the model through time by the firm or in this case accounted for by the Rensch/Paris differentiation rather than assume the differences are due to alteration by former owners –although ultimately there may be some of those encountered as well! As the data base is enlarged the greater the confidence that can be placed in this classification.

There are similar though differing phases in the development of the *Tour de France* to those identified for the *Continental/Professional* due in part to the changes in cycling, either in fashion, in racing development, technical development and of course in response to economic pressures. The first phase was the development from the *Continental* model of the all new lugless frame that Rensch wanted to see bring continental efficiency and style to British cycling.

The second phase was the suppression of development due to WWII but the subsequent introduction of new features, whose origins and inspiration are not yet fully divined, and which accompanied the birth of PARIS – embodying the same continental drivers but with those discrete characteristics that now together define the marque. The third phase is the early post war expansion when this model became so dominant in a world where cycling and road racing sport in Britain was blossoming as never ever before and its popularity was high with its mix of exotic features, bright colours and the impetus of a racing team to drive it forward.

The fourth was the New Welded model with changes in fittings as more and more continental accessories were coming onto the market and the frame styling was altered just as the old guard of the firm was moving on.[1] The fifth phase is the terminal stage: the cycling boom in Britain was fading as the post war motorcycle and motoring industries recovered from their immediate post war difficulties of material resource allocations and the economic depression lifted. The sixth and last phase is the introduction of the Paris Lightweight and later the Condor Paris retro models, perhaps an example of pure fashion and marketing élan driving the situation.

In the *Tour de France* the features that we need to keep in mind are similar to those of the Continental/Professional model and are :-

- Front fork crown, may be epaulette type with a dagger (ECD),a similar pattern but with the dagger long and bold and like a nail (ECN), the twin plate crown (TPC), the flat top epaulette with slot underneath and two concavities(FETC) and the Nervex crown (NC).

---

1   The bilamination pattern of this model seems to have been a very close copy of the 1939 Oscar Egg Super Champion model seen in 'The Competition Bicycle' by Heine J 1998

- The head badge or emblem, either the Rensch brass (RB) or PARIS Alloy or brass (Pal or PBr), PARIS Eifel Tower (PET) or PARIS Large square (PLS) badges, the Rensch or PARIS diamond transfer (RD, PD) Paris Lightweights Paris laurel wreath (PLaur) transfer, or the Condor Paris metal (CPM) badge.
- The top eyes (seat stay tops) either short chamfered (SCH), long chamfered (LCH), tapered and curved -short or long (STC or LTC).
- The frame build either lugless (NoL), Bilaminated pattern i.e. Bil(ET0 to 4, ETMod, RTP-SW, OW) or lugged with Nervex (N) or other (X)
- Chain stay type either special rigid (SR) or Rensch elliptical (RE)
- The front/rear dropouts either (Osgear no25 type in short medium or long spike(OGS, OGM or OGL) or Plain/Simplex (PS)
- Finish i.e. box lining single/double(1BL ,2BL), stencils (Sten)

Feature	Phase 1	Phase 2	Phase 3	Phase 4	Phase 5	Phase 6
Fork crown	ECD	ECN	TPC	FETC	NC	TPC
Head emblem	RB or RD	Pal PD	PET PD	PET/ PLS	PLS	Plaur/ CPM
Top eyes	SCH	STC	LTC	LCH	LCH	LCH
Frame build/ bilaminations	NoL	Bil ET1	Bil ET1	BilET-Mod	N	Bil ET4
Chain stays	SR	SR	RE	RE	RE	New
Dropouts	OGL	OGL	OGM	OGS	PS	Camp
Finish	1BL	Sten	Sten	2BL/ Sten	-	1BL

Note :- The initials for the feature details are explained in the bullet points listed above the table

Chapter 8: Champion du Monde

This top of the range model is difficult both to identify and to understand where it should fit in the firm's range in terms of their objectives for it – possibly it was purely an ego trip for Rensch himself[1]. It was only catalogued post war and was then sold only as a Rensch model[2]. The question is : Did Rensch intend that the Rensch *Champion du Monde* (*CdM*) should take the place of that first, pre war diamond frame *Galibier* which never took off as a best selling flagship model?

The Rensch *CdM* was certainly priced as PARIS's top priced diamond frame, just beaten in the price stakes by that other new model, the strut frame *Galibier*, and in the furore of success of that machine perhaps the *CdM* never achieved the sales and status that was (or might have been) planned for it. It was first listed in the 1947/8 A3 size catalogue "Introduced as the result of the demand for the best possible, in quality and workmanship. The outstanding points on this super production are the fine lug work and beautiful finish which makes Rensch Cycles so outstanding." The specification varies a little between the three versions of these catalogues but goes on "-welded together with Rensch special brazing process … all frame lugs are cut to a very special design and lightened to a minimum …" The shape of those "lugs" or other features of the frame –such as transfers or other means of identification cannot be known because the model was not in fact illustrated in the catalogues or any of the firm's publications nor indeed was it reviewed in any contemporary magazine or advertisements. The specification went on…"Small section seat stays specially shaped at the top ends. Forks - Rensch Continental with special unique cut-out oval section fork crown… or Continental *Tour de France* type in 531 steel, with unique cut out section fork crown of two plate design. This high class production can be had to customers own specification."

All together rather a mystery then, not helped by the fact that with two exceptions none of the machines in the V-CC Register had their original finish or had come to their current owners with any shop receipts that identified their frame number as a *CdM* model.

As it happened photographs of the single definitive *CdM* model had unfortunately been lodged with the previous Marque Enthusiast and passed to the current ME without any identification of either the model or the owner. Only recently has the owner been found , when it became apparent that the machine shown was a *CdM*. It is shown in Figure 61.

1   Tom Board told Mick Butler, who in 2006 retold AJES that the firm's lore was that Rensch was the only person who was allowed to make this model. Harold Jones in 2010 felt that Rensch wanted to make them to emphasise his hold on his firm.just as he created the Rensch Team after the PARIS Team had been closed down.
2   There is in existence however, one machine which is a true CdM but which has unaccountably been badged as a PARIS rather than a Rensch.

Figure 61 Rensch-Champion du Monde #6480 shows a twin plate crown as seen below.

Figure 62a: Head #6480   b: Fork top #6480

The ornate bottom bracket and the high quality build of R-*CdM* #6480 has suggested that this machine could in fact be the *Superbe* version (see Figure 63). May be *CdM* frames which do not have all joints of the frame so adorned would constitute the standard R-*CdM*?

In the later days of the firm the *CdM* remained available and one or two machines are on the register such as #7355 the head tube of which is shown in Figure 64 with lugs that appear to be Nervex in origin though they may have been modified in-house by PARIS. Yet other machines built with Nervex Pro lugs were also sold at this time in the closing days as seen in Figure 65.

Figure 63 Bottom bracket bilaminations of #6480

Figure 64: (left) Head lugs of CdM #7355

Figure 65: (right) Head of Rensch #8871

Chapter 9: Rensch Continental Path and PARIS Path

In the first 1938 catalogue this model is the Rensch *Special Continental Path*, Model 5, "produced to meet the needs of the real sprinter". It had a short wheelbase (40½in), a top tube of 22¼in and steep head and seat angles of 75°/73°. Model 5 had a brazed frame which had 'lugs cut out to a unique design and filed down to a minimum', although it could also be bought as a lugless welded frame (Model 8). This machine had front forks with a twin plate crown and reading the catalogues, at that time this was therefore the only Rensch model to have this style of front fork top. As befits a track bike the forks had ⅞ inch round blades with 'Continental' rake. Using the wording of the catalogue the frame was made of "light section Reynolds 531", it had "very small section seat stays with special rigid chain stays and track ends". Its range of listed finishes was slightly more limited than road machines being offered in Blue, Green, Red or Silver, with seat tube colours and chrome ends. There was no illustration in the catalogue at this time.

It was built for 27 inch wheels with a bottom bracket height of 11½in and the recommended wheels were 27 x1 inch Maplewood rims on Constrictor light steel hubs with double butted tied and soldered spokes. The transmission was 1 x 3/16 inch block chain and Chater Lea or BSA inch pitch block chain sets. Any shape of steel bars could be supplied on a special Rensch brazed up extension to the customer's requirements. The aims of the upright build and the rigidity of the frame were to give it responsiveness to make it the sprinters' ideal mount. In the second catalogue in 1938 the model was again not shown and had become just the *Path* model, No 5a. It sported a Brooks B17 Sprint saddle and now Sibbitt bars on a 2 inch extension were specified.

In the 1939 catalogue the model was illustrated for the first time and the catalogue speak has moved up a notch too. "This superlative production has been designed to meet the needs of the real trackman...is the outcome of years of painstaking care etc " Purchasers are urged to advise whether the bicycle is to be used for cement or grass tracks or both. The frame is now stated to be built throughout with Reynolds double taper butted alloy 531 tubes made especially to Rensch specifications with pencil seat stays and special rigid chain stays and a choice of brazed or welded frame. The frame dimensions were as previously given but the front fork rake was 1½ inch and the choice of bars BSA Continental, Sibbitt or Baileys, all at 17 inch wide on any extension. Figure 66 shows a handsome deep drop Toni Merkens stem could be fitted.

Post war models were only available as PARIS Path in Reynolds 531 or Accles & Pollock's Kromo, specified as double tapered tubes. The early single page brochure picture and the specification remained as in the style of 1939 but from now on only welded construction was offered. The catalogue now

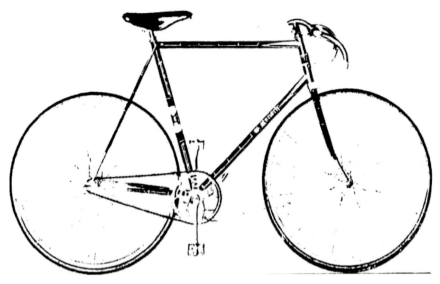

Figure 66 Illustration from the 1939 catalogue

Figure 67 An early post war PARIS Path in original finish #1432 – a purple colour!

stated that as with the other frames an alloy seat pin and the Bayliss Wiley Patent Oil Bath separate bottom bracket were specified.

Figure 68 a   Fork tops of #1432   b   Head badge #1432

Figure 69 Unique down tube on hand painted Rensch insignia on PARIS #1432

The A3 post war brochures repeat the familiar 1939 words and specification which remained unchanged throughout through all the three versions, though the price went up from £12 12s 6 in 1946 to £13.18.6 in 1947/8 to £14.18.6 in 1952. The machine in Figures 68 and 69 was finished with beautiful purple enamel –so post war, the colour choices were greater! The model retained its twin plate crown and round track forks to the end, with the Path's twin plate crown being smaller and neater than the ample and generous road version.

Figure 70   Path model from the 1952 catalogue

Figure 71 The 1948 London Show exhibit of a Path model

Figure 72 The 1948 London Show Path with its beautiful *ET3* bilams –to die for!

Chapter 10: Galibier Strut-Frame Model

In 1939 Cycling[1] had carried
an article about a *Galibier* strut-
frame model that was under development, though little more
was ever heard about this design
at the time. However by 1946 a
number of machines were to be
seen around London bearing the
PARIS name on the strut, and
Figure 74 is a photograph shown
in *Cycling*[2] at the time. Was this
perhaps a case of PARIS staff
intentionally wetting the public
and trade appetite for the new

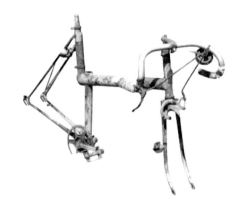

Figure 73 A PARIS *Galibier* Ancestor ?

marque and this new model?
As a follow up to that welcome publicity PARIS sent several publicity items
to *Cycling* – which have been described earlier in the section on the firm's advertising items, described in pages 30-32. In the article in Cycling which followed receipt of the firm's 1947 brochure[3] the reporters noted that "A few of
these machines have been in
general use for some eight
years, being used for both
touring and racing, and
the testers have been completely satisfied with their
performance." Adoption
of the *Galibier* model by at
least one of the riders in
the firm's sponsored team
in 1947-48 quickly brought
it to the public's attention.
The *Galibier* was said to provide a comfortable ride by
"eliminating 'whip' and allowing a certain elasticity to
absorb road shocks thereby
improving   road   holding

An unusual lightweight shown in London recently. The unorthodox design
includes a stout central tube member and a twin top tube. The weight
was reported as 12 lb. These models are not on sale in Britain.

Figure 74 A London street scene August 1946

1   The article has been reported by F Hernandez but cannot currently be located.
2   *Cycling* 28 August 1946
3   *Cycling* 26 March 1947

properties" Thinking about the frame amongst riders was partisan, with many claiming the bottom bracket was not rigid enough. It was unfortunate therefore, perhaps even a reason for the commercial failing of the firm, that frame break- ages in the highly stressed main tube of the *Galibier* gradually caused this expen- sive model to be avoided by many clubmen. In fact there appears to have been only one serious breakage which is described in the final section of this history when recounting the part played by Clive Parker, a nephew of Harry Rensch.

At present all the evidence appears to suggest that the successful and sur- viving strut frame *Galibier* model was inspired by and largely derived from a small production or prototype strut-frame touring bike made in 1935 by a French specialist bicycle maker, Jacques Schulz[1]. One of these bicycles, looking suitably futur- istic, complete with large diam- eter strut and bilaminate joint strengthening but without any top-tube, was exhibited at the 1935 Paris Show. This model was reported with an illustra- tion in the English cycle press[2]. Rensch was known to visit the Paris Shows and could have seen it there and indeed may well have met Schulz[3]. Norman Tay- lor[4] believed that in Rensch's trip to France in 1938, Rensch may have visited Schulz in his work- shop and discussed the 1935 show model strut-frame there. *The Cyclist*, a pre war competi- tor to *Cycling*, was aware of the model in 1938 and included the photograph shown in Figure 75.

An unusual machine seen in Paris. It has an exceptionally large diameter top tube and a small extra handlebar so that the rider may sit upright and steer when he wishes.

Certainly a limited number of these Schulz machines were known to be in circulation in England, and one was even seen later (after the war) in Maclean's

Figure 75 Item from The Cyclist 1938

1   The earliest reference to this assertion is H Stone in Cycling Plus for May 1996
2   Cycling 16 October 1935 p430
3   The impression given to Ken Janes by Rensch in 1947/8 was that this was in 1936.
4   Undated note by Neville Ireland in file passed to AJES in 2005. Norman Taylor was one of the
      Taylor Brothers who had made the Jack Taylor bicycles.

shop in London[1]. Figure 76 shows a Schulz advertisement and in Figure 75 such a machine can be seen together with a standard PARIS *Galibier* for contrast.

SPORT-VITESSE
LÉGÈRETÉ
STABILITÉ
CONFORT

l'Armature Souple
Jacques SCHULZ

La bicyclette du cyclotouriste par ses qualités

mécaniques remarquables et le fini de sa fabrication.

12 bis, rue de Plaisance, **la Garenne-Colombes (Seine)**

Téléphone : Charlebourg 21-72

Figure 76 Advertisement for a Schulz bicycle in 1935 – then a touring bike design

Figure 77 Showing a Schulz and *Galibier* 2246 (with modern fittings) for comparison, taken at a V-CC meeting sometime in the 1990s Photo courtesy Scotford Lawrence

1   Conversation with H Jones February 2006

At least one Schulz has survived and is in captivity[1] Figure 78 shows a detail of the main strut where, in this esoteric design the designer provided a storage for the bicycle tyre inflator, with the 2.3 inch diameter main strut being penetrated by the lower seat tube which then had a screw cap.

The first Rensch strut-frame bicycle which appears not to have had a model name or a top tube(s) of any kind, seems to have been made sometime between 1939 and 1941 if the now mislaid journal describing it can be believed. The model was improved during the war with a small number of trial frames being reported

Figure 78 A detail of the Schulz main strut

to be in circulation[2]. These were remembered as being without the twin top tubes and having an oversize 2 inch main tube, and as being badged as Renschs[3]. One frame which is certainly of this general type is the machine shown in the first figure of this chapter (Figure 73) on page 81. This machine is badged as a Rensch and has an extra large (2 inch) main strut and no top tube(s). It is assumed that it is a direct ancestor of the subsequent production machines. Its Rensch head badge, non standard bilaminations and the vestiges of the diamond shaped Rensch seat tube transfer can be seen in Figure 79. It is currently owned by the original owner's son but was bought secondhand in 1951 so its critical early history is not known, though it saw club competitions in the early 1950s.

1   *News and Views* 265 June 1998
2   *Cycling* 28 August 1946
3   J Coulson *FCOT* No 150 p106 2002

There were reports of several Rensch badged *Galibiers*[1] being raced during the war in bright orange and red livery and perhaps this was one of those machines. The bilamination pattern, though not very clear in the photograph in Figure 71, can be seen enlarged in Figure 79a) below, appears similar to though different from those found on several early Rensch CRR frames cf #1211 and is quite different from later PARIS head tube treatments.

Figure 79 a Head bilam on Ancestor b: Main strut bilam of Ancestor

Note that like a Schulz machine, this Rensch *Galibier* has the lower seat tube penetrating the main strut, and this strut remains at 2 inches, which is still somewhat larger than the 1½inch diameter strut of the later PARIS *Galibiers*. Apparently no frame number could be found on this frame so just how much earlier it is than the currently earliest known *Galibiers* it might be may never now be known.

One other machine, possibly a Schulz but just possibly also an early *Galibier* variant was reported on the road in 1945 and then achieved stardom as shown in Figure 80 .

It can be inferred from the writing within Figure 80 that there was no recognisable head badge or name on the down-tube and that it was apparently completely lugless. Of course it could easily have been a Schulz – or indeed by A.N. OTHER and not a Rensch product - but the location where the bike was seen is close enough to Rensch's home area to make it appear quite likely to have been some sort of experimental machine. It does appear to differ from any known Schulz – they had a parallel sided main strut and were obviously

1   F Hernandez conversation with AJES in 2006

THIS UNUSUAL CYCLE WAS SEEN RECENTLY IN NORTH
WOOLWICH. THE CROSSBAR WAS ABOUT 3" DIAM. AT
THE REAR REDUCING TO
2" AT FRONT IT APPEARED
TO BE AN ALL BRAZED
FRAME. E THE PUMP SLID
INTO THE FRAME TUBE
JUST IN FRONT OF
THE SADDLE.
Sent by Mr G.V. Scriven
(AWARDED ONE GUINEA.)

Figure 80 Extract from Strange but True No 65, a series of advertising items produced for
Currys Limited and published in Cycling by Wheeler Cycling 9 May 1945 p A18

lugged or at least bilaminated - as can be seen in Figure 76. Whether however, the drawing is entirely accurate is another matter – although from the details noted in the short account in the sketch the observer was clearly able to examine the machine at close quarters.

More recently another early *Galibier*, possibly a Rensch made machine as it has #1202 on the bottom bracket which might be expected to place the machine within the war time period, has 'returned' to light. It was renovated in the 1970's when the later PARIS rectangular type of head badge was first fixed to the head tube. Its resemblance to the earlier Schulz and the 'ancestor' can be seen although there are differences in bilamination patterns[1]. Recently its possible Rensch origin has led to a more correct head badge.

A typical *Galibier* drawing probably taken from a 1947 catalogue and a finished machine dating from

Figure 81 *Galibier* #1202 built without a top tube and refinished and re-badged in 2011.

1   The owner describes the build quality as poor and the frame as being very heavy. He has added the lower head bilam in honour of what might have been but originally the head was lugless and the main strut bilamination a plain sheet– not a good sign for it to be a genuine Rensch made frame.

1948, are shown in Figures 82 and 83 below for contrast.

As with the detailed construction of the diamond frame models there were to be several variations in the details of the *Galibier*. These are discussed in the last section of this chapter, but essentially the Rensch made PARIS *Galibier*

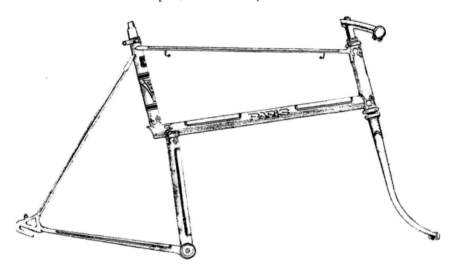

Figure 82 Drawing of an early *Galibier* frame dating to about 1947

Figure 83 Unknown *Galibier* thought to be about 1948 with traditional colour fades

machine remained unaltered through its period of production from 1946 to 1952/3. The only identifiable changes being in-house fashions as the favoured style of bilamination patterns changed, changes in fashion in the paint shop with less box lining and more subtle colours and finally changes induced by equipment suppliers such as Simplex, Agrati and Campagnolo dropouts replacing the original Osgear no 25 pattern. Then of course the *Galibier* story was brought to a temporary close by WB Hurlow who broke up the *Galibier* jigs when he closed down the PARIS Cycles firm in 1953[1].

That mention of the cutting up of the jigs is perhaps significant –it certainly illustrates the powerful emotions that the *Galibier* raised –and still raises today as of course it is still with us. The account of this model so far has probably been detectably on the side of the *Galibier* admirer; but it is certainly the case that there were many for whom the design raised scorn for its stated design aims and who denied it achieved them and bore unconcealed hatred of it and its high sales values. Amongst cycle collectors it, like a number of similar 'different' designs, has always been a popular choice.

Rensch himself was deeply involved in the evolution of the *Galibier* right through the wartime period, and we must presume that its choice and development if not its initial conception was down to him as the then driving force behind the firm. We are told that eight or more prototypes were available through the war period and keen young clubmen such as Tom Saunders and Osborne were encouraged to test it. When Clive Parker, a young nephew of Rensch was drawn into cycling in 1947 he was given the opportunity of racing the machine which he did with gusto before being able to race with seniors in 1948. He was by that time already working part time in the firm as a trainee frame builder whilst riding each afternoon with the PARIS team and his mount was commonly a *Galibier*. He can be seen in Figure 84 on his way to winning the 1947 London Junior Road Championship.. Rensch was probably very proud of his nephew and certainly at this time all was looking good. It was not to last though. Many observers commented upon the bottom bracket movement on the machine being excessive under hard racing conditions and criticised the machines design desiderata. Rensch considered some flex here as acceptable but many pundits claimed prescience when in an unfortunately very public place Parker himself had the misfortune to break the bottom bracket of his *Galibier* when leading the field on a stage of the 1948 Brighton to Glasgow Six day race. The fact that he was photographed whilst in a fit of pique and kicking his broken bicycle in disappointment did not help the cause of the *Galibier* and doubtless was part of the story of his departure from the Team the following year.

The second and now the third lives of the *Galibier*, which were due to the enthusiasm first of all of Michael Kemp and Monty Young and their associates between 1981/7 and now, from 2006 onwards, by Monty Young under

1 Telecon J Wilde with AJES in 2009

Figure 84 Clive Parker leads the pack on his Galibier at an Elstree road circuit.

the Condor Cycles name, are now well known and have been briefly described earlier on pages 23 to 25. A typical product of the first phase, Paris Lightweights, is shown in Figure 85.

These frames were all built by Tom Board who had to build them freehand, as the Rensch jigs had gone the way of Hurlow's intransigence. Improvements were incorporated to take modern alloys into account for the seat tube

Figure 85 A
Tom Board
built Paris
Lightweights
Galibier #1411

though the Bayliss Wiley Oil Bath bracket had to be lost. Nevertheless a fine frame was produced with excellent new transfers reflecting the best of the older designs such as the Eifel Tower as the seat tube emblem and the laurel wreath transfer on the head. After Paris Lightweight Cycles themselves closed in 1987, there were a number of *Galibiers* built as custom builds through Condor Cycles into the 1990s after which Tom Board ceased to build for this firm. Then in 2006 Condor Cycles, still directed by Monty Young, re-introduced the model as a limited number custom machine. It was of course still built in Reynolds 531 with a twin plate crown and those iconic bilaminations.

With such a history and status this model has over the years attracted a number of copyists. Not surprisingly some were established frame builders who relished the challenge of building such a complex frame as the *Galibier*

Figure 86 The 2006 Condor Paris *Galibier* prototype. This *Galibier* is now in limited production as a custom build.

but others were from the band of profiteers who were attracted to being able to cheat –almost inevitable where high valued artefacts are involved. Tom Board himself made a few after he had left Condors – perhaps a case of old habits die hard, or there was a need to show he still had the skills! Tom even built at least one *Galibier* tricycle – a machine that remains in constant use today. Most of the copies can readily be identified as simply obviously lacking the build qualities of the Rensch and later Paris Lightweights/Condor period machines. One which was up to scratch was the frame made by Jack Taylors, seen in Figure 87 whilst Roy Cottingham in his later frame building period is reputed to have made a cracker and Rotrax built two at least one without a top tube –harking back to the early days.

Figure 87 A competent copy of the *Galibier* by Jack Taylor Cycles

Chapter 11: PARIS Sport

A fine problem! The PARIS Sport is a chimaera[1]- a machine that was never mentioned in any of the firm's catalogues, was not reviewed in the contemporary cycling press, and no private secondhand sale advertisements have yet been found when the small ads in Cycling from 1941-1954 were examined for this study. Yet at least five machines bearing both PARIS insignia and the PARIS Sport transfers are listed on the register!

The machines frames are relatively normal PARIS products, though as with other catalogued models there is a wide range of detail differences between them. They are have orthodox diamond frames with frame numbers that allow them to fit perfectly well within the PARIS series putting the model if it was one as beginning in 1949 and ending late 1951. Theories include this model being a venture that came about when someone in the firm wanted to create a fresh market – perhaps in the late 1940s the aim being to attack the high street brands and try to market a "sports" machine to a wider world than the clubs – and road racing clubs at that – with which PARIS Cycles had become associated. The problem here is that if this was a major player in the firm would not a promotional letter to the press have been simple and desirable enough to arrange? Another theory has been that when the firm was closing in 1952, two ex PARIS frame builders set themselves up near Croydon or Mitcham and up to about 1955 either made their own Paris-style frames or else simply refinished earlier unsold frames as PARIS SPORT. There is no firm evidence[2] now that this did not happen, but equally well might one not have expected that by now some one would have come forward to claim some sort of glory? Indeed even the firm under WB Hurlow in his last days might have cobbled unsold stock together – but if they did - why no publicity? Hurlow was actively advertising PARIS products as late as 1953.

What can the machines themselves tell us? The frames show mechanically very little if any difference to the normal product. There are some completely lugless frames, frames with the early Eifel tower bilamination pattern and frames with the later "New Welded " bilaminations. What does distinguish the machines is that they have PARIS SPORT transfers as well as sharing standard model transfers or badges. Owners have not always been forthcoming with detail descriptions of their machines but the pictures below show some interesting features.

A number of PARIS machines carried Reynolds 531 transfers and of course all the firm's catalogues refer to butted R531 as being the tube set used for the top models, but one at least of the known PARIS SPORTS (#6030) carries a Kromo transfer. This has itself led to another possibility based upon

---

1   A chimaera was a mythic beast composed of two otherwise distinct animals –read models in this case!
2   There is no 'evidence' at all for this supposition, its origin is unknown; it is just one of those possibles that seem always to have been around

the first theory being suggested – that the model was introduced when Accles & Pollock Kromo steels were first marketed after the war. There are also a number of other special PARIS SPORT transfers. The first of these first is an attractive "cartoon rider" which shows a mass start rider, complete with spare tubular over his shoulders, and PARIS SPORT spelt out on a half shield below his torso. The PARIS name on the shield was not the traditional special font the firm usually used and the artistic style of the drawing of the rider is quite different from anything else produced by the firm. Does that raise a question over who commissioned this artwork? This transfer was, on different machines of course, used as both a head and seat tube insignia.

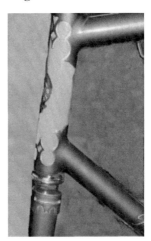

Figure 88 a "cartoon rider" transfer on #6030 seat tube b Kromo transfer on #6030

Figure 89 "Cartoon rider" as head tube transfer

Figure 90 PARIS SPORT in script font on #6789 a lugless frame

The very closeness of the frames to the other PARIS products and the frame numbers appear to favour the first theory, that the model was a mainstream product of the PARIS firm, but, or so goes the counter-argument, skilled frame builders might just have been able to continue to make copies, and if the machines are just refinishes then who can say? It remains possible that it was a venture that was carried out by WB Hurlow when he had the job of liquidising the remaining assets of the old firm for Mrs Rensch. Even a venture by one of the several larger cycle dealers who had carried stock of PARIS models prior to their demise. Finally there is the suggestion that Mike Beazley made when discussing his time with the firm[1]. The reception area of the firm had a large collection of transfers for sale and buyers or owners bringing their bikes in for a refinish could choose whichever transfer they wanted to put on their frame. This would account for some machines having PARIS SPORT and another model name such as TdF on the same frame.

Strangely the name Paris Sport was also used on a few frames made by John Robertson of Edinburgh in the 1950's, but this venture owned nothing to the Rensch inheritance, was quite unrelated and Robertson then built under the name of Robertson or Milano[2]. [Even weirder for English enthusiasts is the fact that yet another firm Paris Sport Cycle was set up in New Jersey USA probably in the 1970's[3]. The main frame builder for this marque in the late 1970's was Francisco Cuevas, though its owner Mike Fraysse originally employed Pepe Limongi. Certainly Cuevas frames carry his name on the chain stay, and as a master builder from Barcelona where he began in 1928 and then Argentina before reaching the US in 1969, he built his frames free without a jig. It is unlikely that any of these high end frames have ever been sold in the United Kingdom. However it appears from a later frame builder, Dave Moulton, who worked as a guest builder with Paris Sport Cycle in 1980 and 90s that the firm did import batches[4] of "Paris Sport" bicycles from France and that some of these may have reached the United Kingdom.

This possibility could explain the origin of the frames owned by Robin Humphreys and purchased by him from a cycle shop that was closing down later in the 1990s. Details can be seen in Figures 91 a-c. These are clearly very much more modern bicycles which carry the PARIS SPORT name. This is an adequate explanation for these later frames, but the reader will readily understand that this cannot in any way explain the existence of obviously late 1940 and early 1950s PARIS frames from being badged as if they were a new model or even make of bicycle.

Robin Humphreys also has an unused set of PARIS SPORT transfers that he bought via the internet and are shown in Figure 92.

The Paris Sport of the main Rensch and PARIS Cycles period remains therefore a conundrum, those who like order seeing a mystery model, whilst those more laissez-faire, just see it as the result of the firm supplying what individual customers wanted.

---

1   Telecom M Beazley and AJES in 2008 and *Boneshaker* 178 pp32-37 2008
2   Telephone conversation Robertson/Ireland 2003
3   Kolin MJ & de la Rosa DM The Custom Bicycle, Rodale Press 1979
4   Article on Paris Sport N&V 339 2010 and subsequent correspondence

Figure 91 a Head view b Down tube c Side view of head of modern Paris Sport

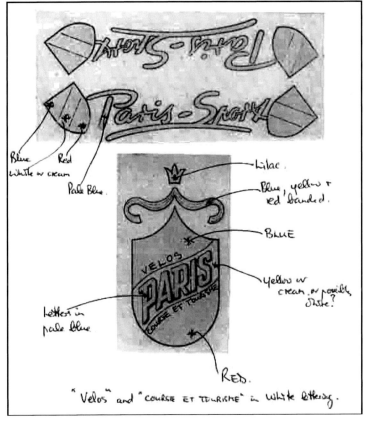

Figure 92 Transfer set including a shield pattern that has not yet been seen on a machine and whose origin remains a mystery.

Chapter 12: Ladies Models

When considering this small group of models we have to bear in mind that only three ladies' models were ever catalogued. Only one of them was ever illustrated though there were in fact four types, one of which had no name. Perhaps some clarification is in order?

It was not until the 1939 catalogue – when the firm probably had a new management or at least a new publicist – that the firm listed a catalogue model for ladies. There may of course have been ladies' bikes that were custom made in earlier years – just as from the later years at least one ladies' *Galibier* strut frame is reputed to have been made and has survived[1].

In the 1939 catalogue then, a white on black illustration of a ladies' model appears rather incongruously on the same page as the Continental Path illustration. The model is entitled the Ladies Model; and as can be seen in Figure 91 it had an orthodox ladies open frame with dropped top tube and the two main tubes not parallel to each other. The frame was welded (lugless) the front forks can be seen to have the central dagger crown and the transmission was by Williams C34 and a derailleur of some sort. Two brakes on dropped handlebars –a club girls model without a doubt

Figure 93 The 1939 catalogue linocut illustration inverted from a linocut for clarity

---

1   Although persistent rumours of this machine still occur it now seems likely that the machine seen was more likely to be a pre-production *Galibier* built without the top tubes but with a larger main strut. It could have been frame #1201 as seen in Figure 81 on page 86.

The sad remains of the only known surviving PARIS Ladies model, the orthodox slant tube type, are shown in Figure 94.

Figure 94 PARIS Ladies #1776- rusty remains of a 21 inch frame but note the PARIS version does have the post war twin plate crown front fork and did have the elegant tapering seat stay tops.

Strangely however, the 1939 catalogue has no mention in its text or even a price for this orthodox slant tube machine. What it did have was a listing and description for a different ladies model! This was the **Dame Sport** , subtitled "*the Super Ladies Sports Cycle*". The description for this other new model was on a separate and later page from the white on black drawing. Whilst there was no illustration it was clearly not the orthodox Ladies Model ! This Dame Sport was a distinctly different model from anything which had gone before. The catalogue explained – "This model has been introduced into our list for the benefit of customers that require a better and smarter ladies cycle." So much then for the sales of the first Ladies Model that had apparently only just been introduced in that same year.

That these were indeed two different models, the specification for the

Dame Sport went on "The frame is of open design with the brake cables hidden in the frame. Another special feature of this model is the twin top tubes giving a very neat appearance.... Designed on continental lines" Clearly then not the orthodox frame of the Ladies model.

It is interesting to ponder - was this the first time out for the twin tube top tube idea with its clever integral brake cable ends – which were later to appear on the *Galibier* strut frame? Was this in fact a mixte design frame as cyclists would later learn to call a continental open frame (one with a normal single lower down tube from head to bottom bracket) – or was it similar to frames already adopted for special models by Centaur, Moorson, Royal Enfield and Grubb ie a completely duplex open frame design? Apart from this the frame was a typical welded Rensch product and according to the catalogue used double butted 531 tubes with 41 inch wheelbase and parallel 70°/70° angles, built for 26 x 1¼ wheels. Its fork had Russ type "abrupt offset rake" and its crown was chrome plated. Such a pity that no illustrations or examples of this 1939 offering have survived.

After WWII the PARIS 1947/8 A3 size catalogue showed a decidedly curvaceous ladies open frame machine the *Type Dame*. So now we have illustration and specification and surely this must either be that same *"Super Ladies Sports Cycle"* of 1939 or at least the very least a development of it? The *Type Dame[1]* can be seen to have been a radical, to quote the catalogues "continental," design, though it was an orthodox mixte style as now understood just beautifully styled.

Figure 95 Catalogue illustration of the *Type Dame*

1   The designation *Type Dame* must have been chosen to emphasise the continental style of this model and was accompanied by the *Type Homme*, a male equivalent. There are no surviving *Type Homme* bicycles – perhaps Englishmen did not care to be so identified?

It can be seen in Figure 95 that it approached the classic continental mixte style with a single down tube – but amongst the highlights of this sensuous machine were those gorgeous double sweep top tubes and the delicious little lower loops which joined them in mid dip to carry the rear brake cable– this 'modele' lived up to the expectations of its new name! Different and so curvy!

The illustrations in the A3 catalogues show that the twin top tubes were long curving twin tubes than swept past the seat tube (in the same manner as the more normal mixte style) before joining the rear drop-outs – now also with rapid taper chain stays and the whole ensemble was said to be made from Accles & Pollock Kromo.

Figure 96 The sweeping curves of the laterals and the lugless construction of this 1947 PARIS Type Dame #3230 can clearly be seen.

The frame angles were now less relaxed at 73°/71° and the fork was different though the Russ pattern shape was still offered. The catalogue illustration also sported the curvaceous PARIS luggage rack that was also sold separately, but which looks to have been designed by the same hand? Would that have been the same hand that designed the pre war *Sport Dame* and the Rensch multi-tube tandem, possibly even the twin top tubes of the later main strut *Galibier*? Could this have been Rensch or was it Dusty Miller who was to become Rensch's most trusted foreman frame builder and latterly the specialist, may be the only, tandem builder apart from Rensch himself? [1]

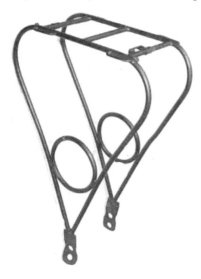

Just as with other PARIS models the ladies machine seems to have had its evolutionary changes, on top that is of the changes we have already noted between the ladies model and the pre war and post war *Dame Dame* and *Type Dame*. Shown below are two of three later style machines, the first of which has not, and the second of which has, survived.

In order to avoid confusion I propose to use the name *Dame Moderne* for this uncatalogued frame shape. The records in the register show that the Ladies model illustrated above (#1776) would have been made in mid 1947 but that all other known *Dames* were built in 1948.

Before leaving this section on the *Type Dame* it is interesting that in Cycling in July 1946[2], and therefore somewhat earlier that might be expected, was a private advertisement for a secondhand Rensch

Figure 97 The matching curves of the PARIS luggage rack offered on the *Dame*

:- *Rensch multitube solo, 22in, 74/72 degrees oval forks, 2¾in Bluemels, North Roads, B17N, callipers, Endricks, red-silver finish £11, or frame only £6. 6s.* Was this a prototype we have not yet heard about, or could it in fact have been a surviving *Sport Dame?* The only other named "multi tube" Rensch frame was a tandem which this frame definitely was not. Just conceivably "multitube" might be construed as a *Galibier* because of the many differing tubing sizes in use, but it would have to be a very early one and this would have been the earliest known *Galibier* small advertisement. If this was the case; a *Galibier* with North Road handlebars?

There again that could take you back to the Schulz – could it have been a Schulz that Rensch had bought in from which to take measurements for his own production?

1   This is of course just another piece of speculation but the fact remains that the better known post war Rensch tandems had twin lateral tubes and the top of the range ran to twin tube drainpipes as well as twin laterals and additionally had curvaceous support tubes of an ornamental appearance; the suspicion is that only Dusty Miller could have made these frames -so did he grow up and then grow old with this exhibitionist frame work?
2   *Cycling* Gents For sale section 10 July 1946 page 8

Figure 98 One frame that did not survive- Chris Edmonds and his mother seen in 1949 on a later ladies machine Dame #4547 (*Dame Moderne*) Is that a dainty separate chain guard we can see below the straight part of the lateral tube?

Figure 99 A recently renovated example of the later straight tube *Dame* or *Dame Moderne*.

Chapter 13: Social Cycle

This really was a special model, and was arguably Harry Rensch's last "throw".

Doubtless many other firms had made such twosome side by side bicycles in the past, and such recreational vehicles had been serious transport offering in the 1890's whilst an Austrian one was shown in Cycling in the later 1930s. Harry and his wife were known to be regular visitors to Butlin's new holiday camp at Southend. Perhaps Rensch was invited to produce such a vehicle, or offered his own design to the management, all that is currently known is that the firm showed this somewhat 'out-of-the-run-of-the-firm's-business' model at the 1949 London Show. May be it was actually just Rensch making a desperate bid to make a product that would make money for the firm and get it out of the economic doldrums that it appears it (and nearly all the smaller special bike makers) were then beginning to enter. Whilst looking at this machine in Figure 100

The " Social Cycle " now being produced by the Paris Cycle Co. (129 to 133, Stoke Newington Church St., London, N.16) as an alternative to the more usual tandem bicycle. The model is built to lightweight standards and will accommodate two adults and a child. The two transmissions operate independently but only one rider can control the steering.

Figure 100 Shown in Cycling "Trade News" 22 June 1950 page 557

give a thought to the bending of the main frame tube (chassis might be a more appropriate term here!) which can be seen below the foot protection board in the photograph. Bending this thick bore tubing was a task that required three men with a five foot long lever on a gargantuan permanently fixed bending machine that Rensch had to devise and had mounted outside of the workshop (because of the space needed to carry out this operation) in the open yard of 133 Stoke Newington Church Street[1].

1   This location is shown in Figure 111 in Chapter 17 of this history. .See also Boneshaker 178 2008 p34

Chapter 14: Tandems

The first Rensch 1938 catalogue listed three models :-
Tourist; Brampton fittings and No.9 tandem frame
Road Racing: HM tubing with SA KSW 3 speed hub
Continental Road Racing: 531 tubing, Chater Lea fittings 60 in wheelbase, Airlites, Cantilevers, Brooks.

This list was at the bottom of the last page of the catalogue which then stated that complete specifications were available on demand. The catalogue had listed the Rensch solo frames as No 1 to 8 so the Tourist tandem with frame No 9 was clearly the first of the firm's tandem frames. The second 1938 single page brochure has no mention at all of any tandem.

In the 1939 catalogue, from the Old Street address, tandems are first actually mentioned in the main text of the catalogue. In its Introduction, where the firm's policy of making welded frames is described, is a reference to solos and tandems. There are no illustrations of the three tandem types in this third catalogue and the order is different from the 1938 catalogue, but at least two of the machines can be recognised from the earlier list.

Tourist – In the 1939 catalogue the specification of this tandem was similar to the *Manaco* (see next model below) but built in unspecified Reynolds tubing and unnamed but possibly Brampton lugs *"filed to a minimum, no thick lugs like doorsteps!"* at three quarters the price of the Manaco. *"Although it a touring tandem it will be found quite suitable for racing. A machine you will be proud to own."*

Manaco – an orthodox frame built in R 531 as either double diamond or with lateral tubes and with triple rear stays. Used Chater Lea lugs but *"cut out to a superb design, filed and polished"* whilst a short wheelbase with curved seat tube was on offer which doubtless would have given a 60 inch wheelbase. Wheels were 26 x 1¼ on tandem hubs and Binda steel 18 in bars were used at front with 19in wide Baileys to the rear.

Continental Road Racing – *"designed by us to meet the needs of the clubman requiring a real Continental style tandem. Something that is really different from the usual British lines."* All welded and *"built completely of twin tubes manufactured for Rensch by Reynolds in 531"*. It was built with a 59½inch wheelbase with curved seat tube at 73°/71° for 26 x 1¼ wheels.

It appears that the new *Manaco* (a name which was in fact dropped after 1939) was the same model as the previous Road Racing machine of the 1938 catalogue though now made in Reynolds 531 and of course the Tourist , the budget machine, was almost certainly the same as the 1938 Tourist.

It begins to look as though that the designer of the new *Continental Road Racing* tandem had also worked on the *Sport Dame* then the *Dame* and might then have gone onto the post war tandem designs, was it Rensch himself?

Figure 101 The only tandem model and style illustrated in the post war A3 catalogues.

In the post war catalogues this top of the line multi-tube machine is illustrated as 'The Rensch Tandem" – see Figure 101 above having the same by-line as that reported above for the Continental Road racing Tandem model with the addition of "This type of tandem is very popular at the moment on the Continent, and quite a selection can be seen at the shows, both in France and Belgium". The model had a curved seat tube frame with twin laterals running from the top tube just before the steersman's seat tube to the rear drop out and from the middle of the head tube to just in front of the stoker's bottom bracket. The drainpipe of the frame was that jewel of the lightweight tandem a flattened oval section. A more expensive version "as above but with superbly cut out lugs at all joints" was some £4.15.0d more. Similarly control cables could be hidden in the tubes if preferred. Figure 102 shows the more elaborate frame that could be built but whether this was actually what you got for your extra £4.15.0d we do not know –but it would have been worth it!

The tourist tandem reappeared in the last post-war A3 catalogue now offered as a PARIS Tourist tandem with the description – straight seat tube, less lugs, by which was probably meant that it was the standard lugless machine without any bilamination embellishments; it cost £5. 0s 0d less than the Rensch version. Figure 102 shows another late PARIS tandem of 1952/3, a period when most frames where probably custom built by foreman Dusty Miller. This had head bilaminations but was otherwise lugless but now the curved seat tube and the

Figure 102 A late touring PARIS tandem with luxury touches

Figure 103 a Head   b: the oval stove pipe has been replaced by duplex tubes to
bilaminations   match the twin lateral frame construction

glorious oval or elliptical drainpipe has been replaced by duplex tubes – this must have been a road racing machine and was ultra light at 13 lbs for the frame.

It is interesting that of the tandems that are on the V-CC Register just two were made in 1948, and all the rest are 1952/3 machines with frame numbers greater than 7000. No pre war Rensch tandems seem to have survived and half of those on the list are single tube machines, with a few of the twin laterals.

Triplet – offered as a frame only in the later 1948 catalogues without any description. Just one machine is known to survive and was seen in the 1980s in Surrey though not since then.

Figure 104 Custom PARIS tandem with special small rear frame

Figure 105 Paris USWB tandem frame #8308 – the height of elegance

There have been persistent reports that Rensch retained the difficult job of tandem building for himself and then latterly to his foreman, Dusty Miller. This is probably true and certainly tandems were incredibly popular (when compared to the interest in them today) and Rensch tandems and then PAR-IS tandems in the secondhand cycles market were indeed numerous. In the period from 1950 onwards when Rensch was ill and beginning to leave the firm, the firm was actively advertising only its tandems –was this because they provided the best income or was it because Dusty Miller remained at his post when most of the other frame builders in the firm were either ineffectively managed or plain incapable of quality work?

Chapter 15: Minor Rensch Models

Grand Tourist

This model was a pre-war model that appears to have been continued – in spirit perhaps - by the post-war *Type Homme* model. In the first 1938 catalogue this was available both lugged and welded, as models 2 and 7 respectively aimed at the fast tourist and using unspecified Reynolds tubing –probably HM grade with a wheelbase of 41inch and 10½ high bracket on 26 x 1¼inch steel Endrick rims and Bayliss Wiley featherweight hubs. The saddle was a Brooks B15 and transmission was Williams C1000 and choice of Osgear or Simplex. In the later 1938 catalogue the model is 4a with either construction available and described as Upright design and short wheelbase using Reynolds 531 with the specification unchanged except that the chain set was now a C35. In the mini-review of Rensch bicycles in The Bicycle[1] in 1938 this model is given almost as much exposure as the *Tour de France* but subsequent marketing would suggest that this touring market was difficult for Rensch to exploit –perhaps his sales boiled down to being just a function of what local clubmen wanted.

In 1939 when reportedly the model "has been an outstanding success in the 1938 season." only a welded version was on offer with the same specification as before but now a seat tube angle of 70° was quoted where none had been stated before. Post war this model does appear to have been continued. Just look in the A3 fold out catalogues where there is just such a lowest priced gents model and this one too has the aim of the "needs of the fast tourist and clubman". Post war the *Type Homme* now has welded Accles & Pollock Kromo best quality steel tubes for its frame and being named as the *Homme* – it was a natural partner to the *Type Dame*.

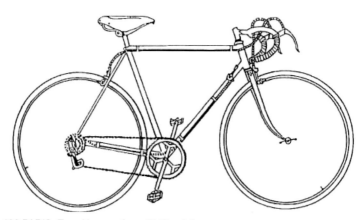

Figure 106 PARIS Type Homme from 1948 catalogue.

1   The Bicycle 18 January 1938

The illustration, for what its worth, as it is more diagrammatic than any of the others, shows no separate seat pillar clip even though the frame was drawn as if lugless, and interestingly whilst the front forks are stated to be twin plate crown, the drawing is unconvincing on this point. This type of fork crown would have been a feature shared with the 'continental styling' models such as the *Professional, Tour de France* and the *Type Dame*

Tourist and/or Club

This model was only on sale as a pre-war H Rensch model and was the lowest priced gents bike, "specially designed for tourist and clubman." It may have been difficult to distinguish this model from the Grand Tourist except for its 42 inch wheelbase but it was almost three quarters of its senior sibling's price and used an unspecified Williams chain set. It was not mentioned in the second 1938 catalogue and was probably quietly dropped in early 1938, perhaps because the firm was looking to move into higher quality and price markets.

Pyrenees/San Reno/Triple Purpose

These three models appeared only in the 1939 catalogue and strongly suggest the presence of someone new to the Rensch management, may be someone whose ideas on the marketing needs of the firm did not succeed : perhaps just because the war intervened. As it happens none of the surviving H Rensch frames or bicycles on the V-CC register have been identified as being of any of these models, so no great time need be spent on them. However, in case identification errors have been made and existing machines wrongly assigned to one or other of the better known models, the key characteristics of these three late 1930s models are listed in the following table.

Feature	Pyrenees	San Reno	Triple Purpose
Stated aim or market	Best quality lugged frame - fine lugwork, a light and responsive mount	Fast touring continental touring, although attractively priced same quality as other Rensch cycles	For clubmen all-round racing, extra track forks available
Frame construction	Brazed DB 531	Brazed special filed lugs DB 531	Welded or continental lugs DB 531
Frame build	WB=41¾, 74°/72°; 11in high on 27inch wheels	WB=41¾, 70½°/72½°; 10¾in high on 26inch wheels	WB=40¾ or 39½, 73°/72°; 11¼in high on 27inch wheels
Wheels	Tabuchi 27 x 1 in for tubs	26 x 1¼ chromed	Tabuchi or Maplewood sprints
Chain stay	Rensch section	Not described	Special oval section*
Fork crown	Unique cut-out oval section fork crown	Special drop forged crown	Continental cutout
Handle bars	Tour de France reinforced 1in alloy	Binda chromed steel	Any shape choice
Price	£15 17s 6d w sprint £13 19s 6d w HPs	£10 17s 6d complete	£12 7s 6d with sprints £11 6 s6d with HP

*One interesting point – may be just another of those possible false leads caused by the inconsistencies of copy writers for the catalogues – is that suddenly in the small print of the Triple Purpose model (a model name similar to the Dual Purpose used by Selbach) is the statement – "Special oval chain stay, fitted only to Rensch welded cycles. The section of these chain stays give clearance for 27 inch wheel with large size tyres and at the same time do not interfere with the rigidity of the cycle." Now was this introduced just for this model - many Rensch bicycles had multiple uses – or was it in general use but simply had not been claimed before? Could it even have been just a bit of sleight of hand by the copywriter –and the fitting itself was just the regular (to the Rensch firm) Rensch elliptical chain stay?

This handsome Rensch feature became a well-loved PARIS feature after the war, when it was referred to as Rensch elliptical chain stays. We need to examine pre-war chain stays! How did these chain stays compare to the others – remember the frequently used mantra for many other models - "Rensch section chain stays" and the other common entry -"special rigid chain stays"? Certainly the early welded Rensch #145 did not have the oval or elliptical chain stays – its chain stays are a type of the rapid taper circular chain stays and indeed the 1939/40 PARIS #1081 also has chain stays very similar to this rapid taper type – though perhaps in this latter case a war time build may explain this feature on this machine.

Before leaving this section lets just look, in the figures below, at a unique but conundrum machine now at rest somewhere in Japan. Surely this machine whose frame's attributes shout Rensch but whose details are not recognisable in any of the models so far described could just be either a *Pyrenees* or a *Triple Purpose*? Once it lived in deepest Hereford with a competition cyclist –if only his ghost could tell us what it was that he had bought, owned and raced!

Figure 107 A unique early post-war competition Rensch machine whose detail features are also shown in the figures 108 a & b

Figure 108 a Head bilams; b oiler on seat tube

Figure 109 Bilams at the top of seat tube and on the top tube but simple seat stay top eyes. Engraved RENSCH saddle pin clip

Chapter 16: The Story in the Models

Some comments have already been made about the significance of various models or features of the bicycles as each model has been described, but there is still much to learn about Harry Rensch and the products of his two companies and their successors.

We have already seen how remarkable it was that, right from the beginning, a young man of 24 years with say just four years of reasonably acceptable "qualified" professional life behind him should have been able to start his own business and found it so well with a range of bicycles which were at the cutting edge of cycle design.[1] Then within just one more year he had introduced an even more successful and innovatory process of frame construction eg bronze welding or lugless frames, trained up a new workforce and moved them into new larger premises so that most of his range of machines could now be offered using that process, including the demanding applications such as racing machines and tandems.

There is a whole fleet of small but intriguing features of the frame work of the pre war Rensch machines such as the specially selected make up of the tube sets with double butting used on the top models, use of the special rigid chain stays, pencil seat stays and details as the chain slap protector on the chain stay and chain hook. On the classic post war Rensch models, the *Professional*, *TdF*, to some extent *CdM* and certainly the *Galibier* there were many features and details that "made the marque stand out" and these included the shaping of the seat stay top eye, the roof of the twin plate crown, the curvaceous valance added to the rear bridge abutment as well as frame set design per se. Finally there was the circular ring used as the mudguard eyes something small, apparently insignificant but a detail only ever used on Rensch made frames. At the risk of sounding too self deprecatory, these have been found to be made from robust closed eye cup hooks, selected perhaps by the same frame builders who had used floor nails in their search for a perfect front fork decoration. The major presumption is that these features were devised by Rensch himself in his initial setting up and for the post war changes, during his WWII down time, to provide his hoped for PARIS customers with his own uniquely crafted "continental inspired" product.

Where did Rensch get these ideas and designs from? We know from the testimony of Ken Janes that Rensch was a keen visitor to France and well read in terms of cycle sport.[2] There is an intriguing possibility that Rensch first saw the way he wanted to go when he was employed by Hobbs of Barbican sometime in the early 1930s. However, his Rensch designs were not a slavish

1 Some of the other founders of cycle firms came from a successful competition background –Grubb, Selbach or Meredith. Rensch however was a technocrat.
2 Working with PARIS Cycles, *Boneshaker* 175 pp 36-44 2007

copy of the beautiful lugwork that Hobbs pioneered on their *Continent* and *Continental Superbe* machines of 1937, rather he saw the added value such work brought to the basic machine and wanted to do something similar though different. It was the germ of the "Continental" design and frame embellishment that he saw whilst he was with them that he picked up, but its fruition on his own bicycles was solely of his own making.

There is a further interesting possibility here, developed after examining some details of a 1936 Reyhand bicycle[1]. This model appears to have a front fork with twin plate crown and its seat stay top eyes made by curved tapering ends –similar to the new frame features which appear on the lugless PARIS frames introduced by Rensch. The plain front head tube even has an understated diamond shaped name plate –just as used for the prewar Rensch firm and later fitted on the *Professional Road Racing* most of which carried only a diamond shaped PARIS transfer rather than a head badge. There can be no proof of a causal relationship at this distance in time, but the reputation enjoyed by Reyhand for fine machines would make any borrowing by Rensch of such details not unexpected from a man known to follow Continental styling. It seems not unlikely that if the unusual strut frame Schultz machine was the inspiration for the main strut *Galibier*[2] then the Reyhand could have been the 'model' for the Francophile Rensch's new string of diamond frame bicycles which came out only after World War II

Other questions arise, for example the timing of the introduction of the diamond frame *Galibier* model. This model only had a short run from sometime in 1938 to the outbreak of war in 1939, and perhaps few or even no bicycles of this type were ever made, perhaps inevitable with the extreme uncertainties and economic pressures of this period. However, just what created the situation in which this model did come about and what was Rensch hoping to achieve with it? Here we have a small firm with an exemplary record of succession innovation and an existing fine top of the range model, the *Tour de France*. Was this new model, which was apparently in excess of both demand and the capability of the firm to supply it, intended to compete with the likes of Hetchins –who were just then actively promoting their sales by sponsoring the 1937 and '38 Wembley 6 Day teams[3]? We do not know, as no Rensch business strategy has ever come down to us.

Whose concept was it to introduce, at the same time as the still born diamond frame *Galibier* and a yet another move to a new shop nearer to central

1   Heine, Jan and Praderes, Jean-Pierre; *The Golden Age of Handbuilt Bicycles*, Vintage Bicycle Press, Seattle 2005

2   The Schulz machine can be seen in Figure 76 to have used large sleeves joint reinforcements which were probably bilaminations. Could Rensch have seen this technique first on the Schulz and introduced it pre war first to his prototype main strut machine and then to the other solo PARIS machines?

3   Ingram, Len in Hetchins, *Lightweight Cycles Catalogues Vol 1* JPMPF 2005

London, not just of this new model, but also a new catalogue and four other top line new models, the *Pyrenees, San Reno and Triple Purpose* and the *Sport Dame*, which were presumably an attempt to build on the Continental connections? Just consider that this flurry of activity must have come at a time when Harry Rensch was courting his future wife. How could it be that, only a year or so after he had just expanded his shop and business for the successful introduction of bronze welding, these additional models were created, each requiring their own design changes. Who would want such additional work load? Several of the features referred to above that would become archetypal features of the marque made their first appearance at this point – or at least there are references to them in the new catalogue. These are just the sort of features which could be the signature of a gifted frame designer/builder – but if they were, could they really be all down to Rensch still just 26 in 1939, with all his other concerns? And don't forget to ask yourself who had the inspiration for that other pre-war and perhaps also still born *Sport Dame* whose duplex top tubes did appear on the post war Type Dame and are perhaps reflected in the top tubes of the main strut frame *Galibier*?

Could some of these tantalising new features have been down to say, Les Ephgrave, who would have been finding his feet in the firm in 1937/8? He had joined Rensch by 1936/7 but he left the firm before the beginning of the war. Could perhaps AE Metcalfe have had a role here? After all Metcalfe was recorded as being very friendly with the Rensch's and may well have joined the firm in the 1938/9 period: he was certainly with them post -war. Metcalfe at least might have been part of the business building side of the firm as he knew the clubmen's needs being an active racing man and later left PARIS in 1948 to found his own business, whereas Ephgrave, who himself went independent in 1948 after working for Claud Butler, was always an inspirational artist in metalwork. Thinking of the elegant tracery of tubes in the last Rensch tandems could Dusty Miller have a much greater part in the history of PARIS frame design?

A third more prosaic wild card scenario is that, are we seeing outside influences here? Could it be that a number of the new features mentioned above came to be introduced by Rensch because they were suggested by trade sources such as Reynolds? Reynolds were the makers of tubing sets for most lightweight cycle frame builders and a number of the frame tubing and front fork features in the Rensch range are close to features seen in the Hobbs' Continental range of 1936-8. Could there have been a tacit agreement between supplier and client organisations here similar to that which earlier had existed between Granby and Selbach over taper tube frame sets?

Checklist of known Rensch and Paris models and the recorded surviving machines from the Veteran-Cycle Club Register August 2012.

Model name	Number known
Rensch *Continental Road Racing* PARIS *Professional Road Racing*	4 23
PARIS *Tour de France*	91
Rensch *Tour de France*	8
Champion du Monde	8
Continental Path	7
Galibier Strut frame model	87
Ladies Model	1
Sport Dame	None
Type Dame and *Dame Moderne*	5
PARIS *Sport*	6
Tandems PARIS and Rensch	22
Triplet	1
Social Cycle	None

Chapter 17: Personnel of the H Rensch and PARIS Firms

This chapter deals with the personalities of the two original firms from the early pre-war days of **H Rensch** to the end of Paris Cycles and records what is known about practical details of working practices. Many details of the firm's staff - the individuals who made it happen - remain a mystery and it seems unlikely that unless one of them has somewhere written down their recollections and these can be unearthed, that anything more definitive can be set down.

For the pre-war period we know very little about the firm's staff except that Les Ephgrave and Jack Jones appear to have been amongst Rensch's first frame welding assistants. Ken Janes has said that EW (Ted) Henderson was to some extent Rensch's right hand man, probably remaining in the Old Street shop after 1939 when Rensch himself was at that time temporarily interned as an alien[1]. After the Old Street shop was bombed in 1940, Henderson is thought to have found work elsewhere for the war effort but perhaps to have remained in the area and may have worked in his spare time for Rensch, perhaps experimenting with the main strut model that would become known as the *Galibier* after its announcement in 1946/7.

Post-war, in the first **PARIS** period, there is rather more though still insubstantial information on the staff of the firm and on the racing team that Rensch supported. A little is known about the team's involvement in mass start racing in BLRC events. A **PARIS** team was started in 1946/7 and continued until at least 1949. Much less is known about the short lived team that wore RENSCH team jerseys.

I have not for that matter attempted in this account to describe the situation in the later Paris Lightweight Company's nor the Condor Paris periods.

The firms' premises

Three addresses for the pre war H Rensch firm were given in the chapter dealing with development of the firm. They were:

1935-37	132 Balls Pond Road London N1
1937-38	246 Balls Pond Road London N1
1937-39	362 Old Street London EC1

No one has come forward who has detailed recollections of the Rensch premises except for the memories of two men who when very young recall visiting them and being treated very favourably by a happy and friendly Harry Rensch. These two are Harold Jones and Monty Young whose reminiscences

---

1   Conversations with Ken Janes 2006 although reservations over Janes' testimony have to acknowledged with the identity of Henderson challenged by John Coulson(Letters, *Boneshaker* 177) and currently the truth about Rensch's wartime status and internment history proving difficult to verify.

have already been drawn upon in Chapters 1 and 2. It is understood that 246 Ball Pond Road has now been demolished and certainly the Old Street, Clerkenwell premises have now been rebuilt and are offices with some residences above. In 2008 on the Paris Origins Ride the ride stopped at 132 Balls Pond Road for photographs of the outside of the current shop –now a nicely random muddle of an ironmongers and the inside was made available for us to look around, although the owner knew nothing of Rensch or his occupation of the premises. Hardly surprising as it was almost 70 years before!

We know quite a bit more about the premises used by the post war PARIS firm, though the information is indirect from examination of the firm's publications and advertisements and latterly from the memories of two members of the firm staff, Ken Janes and Mike Beazley whose recollections have already been cited.[1] Three figures, Figures 111 to 113, have been taken from these two accounts. The first shows the tenancies and occupation records of the three buildings in Stoke Newington Church Street which PARIS used in the post war period to 1953.

The set of drawings on page 120 shows the first memories of the in-

Figure 110 132 Balls Pond Road in 2008

ternal arrangements as remembered by Ken Janes who was with the firm from 1947 to 1948 where the main impression of the firm was the multi storey layout after the property was entered by an approach from the street into the reception area, occupied during the day by Ethel Rensch. Janes remembered a garage on the right of the building where Rensch kept his car – but his recol-

1   References given again for convenience Janes K, *Boneshaker* 175 2007 and Beazley M. *Boneshaker* 178 2008

Evidence from published advertisements in Cycling

Year	1943	1944	1945	1946	1947	1948	1949	1950	1951	1952	1953
129 SNCS									December		
131 SNCS			July / November		August "showroom"	November	July "workshop" / September / November		November / December		December
133 SNCS			July / November	February / July / September / December	March	July / November	July / September / November		November / December		

Evidence from local council records

Year	1943	1944	1945	1946	1947	1948	1949	1950	1951	1952	1953
129 SNCS	No data	Allen Glasswork	Allen Glassworks	Allen Glassworks	Allen Glassworks	Allens to 28 November	All year HH Rensch** House/shop	All year HH Rensch** House/shop	All year PARIS*** Workshop/yard	To 31 March PARIS# Shop/office/yard	Empty by 13 February
131 SNCS	No data	Empty	F Camfield	30 Sep to HH Rensch House/shop	All year HH Rensch House/shop	All year HH Rensch House/shop	All year HH Rensch* House/shop	All year HH Rensch** House/shop	All year PARIS*** House/shop	To 31 March PARIS# Shop and shed	Empty by 13 February
133 SNCS	No data	Empty	1 July to HH Rensch* Workshop	All year HH Rensch* Workshop	All year HH Rensch* Workshop	All year HH Rensch* Workshop	All year HH Rensch* Workshop	To 15 July HH Rensch** Workshop	All year or None PARIS*** House/shop	Empty	Empty

* HH Rensch trading as Paris Welding Company
** HH Rensch and T Rutherford trading as Paris Welding Company
*** Paris Cycle Company
# Paris Cycle Company Ltd

Entry in the 1951 year that all premises are in use contradicts the earlier entry that on 15 July 1950 133 SNCS had been vacated

Yellow indicates property was occupied by Rensch/Paris firm

Green indicates a data error

Presence of witness

Figure 111 Occupancy of 129 to 133 Stoke Newington Church Street.

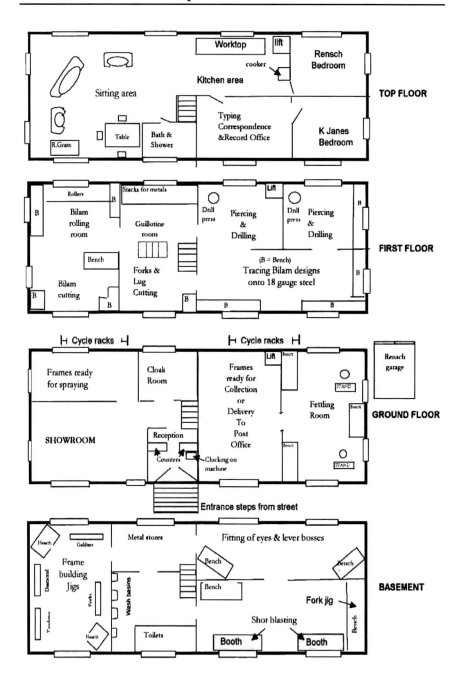

Figure 112 Ken Janes' recollection of the early PARIS building's layout

lections seem only to need one of the houses eg either 131 or 133 whilst the tenancy records in Figure 111 show that in his time (April 1947 to December 1948) the firm occupied 129, 131 and 133 the latter including the all important workshop.

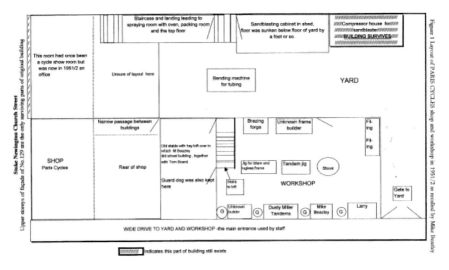

Figure 113 The later situation recalled by Mike Beazley

After this description of the early post war period we can see the later and simpler arrangement recalled by Mike Beazley in Figure 113 from his time in the firm from 1951 to sometime in 1952 after which he left for National Service. In contrast to Janes who as a young man, and the son of a well known lug cutter for Claud Butler, seemed to have the ear of the boss, and who was able to enter via the front entrance, Beazley remembers being just a hired hand and never dreaming of entering via the front entrance, but of being told to come into the workshop via the rear entrance from the side lane and into the inner yard where he could leave his bicycle. In the case of the Beazley layout the entire premises were seen as equivalent to 129 and 131 Stoke Newington Church Street whilst the part he refers to as shop and the workshop (which can be seen as forming the lower part of the drawing) would presumably be 131 with on their right the access lane which Beazley remembers. This access lane was still there in 2009. This layout has its problems too as it makes it difficult to understand where 133 which had been demolished in the 1970s could have been! Beazley was able to confirm that in 2009 the only remaining part of the PARIS buildings structure that he could recognise, apart from the façade of 129 and the access lane, was the ramshackle compressor house.

There are therefore such differences in the two men's accounts of the in-

ternal layout that it would seem unlikely that there is anyone living who can
properly adjudicate between the two situations portrayed. In both cases we
have the best efforts of recall by both men each from some sixty years before
and trying to draw from the imprint in their heads. Neither would have had the
free run of the buildings and their presence in certain parts of the buildings
would probably have caused adverse comment.

Also to be factored in are differences that need to be expected due to the
changes that are known to have occurred between the periods they were each
employed there such as in the early days recalled by Janes the Rensch family
lived up on the top floor of what was 131/3 whilst later Beazley simply remembers that the only occupant overnight was a watchdog in the old stables
area below the cockloft next to the 133 workshop area. At this later period
of course the Renschs had split up and Ethel Rensch was known to be living
near by in Lordship Lane.

It would seem quite invidious to attempt to judge either account but we
should thank both men for their efforts and candour in coming forward with
their thoughts.

Before leaving the workshop completely you may be asking just how were
the machines made and how many were there? The brief answer is that in
the absence of the firm's records we can never be certain. The frame numbers seem to be a chronological run from starting in 1935/6 to ending in
1953 –then approaching 9000. The evidence we have is that which is stored
in the Register and shown in Appendix A2. Do have a look at it there and
watch this space for a more detailed analysis in the future.

The firm's management.

This is another area where a good paper record of the firm's business would
help, even may be a letter-heading listing the principals, but as we already know
in this case there is simply nothing like this to build upon. So we have to make
do with just a few comments made in passing by Ken Janes, Mike Beazley, Harold Jones and MontyYoung.

It does look as though in the early Rensch days of the mid 1930s Rensch
had set up on his own with himself as frame builder and with perhaps a junior
or two to help run any "front of shop" that there might have been in 132 Balls
Pond Road. This would have been when Jack Jones and Les Ephgrave were
taken on and trained up in the Rensch house style.

After the denoument that brought about commercial success of bronze
welding and which would herald an expansion into 246 Balls Pond Road when
bronze welding was used for the majority of the models, the changes in catalogue
model numbers make it look as though there was a new broom at some sort of
mid management level –but although Rensch was always a frame builder he was
also undoubtedly the name behind the firm. It is around this time in 1937/8 that

Les Ephgrave left for Claud Butler –was he disappointed not to have been offered a senior post by Rensch at this time? We will never know of course. Ken Janes[1] has said that Ted Hendersen joined the firm about this time having previously worked for Bates, and perhaps he was offered a management role.

So we move towards late 1938/9 when another move (to 362 Old St) and more exotic models were added to the catalogue whilst Ethel Rensch is known to have been living locally and may be working very closely as well. Could it have been Ethel Rensch, who certainly turned out to have a good business head later on who was the, or part of the, mystery management of the firm in this pre war period? Some one held it together when Rensch was taken into internment[2] in the early months of the war and again Janes suggested that this might have been Hendersen, though once again we can never know.

Moving to the post war PARIS period we have just a hint of more information. In the post war rating books of Hackney there is a first hint of organisation in that in 1945 the earliest occupation of 133 Stoke Newington Church Street is recorded for the PARIS firm when HH Rensch was the listed occupant with "HH Rensch trading as the Paris Welding Company." We know nothing else about the Paris Welding Company, certainly nothing in terms of whether there was a management structure within it, but Monty Young recalls seeing the massive steel plates used for PARIS frame building jigs. Young was told these had been bought as war surplus from the shipyards in which Rensch and many other cycle industry workers had spent their war; it seems possible the Paris Welding Company was a firm created by Rensch to acquire this material. Then, again from the rates records in 1949, the occupant was "HH Rensch and T Rutherford trading as Paris Welding Company." No one now seems to know who T Rutherford was or what role he played within the firm. By 1951 the firm itself (now named in the books as PARIS Cycle Company) is listed as the occupant before changing in 1952 to Paris Cycle Company Ltd. It is understood that from 1951 onwards Harry Rensch was no longer part of the firm which was then headed up by Mrs Rensch. Beazley recalled an older man known as Jock who was the manager in 1951/2 and then it is known that WB Hurlow was brought in as a manager to oversee its winding up.

Mrs Ethel Ellen May Rensch

A very brief mention of the role of Mrs Rensch is given here because there can be no doubt from Janes's account of his daily work in 1947/8 that at this time Mary Rensch (as she was apparently known with in the firm) had a central role in keeping the firm's accounts and perhaps an eagle eye on good workshop practice.

In Janes's account Ethel would be found in a small room next to the recep-

1   Working with Paris Cycles, *Boneshaker* Volume 175 36-45, Winter 2008
2   If indeed there was any internment for Rensch, just at present the jury is out on that assertion.

tion area and even starred in an advertisement for the *Galibier.*

This now famous model was probably
conceived by Rensch in the late 1930's just
about the time that the couple were courting.

What tragedies the Rensch's and their
firm suffered, first in losing their first child,
then the decline in Harry's health and his
later marital infidelities. Which of these
pressure were the cause of the marriage's
instability remains unknown, at which point
Harry and Ethel split, Ethel remarried, the
firm closed and finally there was the loss of
the firm's record books.

Just to close the entry on Mrs Rensch,
she was contacted by one ME (Neville Ireland) in the late 1990s but said that she did
not wish to discuss the firm or its history

Figure 114 Ethel Rensch photographed on a *Galibier.*

and would not comment on whether the firm's records still existed. The contact with her has remained closed.

Figure 115 Could this also be Ethel Rensch with a *Galibier?*

Employees in the shop/workshop	Supported riders or in firm's TEAM
John Adlington	
Slash Beales	
Mike Beazley	
Teddy Binder	
Tom Board	
John Brimmicombe	
Harry Burvill	Harry Burvill- PARIS TEAM
'Stoppa' AH Clark	'Stoppa' AH Clark (Sec, founder PARIS TEAM)
Eric Deeks	
Charlie Galbraith	Charlie Galbraith–Rensch TEAM
Jackie Gutteridge	
	Reg Henderson – Rensch Team
Ted Henderson	
Alan Hockley	Alan Hockley- Rensch TEAM16
Ken Janes	
Jack Jones[1]	
George Kessock aka George Phillips	George Kessock- PARIS TEAM
"Mac" AE Metcalfe	"Mac" AE Metcalfe rode prewar in amateur clubs
Dusty Miller	
Ron Morbey	Ron Morbey – PARIS TEAM
Clive Parker	Clive Parker- PARIS TEAM
Harry Parr	
Vic Payne	
Don Rains	
Ted Rainer	
Jock Rutherford	
Tom or Johnny Saunders	Tom or Johnny Saunders
Bob Stratfall	
Norman Tame	
Bunny Turner	
Willy Turrell	

PARIS staff

The table above lists those people who are known to have been involved either in the shop, workshop[1] or any of the teams. Brief notes on these men follow, some of them woefully short, please do get in touch with the author or the Veteran-Cycle Club if you can help to fill in any gaps in our knowledge.

Notes on individual staff members

Johnny Adlington
Eric Deeks remembers Johnny as a brazer in the late 1940s early 1950s responsible for the rear triangle braze ons and working at a bench next to Dusty Miller.

Slash Beales
'Slash' Beales worked for **PARIS** from 1946 to 1948/9. In talking to Neville Ireland[2] he commented that in his time the firm had twenty odd employees, with up to five frame builders making two to three frames a day, together with lug makers and frame filers and the finishing/enamelling work. Beales left **PARIS** at the same time as Metcalfe and Parker and like Parker helped Metcalfe set up his shop in Caledonian Road. In late 1951 when Metcalfe was closing he moved to Rivett's shop in High Street, Leytonstone, presumably as a frame builder. Later he moved to Stokes and then later to Bates.

Mike Beazley
Mike worked in the firm for a short period in 1951/2, with his recollections being presented in detail an article in The *Boneshaker*[3] . Beazley had previously worked with Aberdale Cycles and though recruited by Rensch did not see much of him – Beazley was of course a youngster and Rensch was probably himself *persona non grata* around the place.

Teddy Binder
Teddy was the main enameller for **PARIS**, presumably under the direction of Harry Parr.

Tom Board
Board was born 8 June 1929 and went to school at St. Josephs in Rugby Warwickshire. His first bike was an old BSA and the first proper racing bike a "Three Spires" which started his love affair with *cycling*. He then started as an apprentice in 1949 with the then busy **PARIS** firm. He has recalled[4] that at that time he was taken on as a frame filer- "That's how most frame builders start, doing all the little bits for the other frame builders. After a year or so I

1   F Hernandez dated 1995, and K Jane, 2002
2   Beales to N Ireland telecon 2003
3   Beazley M *Boneshaker* 178 2008 pp32-39
4   The Name behind the frame *Bicycle* October 1983

built my own frame as a test-piece. It was nothing fancy – just the standard PARIS lugless club frame – but it was OK so I started on full timeframe building." Board spent a couple of years with the firm ending when the firm stopped trading (say late 1952) having been a feature of the firm remembered with affection by co worker Mike Beazley as the only person who could control the large watch dog kept to protect the premises at night. Board then worked at Macleans who were at the time managed by Dick Swann, a well known cycle industry insider and sometime rider for Polytechnic CC. Before long however he moved onto FW Evans because the work at Macleans was unchallenging. By 1971 he had gone solo as an independent frame builder and made frames on demand for

Figure 116 Tom Board seen in 2003

Pat Hanlon. He was a great favourite of Pat's and she always spoke fondly of him[1]. Later he worked as master builder for Condor Cycles. It was whilst with Condors, working with Monty Young that he met Michael Kemp who was an enthusiastic amateur rider who had fallen in love with the **PARIS** *Galibier*. When Kemp found out about Board's earlier experience at **PARIS** and his now well honed frame building skills, he saw a way forward - and together with Monty Young - the **PARIS Lightweight Cycle Company Ltd** was on its way in 1982.

John Brimmicombe

John Brimmicombe worked as a frame filer at some stage in the late 1940's.

Harry Burvill

Harry was arguably the largest of the 1947 PARIS TEAM for the Brighton to Glasgow 6 day event. The team was made up of Harry, Ron Morbey, Stoppa Clarke, Tom Saunders and George Kessock[2]. Within the PARIS team Burvill was also known as Lofty –amongst some quite large people this young man at 6ft 3 really stood out! Some entertaining stories are told by a clubmate Derek (Tiny) Stringer.[3] Derek was later able to buy Burvill's PARIS *Tour de France* from him which was given as an engagement present to his fiancé Beryl who still owns and rides the machine to this day.

---

1   Notes made by Mick Butler 2006
2   *The Bicycle* 30 July 1947
3   See entry in Recollections in www.Classiclightweights.co.uk

Stoppa Clarke

'Stoppa' – AH (Douglas) Clarke - was a man for his times – a lively character who had involved himself promoting the BLRC in London after its forma-
tion in 1942. He was the first Hon. Secretary of the London Section of the
BLRC and much of its early success was down to his efforts. He was a keen
roller riding man and was involved in the first amateur Roller championships
at Collins Music hall. He was perhaps the inspiration for Rensch to set up the
PARIS Racing Team and for the firm to start making and selling PARIS brand-
ed cycle rollers. During the war he had helped to organise the Doomer's Con-
test between various East London clubs, and this, with the London Section
of CTC led to the London Section of BLRC. A V-CC member who wishes
to remain anonymous recently acquired some Paris Team photographs[1] that
record a competition event in 1947, a period when Stoppa Clarke's star was in
the ascendant!

In September 1947 Stoppa was the team leader in the Paris Cycles team in
the Independent Road Championship. This event was sponsored by I.T.P, a

Figure 117 Stoppa Clarke savours the coming awards, and what was Brenda thinking about?

national football pools enterprise, who also sponsored their own team of six
riders in these BLRC events – and all of these I.T.P riders had by mid 1947
individually won earlier races in the series. The race was over 150 miles - a
25 mile triangular circuit ridden six times - organised by the Western Section

1   I clearly cannot divulge his name, but to find out the events shown was advised by Ken Janes
     to write to Dave Orford, doyen of BLRC memorabilia, who kindly also put me in touch with John
     Scott who is currently researching cycle-teams and their management in this post war period, and
     George Bickerstaffe who lived the period and still enjoys recounting it!

can't take this awayfrom him! After finishing first
B.L.R.C. National Independent Road Race Cham-
ip over a gruelling Mendip course. A. H. Clarke
Cycles) wins a kiss from Weston Beauty Queen,
3renda Bartlett. Later he was disqualified by the
and the title went to D. Jaggard (Daytons)

Figure 118 The caption, though cropped badly, says it all! Stoppa takes no prisoners Thanks
to George Bickerstaffe for sending me material about Stoppa's 1947 race at Weston-Super-
Mare

of BLRC. Other powerful teams were entered by the Hamilton, Dayton and
Clement Cycles teams, Bob Thom for Clements having won the same event in
1946. It would be no push over then! The Paris Team came first, second, and
fourth with Stoppa leading them in, but an observer from Dayton Cycles had
seen the Paris Team taking drinks from outside of the official feeding area.

Two days later the results were changed with D. Jaggard of Dayton Cycles (who had been third on the road) winning the event. In the meantime though, to the winner the spoils! As the pair of photographs (Figures 117 and 118) reveals, Stoppa was awarded, on the day at least, with what he plainly enjoyed, from Miss Brenda Bartlett, the Weston–Super–Mare Bathing Beauty for 1947!

Stoppa was always a natty dresser at that time and a "Fair well" biographical note of 1950, when he left England for pastures new in South Africa, fondly recalls his light blue spragging (sic) suit and his propensity to gather controversy around himself![1].

After this time he moved on to TI and Raleigh where he was able to tell them a thing or two about modern lightweight frame design and was with them when Carlton was bought in to really modernise their lightweight system[2]. After that in 1950 Clarke moved away to South Africa. Clarke retired to Spain from where he occasionally visited London to see and enjoy old friendships but he was reported to have died early in 2012.[3]

Eric Deeks

Eric was employed from sometime in 1948 to about mid 1950 when National Service in the RAF took him away. He had been trained by Dusty Miller and was for most of his time in the firm the main fork builder having made forks for all the models by the time he left. He also did a lot of tube mitring and remembers that the *Galibier*s were in his time mostly or all built by Norman Tame.

Charlie Galbraith

Charlie Galbraith was born in 1920 and would have been a school leaver about the time Harry was setting up the Rensch business. How or when he worked with Rensch is not known at present. Galbraith learnt to play the violin as a child and by the early 1940's had become involved in the London jazz scene. He was also known to be a very keen cyclist with touring and road racing in Switzerland and Spain being mentioned[4], but this must have been after WWII. His war was spent in the RAF, where he was lucky to meet 'Professor' Jimmy Edwards in Bomber Command; with whom he learnt to play the trombone. He may have worked part time with **PARIS** immediately after the war as it is known that he only became a professional jazz musician in 1949. He went on to work with Kenny Ball, Cy Laurie, Joe Daniels and Monty Sunshine and at one time had his own band. He also developed an interest and knack of finding antiques particularly fine clocks.

1   Unknown author and publisher, the article is thought to be about 1950, filed by NI in ME's files.
2   AH Clarke in conversation with Neville Ireland 8 August 2002
3   Harold Jones, telephone conversation March 2012."
4   Obituary by John Westwood The Jazz Rag March/April 1997

He was, for a short time at least, part of the Rensch Team, with Alan Hockley.

EW (Ted) Hendersen

Ted joined the pre-war Rensch firm in 1938[1] and it seems not unlikely that this may have been around the time that Les Ephgrave, Rensch's first fully trained assistant left, though of course the firm was being expanded about this time and would move the next year to Old Street and publish its new enlarged catalogue. Janes recalls that Hendersen had been trained at Bates of Plaistow, and thought that he probably continued to work with Rensch may be at his home in the evenings on small scale frame production through the war. Janes says he moved to Norwich after the war, and managed or owned a well known cycling shop in Anglian Square, Norwich was known as *The Norwich Cycling Boutique,* however John Coulson and Harold Jones have stated that this account of Hendersen is incorrect[2].

Jackie Gutteridge

He and apparently his (half?) brother, have been reported[3] to be regular suppliers of filed lugs and bilaminations to PARIS which they prepared in home workshops. They would have been paid a piece rate but were not regularly employed. Jackie later became a well known wrestler, under the surname of Pallo which was in fact a distant family name that he admired. A slightly longer account of his life is given under the name Pallo.

Alan Hockley

Rode for the H RENSCH Team as an Independent in 1948/9. Hockley is still alive and living in East Anglia; attempts to contact him have failed so far but perhaps he could be coaxed into filling out some of his story for us?

Ken Janes

Ken Janes, who worked to the last as a lug cutter using just hand tools, is the stuff of legends. He was always happy to regale both current and previous MEs with his recollections as a peripatetic cycle industry artist in metal. In addition he was a soldier of some stature, being large by nature and large by character[4]. It may be the truth was stretched at times by this raconteur, we shall never know now. Ken's father was Fred Janes who had worked for Claud Butler pre war and from whom Ken learnt the trade of lug cutting as a youngster, though Ken felt that his father saw some of his graphic skills as pointing

1   Telephone conversation with K Janes April 2007
2   Coulson J Letters *The Boneshaker* 177 pp 48-49 and H Jones, telecon August 2012.
3   An anonymous note in the files under Gutteridge.
4   A biographical note can be found at www.classicrendezvous/

to more artistic opportunities for his son.
Ken joined PARIS in early in 1947[1] and at
that time stayed with the Rensch family in
digs at their home. Ken learnt his formal
frame and lug work at **PARIS** but quite
soon found the highly repetitive work bor-
ing. The call of the Army took him away
from cycling for a while after mid 1948.
The figure below shows him in the 1954
Tour of the East, in which he came home
in third place.

    Ken had built one or two PARIS frames
as well, one of which he took with him
and kept unfinished until in the 1990's by
which time he had finally found the time to
collect all the right components and have a
good paint job on it. Ken was honoured
for his oeuvre of high class work and in-
novative design for cycle construction by
being awarded the Deuchar Medal of the
European Institute of Cycle Engineers in
Figure 119   Ken Janes on the Hetchins
he built whilst working with them in
1954 in the 1954 Tour of East Anglia

1982 for his work with PARIS and with Hetchins, Ephgrave and Carpenter[2].
It is understood that a frame built with a final lug set has been presented to the
Coventry Transport Museum.

Jack Jones.

    Jack started with Rensch before the war. He went back to work for **PARIS**
from about 1946 to 1948. He told Mick Butler[3] that he had made several
frames for the PARIS bicycle used in the film *A Girl and Boy and a Bike*. A promotional photograph of the Paris Team at the film's opening gala (see Figure
19 page 32) shows a placard with a statement that the actual model used in the
film could be seen in the photograph. Some separate photographs forwarded
by Mick Butler show a typical early *Tour de France* model with the early ET1
type of head tube bilaminations, characteristic PARIS seat stays and rear brake
bridge valance, in other words just what would be expected for that period.
Photographs from the film show that one at least of the PARIS frames ridden
by the hero had the internal brake cable in the top tube. There are at least two
surviving early ET1 frames with this feature on the V-CC register but whether

1   Ken Janes has left an account of his time with PARIS Cycles in *Boneshaker* Volume 175 pages
     34 to 46.
2   Hywell Jarman writing in Cambridge Evening News, 7.8.92
3   Conversation with M Butler reported to AJES 2005

these are the actual machines is unknown. Sometime around late 1948 Jack left to found his own bike marque. He had his workshop in a cellar under the existing bicycle shop operated by Newton's. This has given rise to the fiction that Jack built bikes for Newton's and badged as such. However, Jack vehemently denied ever building Newton bicycles. Jack started building his own bikes with the initial four bikes sold as *Sibleys*- his wife's maiden name. Thereafter he used *Jack Jones* as the marque's name – often shortened to JJ's by their owners. Jack told David Bromback that some 400 frames were made altogether before he ceased building. One old friend, Percy Horton, remembers[1] how popular Jack was with riders and friends at the Paddington track, and Mrs Jones told Dave Bromback how she and Jack used to love their evenings attending the track meetings[2].

George Kessock

The 1947 PARIS TEAM for the BLRC Brighton to Glasgow 6 day event was made up of Harry Burvill, Ron Morbey, Stoppa Clarke, Tom Saunders and this race was lead by George Kessock. George was first overall and was also in the fourth, Bradford to Newcastle stage, altogether winning £40 for the event[3].

'Mac' AE Metcalfe

Mac as he was widely known was an associate of Rensch's before WWII. Mac' was well known – his marriage to Phyllis Pope also a keen club cyclist was photographed in *Cycling*[4] as a race marshal for the West Barnet CC, and he was also an occasional veteran competitor in London area events.[5] It may have been that as a senior man he became a partner in the **H Rensch** firm in the 1937-9 period.. 'He was said[6] to be a co-director with Harry and Ethel Rensch of **PARIS** and was certainly well enough known to be reported in *The Bicycle* as attending the 1948

Figure 120 Photograph of George receiving his award George, whose real surname is Phillips, is currently living in France. (Photograph made available by mystery owner.)

1   Fellowship News 153/22 FCOT
2   DBromback in conversation with AJES November 2005
3   *The Bicycle* 20 August 1947
4   *Cycling* 3 March 1943 p. 174
5   *Cycling* 1 September 1943 p 158
6   Conversations with Dennis Talbot and Harold Jones Spring 2006

BLRC Annual Dinner with Harry and Ethel Rensch, and their other friends Mr and Mrs Day of Dayton Cycles[1]. Post war, whatever his financial involvement in the firm, Metcalfe worked at **PARIS,** presumably in a position rather more senior than working at bench level, until 1948/9. At or about this time it is known that he left **PARIS** to form his own firm in 78 Caledonian Road, London. The 'Metcalfe' bicycles, which were marketed as *Mac Sports,* were not built by Metcalfe himself, but by Clive Parker and Slash Beales, both of whom also left **PARIS** shortly after Metcalfe himself. It is said that Metcalfe took too much out of his own firm's profits and it closed in late 1951. Metcalfe died in a boating accident in the mid 1950's. His son contacted Neville Ireland in 2002 but has subsequently himself died, though it was thought in 2006 that Mrs Phyllis Metcalfe was still alive living with her daughter in the Isle of White.

Dusty Miller
Miller, whose correct full name remains unknown was said by Mike Beazley to have left PARIS in the Easter of 1952. This appears to be confirmed by the fact that his role in the firm could not be recalled by Hurlow[2] who failed to recognise his name, commenting that he thought it was merely an apocryphal name taken out of someone's WWII services musings. However, Miller has been said to have been the foreman-in-charge in the period 1949 to 1952[3] and Tom Board recalled that when Miller did leave PARIS it was to join F Lipscombe, another lightweight specialist,[4] something that was confirmed by HR Morris who knew both men. Miller is also said to have been very much a tandem specialist and this is not surprising because late in the days of the firm – from 1950/1 onwards **PARIS** seemed to concentrate on tandems, perhaps because of Dusty's skills but also perhaps, because a secure market niche had been found. We will probably never know when Miller joined the firm but it seems quite likely that he might have been with Rensch from 1945 onwards.

Ron Morbey
Ron was a member of the 1947 PARIS TEAM for the Brighton to Glasgow 6 day event. The team was Harry Burvill, Ron Morbey, Stoppa Clarke, Tom Saunders and George Kessock. Morbey, who is mentioned also below in the account of Clive Parker, came home in 22nd place in this 1947 event.

---

1   *The Bicycle* 21 January 1948
2   Conversion with AJES 2006
3   N Palmer to P Wray September 2005 and M Butler to AJES 2006
4   T Board and HR Morris to N Ireland 2003

Jacky Pallo(w)

Pallo was the performing name for Jacky Gutteridge[1]. In his last and best known career he was a pantomime baddie for television wrestling in its brief flowering in the 1960s, becoming a well known minor parts actor in his later years. He had become a professional wrestler at age 26 in 1952 having grown up watching his father's boxing gym and went on to perfect acting out the dastardly acts of TV wrestling before making himself unwelcome in the ring when a premature publication of his memoirs revealed too many unpalatable truths of the trade; he became persona non grata where once he had been fated. In his teens he had been a reasonable lug cutter and filer for PARIS –one of the band of out-workers who could take work away and bring back the finished goods if they wished[2]. After his death, when approached by this author, his family appeared to know nothing about this aspect of his life. Colin Skipp[3] described seeing him acting as an accomplice to Bruce Reynolds as recorded in the section for Reynolds later in this chapter.

Clive Parker

Clive Parker was reported to be a nephew of Harry, though was possibly not a direct line nephew. Clive who was 14 in 1943 appears to have left school about that time. He was a keen cyclist, though was initially self taught. Two of Parker's contemporaries, Harold Jones and Dennis Talbot have helped very considerably with this account.

Harold Jones starts these recollections of their intertwined careers. He (Jones) left school (the same school as Parker) in 1944. Parker had already started work in spring 1944 at a small engineering and cycle shop company, Stills of Wood Street, Walthamstow. Parker had chosen to work in the engineering side of the firm. After about a year he moved to another enterprise owned by Stills – yet another cycle shop, though this one was in fact owned run by the brother of the Stills who was his first employer. About 1945 Jones, after a few months of work, joined the CTC's Leyton Section which met at the top of the road in which he lived. It was around this time that Jones renewed contact with Parker, who he recalled as a slightly older school contact, because Parker also joined the CTC. At this period he, like most youngsters, was riding an old sports bike. Jones recalls they rode everywhere on these heavy bikes including visits to Brighton and back. Jones also remembers that it was at Easter 1946 that the secretary of the Leyton Section, Fred Clement, took both lads to see the BLRC Dover to London road race, which they saw as the riders tackled the severe Wrotham Hill. Ever afterwards, and whenever these friends met, Parker would reminisce about seeing Ted Jones leading the pack up that

1   Obituary in *The Independent* 16 February 2006
2   N Palmer to AJES 2006
3   Colin Skipp, V-CC member in telephone conversation to AJES 2012

famous hill and say how that sort of attacking cycling had inspired him. Harold Jones comments that it was only three years later in 1949 that Parker beat Ted Jones in the 1949 version of that race.

Harold Jones thinks that it was around Easter of 1946, doubtless as he and Parker began to mingle with older boys and club members who would have been talking about the sport (and particularly in this area of BLRC and its dashing heroes), that Parker became aware that he had a family connection – one he had not previously known about - who had a successful cycle company and who was making circles in the BLRC pool. Jones says that within a week of hearing about Rensch and his **PARIS** firm's BLRC involvement Parker was working at the shop. Shortly after that Jones and Parker joined the East London Section of BLRC .

Jones recalls that Parker rode a **PARIS** *Tour de France* when he first rode competitively but that by 1947 he was riding a *Galibier*. Jones says that it was during the 1948 National Road Championship when Parker and a strong Australian rider, Harold Johnson, were away together in the Derbyshire Peaks that Parker's *Galibier* broke its bottom bracket just below the crest of a hill. Johnson was away in a flash and it was the end of the race for Parker. Jones says that Parker was terribly disappointed and though he did not see it, he suspects that the fabled kicking of his disabled *Galibier* by Parker probably did happen.

Dennis Talbot recalls Parker not just as a fellow club-mate, but as one with whom he went on to ride professionally. When they first met in 1946 Parker had already started working with **PARIS**, but was then a Junior un-aligned with any club. Talbot recalls[1] from his own experience just how much membership of a club and training with a club mentor could bring out and improve native talent.

Talbot himself was being brought on in this way by his brother-in-law Ron Morbey, both being keen members of the East London Section of the BLRC. As it happened Morbey was already a PARIS TEAM rider for Rensch. So that when Talbot and Morbey identified Parker as having real talent it was natural that Parker's introduction to club training and indoctrination – and probably time off during the week for miles in his legs - would be supported by Rensch. Talbot recalls how at this time the inculcation of the cycling life, which as he recalls with some awe, included vegetarian menus and early bedtimes to support the regular training rides, was a joy to young lads who were eager to be led in this way. Talbot remembers that Morbey told him that such guided training could give a talented rider as much as a five year advantage over his peers.

Parker became an eager follower and quickly learnt the way forward. Talbot remembers that Parker was always independent by nature - capable of detaching himself from others – he showed even then that he was a self-contained and

Figure 121 Parker about to have a sandwich from Dennis Talbot

'driven' personality. Both Talbot and Jones have commented that Parker was more often than not found to be away from his frame building bench – getting the miles in. In 1947 he won the London Junior Road Championship. In 1948, in his first race as a senior, he won the London Road Championship at High Beach in Epping Forest riding a *Galibier*. Later in 1948 he rode in the **PARIS** Team. Parker really had learnt his cycling skills with **PARIS** both in the workshop and on the road. Parker is seen in Figure 121 at the top of Mott Street in the London Road Championships on his *Galibier* with Talbot about to hand him a sandwich and Jones with the bike in the background.

In 1948 Parker did win the London Championship, and that championship race was won on a *Galibier* he had built himself. He is shown with the rest of the **PARIS** TEAM in the last photograph. In his first big road stage race the 1948 Brighton to Glasgow he was first in the fifth and penultimate stage, coming in 6th overall behind

Stoppa Clarke[1], but contributing handsomely to the PARIS TEAM's win. As already noted Talbot has commented that Parker had a way of taking time away from the bench to get the miles in. It is not known what Rensch thought of this behaviour but there were changes beginning to get underway in PARIS affairs at this time. 'Mac' Metcalfe who was an old friend and possibly a financial partner in **PARIS** must have been getting ready at this time for future changes. Sometime in 1948/9 Metcalfe left **PARIS** in order to set up his own firm, and it appears that he took Parker with him. It seems likely that Parker's frame building skills were essential to Metcalfe who also took on Beales from **PARIS**. It is probable that Parker, who about this time became known as a BLRC Independent rider, was able at Metcalfe's to take even more time out on his bike and away from the bench. Doubtless, as Parker was clearly an experienced and fully skilled frame builder, he would have been employed on piece work and have been able to choose his own hours for working for Metcalfe. Parker is known to have ridden his last races in the **PARIS** Team colours in the 1949 Brighton to Glasgow and then, in the Tour of Poland in which he damaged his Achilles tendon, had to retire from the race.

In 1950 Parker signed for the Dayton Team. Freddy Derman, manager of Dayton Cycles was coincidentally Secretary of BLRC. This team continued in 1951 with team mates such as Dave Bedwell. Harold Jones who had ceased riding competitively by then recalls that Parker had also taken to ballroom dancing and was throwing himself into it with his accustomed single mindedness. Jones did not share this enthusiasm and these two friends drifted apart. Jones did keep in touch when Parker was working at Metcalfe's by occasionally seeing his friend at work in the cellar in Caledonian Road that was the Metcalfe premises. In late 1951 Metcalfe's business closed so there was no winter employment there for Parker. Beales, who had also been with Parker at Metcalfe's had already started to work with Rivetts, the famous Leyton-stone cycle shop.

Parker kept himself 'super fit' in the winter of 1951/2 by working with the Forestry Commission in Epping Forest before himself signing for Rivetts track team at Herne Hill in what became known as the Johnny Dennis Herne Hill School. Parker also rode on the Continent for Rivetts –one of the small post war band of English riders who successfully joined the continentals at what had been their own game. The advertisement for Rivetts shown in Figure 122 shows

"**R**IDE **IVETTS** WITH **CLIVE**"

We will gladly quote you for a Frame Set or Complete Machine to the identical Specification

A postcard to us will be sure to bring you this specification together with OUR FREE MAIL ORDER PRICE LIST of Equipment and Accessories (English and Continental)

Figure 122   Parker racing in Rivetts colours

Parker in the World's Professional Road Race in Luxemburg in August 1952.[1]

During this year Jones recalls that he and another old friend Neil Palmer acted as mechanics for both Parker and Talbot in this team at Herne Hill.

It was sometime in early 1953 that Jones and Parker finally drifted apart. Parker and Talbot who were also loosing contact with each other as a result of courtships were both married in that year and Parker moved away physically to south London. Then also in 1953 Parker signed for the Hercules professional team although Talbot joined him there in the same year. The rest of the story does not concern this PARIS history[2], but Talbot and Jones are still very much alive and riding. Parker, after a second career as a cheddar cheese wholesaler/retailer and a lay preacher much loved by his flock, died untimely and very suddenly in June 2005. Latterly he had loved to recount his youthful exploits, though few of his flock knew any details of his early career, and he never returned to cycling. Talbot, recalling his boyhood friend, who he had just re-found in early 2005, remembers with great sadness that Parker was not uninterested in trying out cycling again when they spoke just a few weeks before his death.

Harry Parr

The role of Harry Parr within the firm is poorly known at present. Ken Janes has described how successful some of the artistic sign painting by Harry Parr was –he particularly recalled being told about the Mackintosh's delivery vans with huge painted sides depicting Quality Street Chocolates and toffees with their gaily painted Regency scenes of ladies in ball gowns enjoying the toffees[3]. Bill Hurlow in 2006 remembered that at the end of the PARIS firm it was largely earnings from Harry Parr's enamelling division of the firm that were keeping the firm going. When Hurlow[4] was completing the last of the PARIS stock, this division which was by then either owned or certainly separately managed by Parr, who may have been the manager known to Beazley as 'Jock', refused to carry out frame finishing of these last frames and Hurlow had to find other frame finishers for these last PARIS machines. Harold Jones believes that it is 'Jock' who can be seen with the PARIS racing team in Figure 125 in the last chapter.

Vic Payne and Don Rains

Both of these men were recalled as frame builders for PARIS by John Coulson[5] who knew them when riding with various clubs, Raines during 1949/50 and Payne much later in the 1990s. Neither at the time offered Coulson any details of their roles in the firm.

1 Advertisement presented to Peter Underwood by Neville Ireland in 2004, origin unknown.
2 An account can be read on http:/www.classiclightweights.co.uk
3 Mackintosh launched *Quality Street* in 1936 so this story reported to AJES by K Janes in 2007 must have been PARIS shop talk folklore!
4 WB Hurlow telecon 2006
5 Letters to N Ireland July to December 2002

Ted Rainer

Rainer worked for Rensch in the Balls Pond Road enamelling section and was their box lining artist.[1]

Bruce Reynolds

Reynolds worked or shirked in PARIS for a short time as a trainee rider/ tube filer preparing tubes for the frame builders[2]. It was quickly apparent he had no application for riding competitively and when found double dealing both his own father and Rensch over a PARIS bike, he was quickly dismissed. A slide into crime merely gathered pace whilst being with Claud Butler's and he eventually became one of the Great Train Robbery mob. He was last seen sometime after having been released from jail approaching the Lotus company with a paper carrier bag full of used five pound notes, where he bought a new Lotus Cortina. At this time he had as company Jacky Gutteridge, who was doubtless acting as his back up. See Pallo.

Jock Rutherford

Mike Beazley recalls[3] a senior manager who headed up the firm under Mrs Rensch in 1951 and who was known as either Mac or Jock –a Scots term anyway! Mike recalled him as having dark brown hair and a moustache and as having a reputation as having been a fine frame builder in his younger days. It appears this 'Jock' could also have been Harry Parr! A T Rutherford was named together with Harry Rensch as the rates payer on behalf of the Paris Welding Company for 131and 133 Stoke Newington Church Street in 1945 and '46. Whether or not this is the T Rutherford that someone had told Neville Ireland had some involvement with the firm remains unknown.

Tom Saunders

Tom or Johnny Saunders was well known to the Rensch/Paris firm and as mentioned already Ken Janes remembers seeing him and Tom Osbourne riding *Galibier* machines prior to WWII in 1939/40 – so was obviously part of the inner circle! Tom Saunders was fourth in the 1947 Grand Prix de La Bastille, a BLRC Battersea Park criterium race held over 31½ miles.[4] Tom was also in the first PARIS TEAM created for the third Brighton-Glasgow 6 day BLRC race 4 – 7 August 1947. This 1947 PARIS TEAM was Harry Burvill, Ron Morbey, Stoppa Clarke, Tom Saunders and George Kessock.

1   Note by Bryan Clarke to P Underwood February 2006
2   Reynolds B The Autobiography of a Thief. Virgin Books. Thanks to Ian Rodwell for this reference
3   M Beazley *Boneshaker* 178 2007
4   *The Bicycle* July 16 1947

Bob Stratfull

Several informants have identified Stratfull as working for the firm but what precise role he played has not been recorded. However Eric Deeks remembers his work bench was in a corner near to the frame jigs and next to that of another framebuilder worker known as Larry who was in 1949/50 the next senior frame builder to Dusty Miller. Stratfull went on to work for Hetchin's where Len Ingrams has records to show he must have assembled and brazed up hundreds of Hetchin's frames under the eye of Jack Denny during 1957 to about 1959. After this time no more more is known.[1]

Norman Tame

Eric Deeks has said that Tame was the frame builder who concentrated on the *Galibier* model when he himself was there. None of the *Galibier*s on the V-CC register and which were made in this period, 1948 to 1950, are reported to carry any frame builder marks, only the frame numbers being recorded. Eric remembers that his work bench was next to Tame's and on the other side of Tame was Miller's bench. Tame is thought have moved on to Claud Butler and to have become a team manager for Holdsworth[2]. He is believed to be still alive and we would be delighted to hear from him.

Bunny Turner

Bunny was remembered by Tom Board[3] as being involved with the firm in its closing days and perhaps building tandems with Dusty Miller. Tom remembered that afterwards Bunny also worked for Condor Cycles, but this has not yet been confirmed.

Willy Turrell

Willy Turrell was quoted by John Lattimore[4] as likely to have been a lug cutter for PARIS between 1946 to 1953. Apparently Turrell went on to work for Maclean and Holdsworth.

1   Len Ingrams, telephone conversation with AJES March 2012.
2   Uninitialled notes in ME's collection.
3   Telecon AJES with TB in summer 1994
4   N&V 296 Discoveries p 80 Aug/Sep 2003

Chapter 18: The Rench and PARIS TEAMS

This account is largely drawn from reports in *The Bicycle* and *Cycling* of the period, and photographs made available by a Veteran-Cycle Club member. Perhaps more information is still locked away in people's memories and it is hoped this text will jog some more out.

The 1947 PARIS TEAM for the Brighton to Glasgow 6 day event was led by Stoppa Clarke with Harry Burvill, Ron Morbey, Tom Saunders and George Kessock. The team is shown in the photograph below, with, on the left in white overalls Mac Metcalfe, and most importantly on the right in white overalls, a very rare shot of Harry Rensch himself.

Figure 123 The 1947 PARIS Brighton to Glasgow Team

Clarke came 15th in the 1947 Brighton to Glasgow 6 day event, but had improved for the fourth Brighton to Glasgow in 1948 where he came second overall, winning the yellow jersey on the third stage. The 1948 PARIS Team was first in that race. A rare picture shows Clive Parker leading a Dayton competitor Tom Saunders in the Newcastle to Edinburgh stage of the 1948 Brighton to Glasgow race[1].

1   The North-Eastern Cyclist, Vol 1 No 13 (4 September 1947) page 9 courtesy Ken Janes and
     Lewis Hall

W. ('Tom') Saunders receives th e latest news and placings as he follows Clive Parker and Ridley's S'an Blair up towards Carter Bar on the Newcastle - Edinburgh stage of the six-day Brighton to Glasgow BLRC even'.

Figure 124 Parker (Galibier) leading Blair and Saunders who was being briefed by the Dayton Team Manager in the 1948 Brighton to Glasgow

A later 1948 team is shown in the photograph taken in 1948 below :-

Figure 125 The PARIS Team of 1948 at Sandown Park. Left to right are Stoppa Clarke, Harry Rensch, Ron Morbey, Harry Parr (Jock), Ken Janes with goggles over his cotton hat, Clive Parker with his *Galibier,* Mac Metcalfe and finally Lofty Burvill

Appendix 1:
Details of the Frames

This appendix begins with a listing of frame features and an explanation of the terms devised to record these Rensch and PARIS frame details, so that when recording sheets are sent out to members they can be more readily completed. Some of the features mentioned have been illustrated at the end of this section.

A new owner looking at Rensch and Paris frames at a meeting may well go away saying – "But they're all different – Not one the same!" Not so! However, in order that the register of Rensch and Paris frames and machines records these variations of the details, and so that interested owners can see where their machine fits within the R/P envelope of variations, a system of identifying the features and referring to them using just the initials of the names has been devised to keep the register entries short. Eventually the register will also have a full photographic entry so that both verbal and graphic records can be interrogated. Apologies to those who do not like initials –its just they are useful here!

No written records of the firm's construction methods or its individual products survive. There is no doubt that Rensch employed many frame builders during the fourteen odd frantic years that resulted in nearly 9000 bikes – yet despite that variations occur with models as well as between them those in model variations that do exist are relatively minor and appear to be explainable by known "evolution". Whilst in small aggregations no one machine appears quite like another, and indeed all were hand-made, there is a startling uniformity within the model types (with the possible exception of early *Galibiers* and *Galibier* bilaminations). Nevertheless the variations are there to be seen! Some can be associated with particular models, some with the passage of time, yet others could reflect individual craftsmen builders. The observation and collection of a record of these details should gradually allow a better understanding of them and thereby of the why and wherefore of them. The list below describes the key characteristics that can be determined in the construction and style of the frames. Some of these features are seen in the photographs[1]. All the features have abbreviated names as initials (*in bold italics* in text below) to allow their entry in the details register.

Frame construction.

Early catalogues list lugged frames (*Lugs*) but some models were available as bronze welded (lugless). This style should be recorded as *NoL*. Post war frames largely had bilaminations *Bilam* at varying numbers of frame joints with some lugless joints whilst at the close frames were built with orthodox lugs.

Bilamination patterns

Early post war PARIS TdF and *Galibier* models had head bilaminations using the 'Eifel Tower' shape (***ET0,ET1,ET2,ET3,ET4***). The Eifel Tower shape can also be likened to an arrow whose head has three points with a diamond opening or window in the head and a triangle cut out in the base. This bilam pattern is used only on the head tube in the standard TdF but is repeated on most *Galibier* frames on the main strut/seat tube bilamination. Five main types of *Eiffel Tower* bilaminated pattern can be distinguished.

ET0   This shape, on an early frame (1081) made in 1939 may well be a prototype – the tower's arrow head has only a 3mm circular hole and there is no triangle piercing in the base of the spire

ET1   Usually 1¼in high and with sharp points to the arrow head. Two towers at top and bottom of head tube with ¼in separation of the side points along the centreline of the head tube.

ET2   Similar to ***ET1*** but the side points of individual towers are close up (1/16in) on the head. It is currently supposed that this pattern, so far seen only on one ***Galibier***, is an indication that the frame is one of the several series of copies- but by whom is not known, but possibly Roy Cottingham.

ET3   Similar to ***ET1*** but bigger and more delicate in appearance used, so far as is known, was used only on 1948 London show model "Olympian track TdF"which was possibly a special exhibition bike.

ET4   Points on the arrows have blunt ends with small windows in the head and base of the tower which is shorter and more squat than ***ET0 to 3*** and the towers are close up to each other on the head tube with only 1/16in spacing. This pattern is sometimes referred to as Gothic Spires to distinguish it from the Eifel Tower shape and is usually an indication that the frame is an early one built by Ken Janes or one of the later Tom Board built machines* but this pattern has also been used on the 2006** ***Condor Paris Galibiers,*** for which the patterns were cut by Len Phipps.

ETMod   The "New Welded TdF" model of PARIS *TdF* that was introduced in or about 1948 or possibly later had this pattern of bilamination. This style has a short central point with a triangle in the base on the head tube and a side arrow coming in from the edge on each side with a diamond window. This style also appears on some later tandems (Rensch badged top of the range models, and some later (8000 and above) *Galibiers* have been found with this pattern, these machines were built round about 1952 and later.

Bilaminations (continued)

Rensch models have had four recognisable patterns of bilams (*RV, RSP, RTP-SW and RTP-DW*)

RV   This is on early frames and has a Vee band at top and bottom of the head tube. It is probably a lug with bilam extensions

RSP   Has a single massive single point arising from integral bearing holders on the head tube, so these may be true lugs extended by bilams.

RTP-SW Made from a single point which is split and curled back to the sides to give elegant circular pattern shapes with a central triangular window in the base.

RTP-DW Made from a single point split and turned back but wider arms and two smaller windows at the base.

In some top-of-the-line models frames had all four joints of the frame fitted with similar pattern bilaminations – but some had only two or three of the joints treated. Some Rensch tandems also shared these patterns especially *RTP,* and *ETMod* as described above

Tom Board used some differing lug bilam styles, for example *TBPr* is known from his prototype, and *TBItal* used for the Prugnat or similar plain lugs frames. The *ET4* style was introduced by Board when requested by purchasers of the 1980's Paris Lightweight models to use bilaminations of an earlier design. In October 2006 Condor Cycles re-introduced the *"Condor Paris Galibier"* and later the *"Condor Paris Tour de France"* also using the *ET4* style.

Bottom Bracket and seat tube top bilaminations (Diamond frames) - A special pointed pattern was used in the New Welded model TdF and recognisable versions of both *RSP* and *RTP* patterns can be found on RTdF and CdM frames which have these patterns used on the head tube. Note that TdF and CdM frames usually have an oversize top tube at 1⅛in except in the case of late variants of these types that were built using framesets intended for use with proprietary lugs.

Galibier **main strut/seat tube joint** Usually the decoration follows the bilam style used on the head tube but some early machines had plain sleeves which just a single point or a series of slots –record as *Spec* if present. In the case of this unique model the offset of the upper seat tube from the lower seat tube could be altered to allow the length of the toptube to be varied. This MS/ST offset or *MSO* varies from +0.5 to +2.5 inches in existing frames

Saddle pin clamp Lugless frames and most post war *ET1* built TdFs and *Galibier*s had a separate saddle clip *SPC* of chromed bronze, others of steel. Clips with Rensch (*RSPC*) or PARIS (*PSPC*) embossed on them are known but bronze clips with a single annular groove (*GBSPC)* appear to have been most common. Many frames have chromed steel clips with a ring motif

(*SRSPC*) whilst others have an embossed swastika-look pattern (*SSSPC*) and numbers of frames have plain clips (*PPSPC*).

Front fork shoulder

Epaulette types *ECD0, 1, 2, 3,4* where CD stands for central dagger
Twin plate crown=*TPC*,
Nervex fork crown =*N*

Seat stay tops

Tapered long >1¼inch or short, 1¼inch =**TL, TS**,
Chamfered long or short =**CL, CS**,
Concave =**Con.**

Badges

Rensch = *RBr* This brass painted badge has rivets at 1⅝inch (42mm) centres

Paris   Eifel Tower = *PET* This enamelled badge has rivets at 1⅝inch (40-43mm) centres apparently varying between batches of badge– colour of enamelling also varied or has aged differently

Laurel wreath = *PBr* made of brass or aluminium *Pall.* Both have rivets at 1¼inch (31-2mm) centres.
Rectangle = *PLS* This brass painted badge has rivets at 2¼inch (58mm) centres
Paris Sport =*PS* This large, about 2in, enamelled badge may have been used on Paris Sport frames

Transfers

Head   H Rensch diamond =*TRD*
Paris diamond =*TPD*
Paris laurel wreath = *TPlaur*   Introduced for Paris Lightweights Ltd in the 1980s but widely fitted in restorations since then, prefix T
Note the prefix *T* is added to these transfers when placed on the head tube to indicate that they provide the makers badge

Seat tube   Paris 'vase' emblem = *STPV*
Paris Eifel Tower transfer=*ST1* or *ST2* or *ST3* or *ST4*
Paris laurel wreath *Plaur or RD or PD diamonds* commonly used on seat tube contrast bands machines
Paris chequers in a panel =*STChP*
Paris Sport cartoon =*Paris Sport cart*

Down tube
> H Rensch in Gothic block =*HRblock*
> Paris in stencil –single and tricolours =*Pblock*
> Paris in flowing script = *Pscript*
> Paris Sport =*PSblock*
> Gran Prix= *PGP*

Lettering
> *PStens* for any stencilled letters Please note the phrases using the initial letters of the words plus note on location.

Frame numbers
> Small 3.5mm font   = *FNS*
> Large 5.5mm font   = *FNL*

Rear brake bridge

To date most post-war **PARIS** frames (some Rensch) appear to share the trademark teardrop type of brake bridge mount or valance for the straight rear brake bridge. Two types can be distinguished (*RBBM1* or *RBBM2*). *RBB1* is found on all bikes with *ET1* bilaminations and is rounded in style, whereas *RBBM2* is found on machines with *ET4* bilaminations and is somewhat more angular though of generally the same shape. Please record as *Plain* or *Other* in the brake bridge section if your frame does not have this feature.

Pump pegs

To date post-war frames fitted for pumps on the top tube seem to have had a simple round base at about 5/16 inch diameter to the pump peg (*RPP*). On some frames there is a diamond shaped base about ¾in long (*DPP*). It may be that **Rensch** frames have the *DPP* and **Paris** frames the *RPP,* this is yet to be confirmed. Note these points in the frame details section.

Bottom brackets

Note that nearly all Renschs and most Rensch built PARIS frames – with the exception of lugged frames and some late (1952 and 53) exceptions – used a Bayliss Wiley Oil Bath separate bottom bracket. These brackets have a 2BA or 3/16inch cycle thread locator (round head screw) inserted at about 6 o'clock or sometimes 9 o'clock in the frame's BB sleeve which is needed to lock the sleeve to prevent its rotation in the housing. This bottom bracket is not of course unique to Rensch or PARIS, but it can be a useful guide, though as noted any lugged frame will have had a normal proprietary threaded BB lug.

In the next few pages some of the characteristic Rensch & PARIS features are set out, accompanied by the short descriptive code name each has been given. These short names help in allowing the bikes themselves to be accurately defined when this may be needed for precise identification.

However whilst taking in these detail images it is interesting to reflect on how the changes were made over the years —an aspect which can be key to assessing the age or position in the sequence of some machines which may otherwise be difficult to place. For example, is there a transition from the strong single riser of the 1937 Rensch Single Point *(RSP)* lug design to get to the first of the Eifel Tower *(ET0)* emblems of 1939 then onto *ET3* which ended that series in 1948? Was it the same hand that split that single riser into two for the Rensch Twin Point *(RTP-SW)* of the Rensch *TdF* model with its single triangular window and then devised the twin window version or *RTP-DW* for the Rensch *Champion du Monde*? Can we perhaps detect a second hand involved in the styling when the New Welded *Tour de France* came about in 1949 with the *ETMod* style of bilaminations, some of which may be extended lugs? Certainly the Paris Lightweight period brought in new lug cutting skills with the *ET4* style of Gothic Spires bilamination that has also been used by the latest Condor designers.

R.Rensch/**PARIS**

Marque Enthusiast

Alvin Smith Castle Cottage Wigmore Herefordshire HR6 9UA 01568 770327

Harry Rensch

Your name_____

Address _____

_____

_____

_____

Post Code _____

Frame number_____Model if known_____ Frame size(inches)____(bb axis to top tube top

Frame construction [ ] Enter *NoL* if lugless, or *Bilam* if bilaminated or *Lugs* if a lugged frame

Bilamination pattern [ ] Enter *ET0,ET1,ET2,ET3,ET4,ETMod,RV,RSP,RTP,TBPr, TBO*

Lugs [ ] Enter *N, or 1*

Main strut [ ] Enter using the Bilam pattern abbreviations or *Spec* or enter ST offset

Front forks tops [ ] Enter *TPC, HS, N* or for other use drawing ⟶

Seat stay tops [ ] Enter *TL* or *TS, Con, CS* or *CL*

Bottom bracket/seat tube top [ ] Enter appropriate Bilam or lug pattern

Saddle pin clamp [ ] Enter *RPC, PPC, GPC, SRPC, SSPC,* or *Other*

Badges [ ] Enter *RBr, PET,PBL, PALL, PLS, PS*

Transfer if used as a head badge [ ] Enter *RD, PD, Plaur*

Transfers ST= [ ] TT[ ] DT=[ ] Enter *ETT1-4, RD,PD, TdF, Plaur*

Stencils /Lettering   Please record here : [ ]

Frame number font size = [ ] Please enter FNS if small or FNL if large –see notes.

Rear brake bridge valance   = [ ] Please record as either *RBBM1, RBBM2,* or *Other*

Bottom bracket type = Baylis Wiley Oil bath : record [ ] as either *Yes/No*

Frame colour and surface finish :

Other details available – such as oversize top tube diameter at 1⅛in for some models

      - small chainhanger on O/S chainstay ? –some early Rensch TdFs

      - history of ownership etc :-

24/01/2012R&P-ID docfin6Last printed 1/24/2012 11:17:00 AM   3

Figure A1.1   Reporting sheet for use by members

Lugs and or bilaminations
Pre war lugs

A1.2 a **RSP** front   b **RSP** side view
Where RSP stands for Rensch Single Point

Post war bilaminations and lugs

A1.3 **ET0**   A1.4a **ET1** from front   A1.4b **ET1** from the side
Where ET stands for Eifel Tower as the design emblem. ET0 is the prototype; ET1 is used in early **P-TdFs** (1946-49)

A1.4c **ET1** on most Galibier main struts   A1.5 **ET2** has its emblems
                                                    closed up

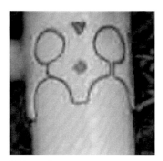

A1.6 *ET3*   A1.7 *ET4*

ET3 has been used on special show models; *ET4* on Paris Lightweight and Condor Paris frames. *ET4* is sometimes called Gothic Spires.

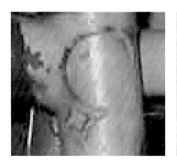

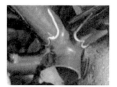

A1.8a *ETMod* on head   A1.8b *ETMod* seat tube A1.8c   *ETMod* on BB
ETMod was introduced for and used on the New Welded TdF (1949-52)

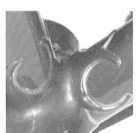

A1.9a *RTP_SW*   A1.9b *RTP-SW* on bracket   A1.10 *RTP-DW*
Where RTP is Rensch twin point and SW is single window DW twin window

A1.11 *RCC*   A1.12 *ROC*   A1.13 *RV*

Where RCC is Rensch close curve and OC is open curve, V is Vee shape

A1.14 *PL-P*   A1.15 *PL-Ital*   A1.16 *ROW*
                                              (tandems only)

Where PL-P is Paris Lightweights prototype and Ital is Italian style. OW is opposing waves

A1.17*ECentdag0*   A1.18 *ECentdag 1*   A1.19 *ECentdag 2*

Where E is epaulette with a central dagger with various variations ECentdag 1 is popularly supposed to have been created using an old fashioned flooring nail as the dagger.

In this collection of bilamination patterns it is suspected that RSP, RCC, ROC and PL-Ital were in origin at least proprietary lug sets, but not infrequently the machines with them have not been examined direct in the steel.

Front fork tops

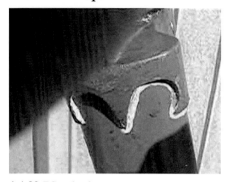

A.1.20 *ECentdag 3*

A1.21 *ECentdag 4*

A1.22 *EFTCent*
Where EFTC is epaulette with fishtail central

A1.23 *TPC1*

A1.24 *TPC2*

Where TPC is twin plate crown with variations of the tricolour pattern (TRIC)

Seat stay top eyes

A1.25 *SS-ST*   A1.26 *SS-MT*   A1.27 *SS-LCC*

Where SS is seat stay top eye ST is short taper, M is medium and L is long,CC is long concave curved

Other frame features

A1.28 Seat tube chequer band   A1.29 top tube TdF transfer

A1.30 top tube Rensch Champion du Monde transfer

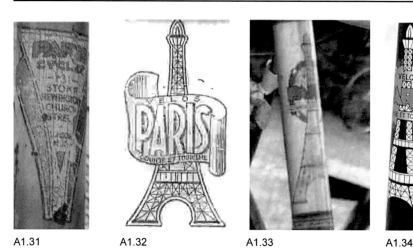

A1.31   A1.32   A1.33   A1.34

Figures A1.31 to A1.34 show the early seat tube emblems; A1.34 is currently available

A1.35 Stencil for top tube of a TdF - differing phrases were used on other models

A1.36 *RBBM1*   A1.37 *RBBM2*

Where RBBM is rear brake bridge type, 1 used on R&P ; 2 used on PL and CP frames

A1.38 *Ellipt* chstay   A1.39 *CSprot*   A1.40 *MGeye*

Where *Ellipt* chstay is the special Rensch elliptical chain stay used on many post WWII models; *CSprot* is the chain stay protector against chain slap offered by Rensch and the *MGeye* is the unique to Rensch and PARIS closed eye cup hook used as a mudguard fitting on nearly all his models

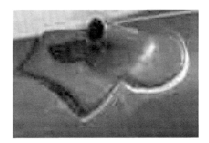

A1.41 Internal brake cableentry point.   A1.42 Stem E1

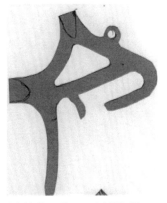
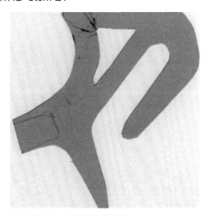

A1.43 Rear Dropout 1936-47   A1.44 Dropout 1948-1949

A1.45 Dropout 1950 -1952   Date ranges for dropouts only approx

Badges A1.46 to A1.53

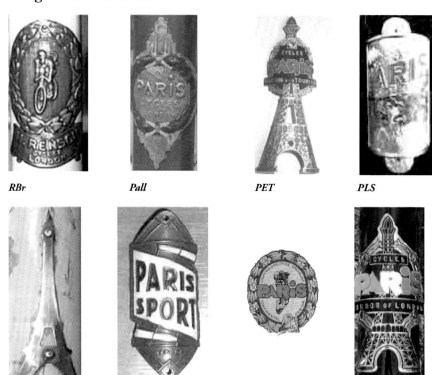

RBr   *Pall*   *PET*   *PLS*

PET-Special   *PS*   *PLaur*   *PCond*

Appendix A2:
Surviving Bicycles: V-CC Register February 2012
The Rensch and PARIS Register

The machines are listed in chronological order with the technical information held for each summarised in the tables shown as Figures A2.1-6. Entries in the register shown in a green font have either a receipt evidence for their manufacture or at least first sale or hearsay of when bought from the first owner. The entries try to give a summary description using some of the initials set out in Appendix A1. Currently many machines do not yet have all their data recorded. Identification packs can be sent out to members on request.

In Figure A2.7 I have shown a reduction on one page of the four register sheets which I have marked up with lines which approximate to the calendar years of production of machines and additionally I have used the 'patterns' which can be detected in the record for each model to mark up what I believe must represent batch production for a number of the models within the firm, with the exception that the *Tour de France* model and just may be the *Galibier* would appear to have been in production on a virtually full time basis. A more detailed analysis of the register data is in preparation for a forthcoming *Boneshaker* article.

Rensch and Paris. Known frames and/or bicycles August 2012 (History)

Frame number (On BB)	RENSCH	PARIS	P Lightweights	Other origin	Rensch CRR	Rensch TdF	Rensch CdM	P Professional	PARIS TdF	PARIS Galibier	Path	T. Dame	Ladies fr	Tandems (R&P)	Paris Sport	Date known	Seat Tube length in inches
26	y										1						
145	y				1												22
227	y				1												
759	y				1												23.5
966	y				1												21
1002				y						1							
1034				y						1							22.5
1081		y							1							Y	
1129			y							1							
1182	y				1												23
1186			y							1							
1193	y				1												
1200	y						1										
1202				y						1							
1211	y				1												
1282		y						1									
1291	y						1										
1335				y						1							22.5
1363	y				1												
1355		y								1							25
1382		y							1							Y	
1406		y							1								
1411		y	y							1						Y	24.5
1411			y							1							
1420 7	y								1								
1432		y										1					24
"1500"		y							1								23
1502		y							1								23
1549		y							1								
1554		y							1								22
1604		.y							1								22
1650		y								1							
1707		y								1							
1776														1			21
1886		y							1								
1892		y								1							22
1917									1							Y	23
1927		y								1							
1950		y							1								
1952										1							
1969		y					1										
1998		y								1							
"2000"		y							1								22.5
2001		y					1									Y	23
2080		y							1								
2119		y								1							

Figure A2.1 First sheet of R&P Register

Rensch and Paris. Known frames and/or bicycles August 2012 (History)

Frame number On BB	RENSCH	PARIS	P Lightweights	Other origin	Rensch CR3	Rensch TdF	Rensch CdM	P Professional	PARIS TdF	PARIS Galibier	Path	T. Dame	Ladies fr	Tandems (R&P)	Paris Sport	Date known	Seat Tube length in inches
2138	y								1								23
2155	y								1							Y	24.5
2165	y								1								25
2200	y									1							
2228		y								1							
2230	y								1								23
2244	y									1							21.5
2246	y									1							22.5
2321		y								1							
2350	y								1								
2351	y								1								
2380	y								1								19
2475	y								1							Y	22.5
2476	y				1											Y	23
2484	y				1												23
2505	y				1												
2528	y								1								
2566			y						1								
2561	y													1			
2650	y									1							22
2668	y									1							22
2675	y									1							22
2679	y									1							23
2681	y								1								23.5
2682	y								1								
2730	y											1					
2821	y								1								21.5
2900	y											1					23
2949	y							1									
2966	y								1								23
3201	y								1								
3217	y									1							
3228	y												1				20
3230	y												1				20
3311	y									1							23
3401	y								1								21
3422	y								1								22.5
3437	y								1								
3440	y								1								23
3445	y								1								23
3512	y								1							Y	
3559	y								1								22.5
3567	y														1		21.5
3576	y														1		
3625	y								1								23
3664	y							1									

Figure A2.2 Second sheet of R&P Register

Rensch and Paris. Known frames and/or bicycles August 2012 (History)

Frame number On BB	RENSCH	PARIS	P Lightweights	Other origin	Rensch CRR	Rensch TdF	Rensch CdM	P Professional	PARIS TdF	PARIS Galibier	Path	T. Dame	Ladies fr	Tandems (R&P)	Paris Sport	Date known	length in inches
3842		y								1							23.5
3915		y									1						
3939		y								1							
3992		y						1									24
4---??		y								1							
4005		y												1			
4098	y													1			23/23
4266		y								1							
4342	y													1			
4434		y												1			23/21
1948		y									1						
"1948"	y													1			
4437		y												1			
?218		y							1								24
4490		y							1								
4535		y							1								
4547		y										1					
4572		y												1			
4576	y				1												
4588		y												1			
4595		y								1							
4640		y							1								
4666	y								1								
4732		y						1									22.5
4738		y							1							Y	23.5
4768		y								1							23
4825		y							1								23.5
4842		y							1								23
"USA"		y						1									
4872		y							1								23
4883		y								1							
4885		y												1			23/18
"1949"		y							1								
4912		y										1				Y	
4935	y					1	1										P
4957	y					1											
5022		y							1								
5027		y							1								23.5
5073				y					1								
5082	y								1								23
5282		y								1							22.5
5283		y								1							
5116		y								1							
5122	y								1								
5462		y							1						1		
5466		y							1								

Figure A2.3 Third sheet of R&P Register

Rensch and Paris. Known frames and/or bicycles August 2012 (History)

Frame number On BB	RENSCH	PARIS	P Lightweights	Other origin	Rensch CRR	Rensch TdF	Rensch CdM	P Professional	PARIS TdF	PARIS Galibier	Path	T. Dame	Ladies fr	Tandems (R&P)	Paris Sport	Date known	Seat Tube length in inches
5486		y							1								
5527		y								1							
5576		y								1							25
5644		y							1								
5716		y							1								
6024	y													1			
6030		y													1		23
6031		y							1								24
6061										1							
6131		y							1								23
6159		y							1								23.5
6235		y						1									23.5
6299		y								1						Y	23
6306		y						1									22
6334		y							1								23
6355	y						1										24
6375		y								1							23
6450		y						1									23.5
6452	y						1										
6468		y								1							
6480	y						1										
6512		y						1									
6512	y						1										
6524		y								1							24
6564		y							1								
6567		y								1							
6570		y								1							23.5
6573		y								1							
6580		y							1								25
6586		y							1								
6610		y							1								22.5
6612		y							1								23
6624		y								1							
6634		y							1								23
6639		y							1								23.5
6640		y							1								23.5
6671		y								1							23
6677			y							1							
6679		y							1								24
6681		y								1							23
6695		y						1									22
6706		y							1								
6728		y									1						
6731		y							1								
6734		y								1							
6743		y							1								23

A2.4 Fourth sheet of R&P Register.

Rensch and Paris. Known frames and/or bicycles August 2012 (History)

Frame number On BB	RENSCH	PARIS	P Lightweights	Other origin	Rensch CRR	Rensch TdF	Rensch CdM	P Professional	PARIS TdF	PARIS Galibier	Path	T. Dame	Ladies fr	Tandems (R&P)	Paris Sport	Date known	length in inches
6782		y							1								23.5
6789		y													1		
6790??		y								1							
6814		y						1									
6817		y							1								
6850		y								1							23
6929		y						1									23
7003		y							1								23
7005		y							1								
7050		y							1								
7074		y							1								
7086		y								1							
7093	?													1			
7096		y							1								
7140		y								1							25
7168		y													1		
7186		y								1							
7191		y												1			
7205	y													1			23/22
7266 9		y										1				Y	22
&303		y						1									??
7307		y								1							23
7322		y								1							
7355	y					1											
7417		y							1								
7450		y								1							23
7462		y								1							
7555		y							1								23
7563		y							1								
7624 7		y							1								
7640		y							1								
7662		y							1								23
7663		y							1								23.5
7743		y							1								
7788	y					1										Y	
7874		y							1								22
7882		y							1								
7913		y								1							25
7914		y								1							24
7916		y								1							
7985		y				1											
8002	y				1												23
8028		y							1							Y	24.5
8067	y														1		23/21
8107 11		y								1							23
8127			y							1							24

A2.5 Fifth sheet of R&P Register.

Rensch and Paris. Known frames and/or bicycles August 2012 (History)

Frame number On BB	RENSCH	PARIS	P Lightweights	Other origin	Rensch CRR	Rensch TdF	Rensch CdM	P Professional	PARIS TdF	PARIS Galibier	Path	T. Dame	Ladies fr	Tandems (R&P)	Paris Sport	Date known	Seat Tube length in inches
8354		y												1			
8382		y							1								23
8399 11		y						1									22
8434			y							1							23
8435		y							1								
8461		y						1									
8471	y													1			23/21
8594		y						1									
8599			y							1							
8611 7		y								1							
8612		y								1							22
8631 11		y								1							24
8633		y												1			
8667		y							1							Y	
8734	y													1			23/21
8777 3		y								1							
8804 1	y													1			23/22
8835		y								1							
8845	y													1			24/23
8846		y								1							
8851		y								1							
8875		y								1							
8871 7	y				1												23
8888		y					1										22
8894		y						1									23
8913		y								1							
526		y								1							
?548	y								1								
552		y							1								
SMP152		y								1							
None			y							1							
Totals	41	204	12	5	4	8	10	23	92	89	7	6	1	22	6	16	

	RENSC	PARIS	P'Lt	Other	CRR	RTdf	CdM	Prof	PTdF	Gal	Path	Dame	Lady	Tander	PSp	Dated
	41	204	12	5	4	8	10	23	92	89	7	6	1	22	6	16

Grand Total R+P=   245

Total later variations =   23

268   (=Total all machines)

A2.6 Sixth and last sheet of R&P Register showing totals for models and marques

The Register marked up to suggest when batch production was in use

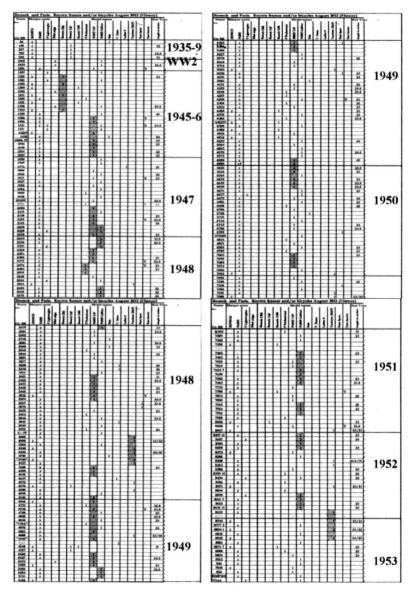

Figure A2.7 The initial analysis of the register –Estimates of year ends showing production in that year with probable batches blocked and shaded. Please do not attempt to read details of each machine -refer to the previous Figures A2.1 to A2.6 for that purpose.

Frame and bicycle age identification.

The first Marque Enthusiast, Frank Hernandez, initially recorded his views on identification in a short account for the Veteran-Cycle Club.[1] Briefly this was

- Type of fork crown e.g. Two plate or Bastide pattern crown used only to 1949.[2]
- Type of badge e.g. Rensch with brass badge, PARIS (started only post early1940's with round aluminium laurel wreath 1947/48, then later but in same period the bronze lacquered Eifel Tower on brass, then finally a larger rectangular badge with a rider honking against a mountain backdrop, both these latter two available 1948 to 1953.
- Most accurate aging is by the four digit frame number under the bottom bracket, e.g. below 1000 = prewar H Rensch, 1000 and on = post-war PARIS and some H Rensch to 5000 in early 1950 and 5001 on and ending 8900 or thereabouts = PARIS and some Rensch up to mid 1953.

As will be apparent from the text of this book and from Appendix A1 there are exceptions to these simple rules, but by and large they still give a good initial appraisal of the machine, with perhaps the style of the lug or bilamination work being the other reliable (and difficult to falsify) criterion. While the easy and cheap feature to copy, but apparently one that up to now never was copied –the round mudguard eye - is also a very useful item.

Frame Numbering and builder identification

It seems most likely that Rensch started numbering his frames without any lettering or differentiation for particular models and continued with this system until the firm was closed. The numbers were a simple se-quence may be starting at 1 or some other low number such as 20. Early frames were stamped

Figure A2.8: Frame number and builder identifier on #8107

1   F Hernandez V-CC News & Views 264 April 1998
2   Mike Beazley V-CC News & Views Noted that the twin plate crown was still available as an option in 1951 when he worked in the firm.

on the bottom bracket across the width of the bracket under the near side chain stay with the head of the frame pointing to the ground. The frame number, but not the builder identification, was also stamped on the fork header tube. This is almost certainly because as we now know from Eric Deek's testimony, there was a dedicated forks builder who made all the forks.[1]

There are a number of post war PARIS frames with marks which the frame builders added as their own identification and this was a mark or a number. In two cases #7460 and 8107 this suffix number was "11" and was placed under the actual frame number as shown below.

The identity of the frame builder who used the mark "11" is tantalisingly unknown. Ken Janes said his mark was a triangle[2].

Estimated production of all R&P models

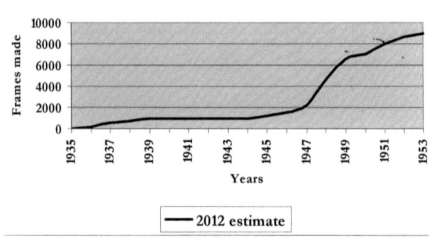

Figure A2.9: Initial estimate of production of the firm

V-CC records of the firm bicycles

As far as we can determine none of the firm's own detailed records of the build or the customer orders have survived. Consequently, how many frames, and how many of each model, were made cannot be known exactly. For example, were absolutely all the numbers (8900 of them) in that sequence actually made? The frame numbers of surviving bicycle frame numbers range in round numbers from #26 to (say) about 1000 to WWII as H Rensch , then post-war as PARIS, PARIS SPORT or Rensch reaching #5000 by sometime in 1950 and end at about 8900 at the end of the Rensch era in 1953.   Unfortunately only about

1   Deeks to AJES in 2007
2   K Janes telephone conversation in 2007

sixteen of the frames on the register (shown in the last but one column on the right in Figures A2.1 to A2.6) have known purchase dates or other good provenance and even in these cases the frames might have been made well before the recorded date of sale. Figure A2.9 shows the current best estimate of frame production assuming all the intervening frame numbers were actually built and that they were built in a plain serial manner.

Some 245 Rensch and PARIS bicycles are known to the Veteran-Cycle Club, though not all are confirmed as still existing in 2012. This is because some have been 'registered', or information about them provided, since the early 1990's. The make-up at August 2012 can be seen at the bottom of the register in Figure A2.6, at present about 2 further machines are reported and added each month. Currently there are no known surviving examples of the PARIS Social Cycle nor have examples been identified of a number of the pre-war Rensch models, however there are now 6 PARIS SPORT machines on the register.

In addition to the above original company frames there are 17 later made Paris machines on the register and the existence of later made Rensch machines cannot be precluded. Paris Lightweight Company frame numbers were of four digits thought to refer to a date of build not a chronological sequence.

Enamelling

The post war years saw the true flowering of the Rensch inspired bicycle by virtue of the success of his colour schemes and in particular the Polychromatic or colour fading that he made so popular. Ken Janes[1] said that the fading was achieved by spraying the adjoining two colours, wet on wet, several times, very thinly, overlapping about 3 to 4 inches. When all dry, blend together with very fine (1200 grade) flatting paper or cutting paste and lacquer over.

The colour schemes were known to include :-

- Red-Silver-Blue
- Red-silver-Gold
- Purple-silver-Green
- Duck egg blue- mid blue
- Other colours that were favoured were :-
- Plain Yellow
- Orange with red contrasts – this was the colour scheme for the Paris Team

---

1   Telephone conversation KJ to R Walker August 2007

APPENDIX 3:

Components fitted to the bikes as derived from second hand bicycle advertisements 1936 –53

This Appendix includes all the known second hand advertisements placed in *The Bicycle* (B) and *Cycling* (C) for the period that the original Rensch firms were operating. Mostly entries for tandems were not included as these have less application for V-CC members and generally provided less information on their fittings. The entries are reported verbatim with contemporary spelling and abbreviations retained. Repeating these here means that nearly 20 years of complete unbound copies of the journals need not be bought by the gentle reader. Such advertisements have usually been lost by binding of journals into bound annuals kept in libraries. Enjoy the history! At the end of each period are tables which summarise the accessories from these advertisements which thus give a listing of fittings used for each period by owners.

1937
- 17 August (B) Rensch Continental 22½ French blue, Glorias, Brooks, Bluemels, Dunlops, perfect condition £5 5s Holloway.

1938
- 4 May (B) Rensch 1937 Continental, upright 22½in ; turquoise blue, Pinder bars, white Bluemels, front Gloria brake, Brooks B17 £5 or nearest Holloway.
- 13 August(B) Rensch 1938¼ Unmarked 22 in 74-71, Conloys, Airlite Continentals, Simplex, Boas, Cantilevers, Ambra Supergas, dural bars,seat pillar etc. Flyer saddle, feeding bottles Chossy bag , Shoes etc Tranmore, Birchwood Rd, Parkstone, Dorset.

1939
- 18 January(C) Latest Rensch 23 inch 531 High Press Osgear £8
- 8 March (C) Rensch (1939¾) 23 inch welded 74/72 Blue flam, Osgear, Glorias, B17 Bindas, Sprites
- 15 March (C) Rensch 1937 late 22 inch 74/72 B17 C1000 Bindas, Tabuchi brakes.
- 29 March (C) Rensch 72/74 Bindas, Tabuchis C1000 Simplex professional Conloys B17 Dunlops Cost £16 Best offers
- 29 March (C) Rensch Continental 22 inch 39½ WB 75/73 all accessories 2 sprints tubs £5.10s
- 8 April (B) Late 1938 Rensch 23 in BAS, High pressures, two Glorias, Osgear Complete £7 10s RE Smith Houer Street, London W1

- 19 April (C) Rensch 22 inch Osgear, HPs, B17 £6.10s
- 26 April (C) Rensch DG tandem Chater all, chrome forks,head and Dos, Cantis,3 speed, Leather bag, capes ,as new £10
- 6 May (B) Rensch TdF Used in 1937 races 21½ welded BSA High pressures Dural rims, guards, bends, stem. Renovated but shop soiled £8.00 18 Chesham Buildings, Duke St Grosvenor Sq London W1.

Some stated accessories or characteristics of pre war Rensch bicycles

Category	Example
Frame	21½, 22, 22½,23: Upright, Welded
Colour	French blue,Turquoise blue
Saddle	Brooks, Brooks B17, Flyer
Wheels	HPs, Conloys on Airlite Continentals, Dural rims
Gears	Simplex, Osgears
Brakes	Glorias, Cantilevers, Ambra Supergas, Tabuchis
Chainset	BSA, Williams C1000
Mudguards	Bluemels, Dural
Toe clips	Bindas
Handlebars	Dural, Pinder
Saddle bag	Chossy
Tyres	Dunlops, Tabuchis, sprints

1940
Not examined yet

1941
Not examined yet

1942
Not examined yet

1943 All following entries are from *Cycling* only.
- 6 January; 22½ Paris frame by Rensch. BSA chainwheel, Bindas, Bulla brakes, Dunlops, Mansfield Ormond saddle, excellent condition, £12 or nearest offer, owner is in Navy. 50 Devonshire Road, Harrow, Middlesex.
- 27 January; 22½ PARIS cycle, built by Rensch, as used in Tour de France, upright Continental, feathered lugs, Ava bars and stem, Bulla brakes, new Brooks B17 alloy saddle, Noweight guards, B.S.A.chainwheel set, B.W.hubs in Endricks, enamel and maker's name as new, perfect condition £20 or nearest offer. Can be seen any evening. Cpl Hall, care of 37 Bell Street, Sawbridgeworth, Herts.

- 26 May; Continental Rensch, dural chainset, Fenucheux(sic) pedals, AVA bends and stem, Simplex Bowden brakes, hooded levers, alloy framed Flyweight Flier saddle, alloy pin, Simplex gears, chrome HP wheels with tyres, Airlite alloy flanged hubs, alloy guards and pump, super machine in showroom condition 25 guineas. Offers London area.
- 20 October; Rensch Continental fitted with Osgear, HP's Tabuchi brakes on alloy bends.
- 8 December; Rensch Tour de France welded 531 21½in frame, Ecla forks and stays, Simplex, Binda's Bulla's, alloy guards, steel rims with pre war tyres, £20 Abingdon.
- And Rensch 22 inch high pressures, alloy fittings. Take another in part exchange .Middlesex.

1944 *Not examined yet*

1945 *Not examined yet*

1946

- 24 April; Rensch 22in frame alloy pedals, pin, guards, brakes (two Lam) Bars Maes on 2 in stem C1000, Flyweight Flyer, 26 in Con-loys, £17 E12.
- 8 June : Rensch Tour de France 23½ frame 41½ in WB, mauve flamboyant 27 in HP rims, SA 4 s peed, B17N 6¾ in Duprat Octagonal cranks, alloy pedals, Maes bends , brazed on Osgear fittings, alloy TdF brakes, condition as new £25, Dartford.
- 12 June; Lightweight Rensch, high pressures, feeding bottle set, racing shoes (9) £15 , Middlesex and
- Rensch 23½- 41½ in Rensch Continental as new, 73/71 Reynolds, 531 26 in HP wheels, alloy brakes, B17, Bluemels, BW hubs, blue finish with chrome head and dropouts, first class road racing machine, cape bag, lamps £20.
- PARIS Mass start, grey 23 -22½, 71 degrees, 73 degrees, Osgear fittings. Offers After 6 o'clock 91 Havelock Road, Dartford.
- Rensch Multi-tube model22 in 74/72 oval forks, 2¾, Bluemels, North Roads B17N, callipers, Endricks, red-silver finish, £11 or frame only £6 6s, Middlesex
- 4 December; Rensch Tour de France 27 in high pressures Osgear alloy bars, pedals, brakes, guards, hooded levers B17, Duprat chainset octagonal cranks £24.
- 11 December; 22½-in PARIS welded, 73-71, new Baileys, GBs, Philites, 26-in HPs, Hardens, tools,cape. £23: also Constrictor gear and clothing.

1947

- 15 January; 1946 PARIS red lustre for £25 as new condition complete with 4 speed Osgear, GB brakes, Maes bars 27 in wheels and a narrow Brooks saddle.
- Rensch 22 inch frame 73/71 angles with BSA fittings, Conloys, hps, BOA pedals and Brooks B17N saddle.
- 12 February; Summer 1946 Paris Professional with Osgear, on steel 27 wheels, alloy Maes on AVA stem and Williams chainset was offered at near £23 .
- PARIS ladies continental 18 inch frame –a welded 73/71
- 2 April; PARIS single speed, Professional £18,
- 16 April; 24 inch PARIS TdF 27 Conloys on Excelto hubs, Loyal hooded lever brakes, Stronglite chainset Lyotard pedals, Osgear Professional 4 speed, 18in Zefal pump, B17 Brooks for £35
- 23 April; PARIS model with BSA fluted chainset, Sport Bowden brakes Simplex du Monde gears, Faucheux pedals –'ideal massed start machine' –for £23.
- Rensch Continental, 22 in frame with 26 steel Endricks, French Sport Fabrique brakes, and Mansfield Sprinter saddle which was on offer at £14. 10s.
- Rensch Continental, fast road racing machine, pre war high pressures, bag,pump, lamp, excellent condition, £25, North Acton
- PARIS Professional Road machine, 22½in 1947, 42 inch WB, Hardens on Airlite Continentals, Conloys, B17N, BSA chainset, Hobbs brakes and guards, alloy Pelissiers, Allez pedals, Osgear four, polished bottles and carriers, only 100 miles hardly needs pedalling, pump,cape,bag,gloves, shoes,shorts ets cost £43, £35 ono, Box 1347 at *Cycling.*
- June; PARIS Tour de France, 22 in, 27 in Conloys, Blumfields, Pellissiers, B17N, Simplex, 3in Phillipe stem, twin bottles, GBs, Allez. Three months old, going in Forces, first from £30. Prestwick.
- July; PARIS Path, BSA fittings 22 in, 74/72, B17, fitted with steels and guards for road use, beautiful condition £12, Brockley SE4.
- 6 August; Rensch 21 in Dunlop rims, Brampton fittings, lamps, leather bag, £14. Hornsey
- 1947 PARIS Tour de France 73/71, 27in Conloys on Hardens, Pellissier, Reynolds 2 in stem, GBs Simplex 3, Phillites, Williams, Mansfield, alloy mudguards and Pump, snip £22.
- Rensch Tour de France, one tube model welded frame, Constrictor rims, Hiduminium fittings, Cyclo 3 speed, perfect condition, £25 E17;

- 27 August; 24 in Rensch £22,
- Prewar Rensch with B17N, Bluemels, Gloria brakes, Dunlops on Endricks.
- PARIS Tour de France 1947 23 in 72/74(sic)Williams, Webb quills, 27in Conloys, Solites, Simplex 3, Pelissiers, Mansfield, GBs on Reynolds 3 in, alloy guards and pump, £30 ono Kingsbury.
- 12 November; PARIS Tour de France 1947 23in 72/74, Williams, Webb Quills, 27 in Conloys, Solites, Simplex 3, Pelissiers, Mansfield, GBs, Renolds 3 in, alloy guards and pump, feeding bottles and lamps, hardly ridden, £33 no offers Bulwell Nottingham.
- PARIS Tour de France 1947½ Durax crhainset, 27in Conloys pre war covers, all aluminium fittings, twin bottles, Champion du Monde four, ideal massed start job, £27 ono Sneinton Nottingham.

Some characteristics of early post war Rensch and PARIS bicycles

Category	Example
Frame	Upright, welded, lugged, Brampton fittings, ECLA forks, 18 –22in
Colour	Mauve flam, red-silver, grey, blue chrome ends
Saddle	Mansfield Ormonde, Sprinter, Flyer, B17, B17N
Wheels	26 sprints, 27 HPs, Steels, Conloys, Bw Solites, Airlite Continentals, Harden, Blumfield, Excelto
Gears	Simplex Champion du Monde, Osgear,3 SA4, Constrictor
Brakes	Bulla, Bowden, Sport Bowden, Tabuchi, Lam, GBs, TdF, Sport, Loyal levers, Lytaloy
Chainset	BSA, Dural, Durax, Duprat, Duprat Octogonal, Stronglite
Mudguards	Alloys, Bluemels Noweight,
Handlebars/Stems	Baileys, North Road, Maes, Reynolds, AVA
Saddle bag/pumps	Zefal
Tyres	Dunlops,
Pedals	Bindas, Faucheux, Lyotards, Philites, Boa, Allez Pelissiers

1948

- 14 January; Rensch 19½inch 3sp Simplex 27Hp on Hardens on 14 January at £25.
- 14 January; Paris TdF Blue'silverSimplex4 KPs with Hardens, Baileys, Durax alloy peds
- 11 February; Paris TdF amber flam 23in 74/72 27 Airlites Simplex 4 C34 £23
- 18 February; Professional 23inch Durax, 27Conloys on Hardens,Durax B17N cost £34. TdF frame 22 deep yellow £8.
- 18 February; Rensch 24inch £10
- 25 February; PARIS 22½ shaded amber lustre 73/71 40½WB £11
- 10 March; PARIS TdF 22½ 27 Conloy sprints BSA chainset, GB B17 £30
- 17 March; PARIS Professional £15
- 24 March; Rensch £20
- 31 March; PARIS TdF 27HPs alloy GBs Highgates, Chater , B17
- 21 April ; PARIS TdF 73/71 41½ 27 Conloys on Hardens Simplex 3 Doherty brakes £30
- 5 May; PARIS TdF 24 27HPConloys on Airlite Continentals
- 19 May; Rensch TdF22 26HP Conloy on Airlite Continentals Durax, Webbs, Osgear, Mansfield Sprint AVA bars £27
- 2 June; PARIS TdF 23 in & Conloys Simplex 4 Durax Ormonde £30
- 16 June; PARIS TdF22½ 26HPs Alloy Chater chainset, peds £22
- 23 June ; *Galibier*, (the first recorded second-hand *Galibier* sale!) - all alloy accessories with harden hubs, cost £35 and now £28.
- 30 June ; Rensch 1938 75/72 HPs on Airlite Continentals, Durax Supercourse, Swallow Bramptons £28
- 7 July; a 1947 **Professional** frame was offered at £8 15s. which was finished in maroon and cream,
- 14 July;; a1948 Paris **TdF** for £ 34 with Cyclo Ace gears.
- 6 October; the second recorded second-hand sale *Galibier*, asking price £35.
- 3 November, then the third, 1948 *Galibier*

1949

Advertisements for Jan – June 1949 not examined yet

- 27 October 1949 Paris *Galibier* 73/71 41½in WB TdF bars B17 26 inch wheels on Hardens, fitted with GB equipment. Cost £43 will sell for £30. Middlesex.

1950

- 5 January; Paris TDF 22 in 73-71 deg 41½, red and chrome, Titan-Maes, Lytaloys, Chater 3/32 Simplex 4 Lyotards, Endricks, Airlites, pump but less saddle £20 Nottingham
- 12 January; Rensch 22in Tour de France, chrome, Simplex 3 B17, 27in alloy HPs £20 Wembley
- 26January; 23 in Rensch Champion du Monde, black and chrome, as new all accessories, £27 10s Sloane square.
- Same date; Paris 23x23 DG Tandem 27 hps B17, Conloys re enamelled. Box No.
- Same date; *1949 Paris Professional Road Racer 74/72 41 in WB cream and chrome 27 HPs, cantilevers, Durax,, good condition £18 Welling Kent.*
- Same date; Paris TdF red,Champion changer, Allez cranks, Elios chain, Regina 14,17,19,21 GB brakes Pelissier bars, Mansfield, cape,pump accessories First class condition £38 nearest, Manchester
- 2 February; 1949 Paris track 21½in 531 red 40½WB sprints 27in No 3 Durax, One GB, Bramption pedals Maes, £15 Acton
- Paris *Galibier*, red 23 74/72 Brooks B17, 27HP on Chater Lea hubs. Pedals, Williams 3 speed Resilion cantivere brakes, £20 or frame only, Hexthorpe, Doncaster.
- Same date; Paris Tour de France all blue 21 in excellent condition 27in San georgios on Gnutti hubs, Simplex 8 Brooks, Maes, 2 GBs 18in Ad Hoc alloy guards £28.
- 16 March; 1949½ Paris TdF 73/71 Superbe Showroom model Continental finish heliotrope.27in HP Dunlops on FBs double chainset, Stella chainwheel, Simplex 4 Brooks B17, S of F bars Gloria brakes, perfect £30.
- *23 March; 1949½ Paris* TdF 22½ inch, 27HP, GBs,Simplex 4, BW hubs perfect condition. Cost £38 sell £27. Stourbridge.
- 30 March; Rensch 21inch BSA, Brooks,Constrictors, 3cog hub, alloy barsand MGs, cape,tools. Enfield West.
- Same date; Paris 23½ Conloys, Simplex, etc, Cost £40 sell £22.
- Same date; Paris 22½ Tour de France frame, green flamboyant,, box lined, Belgian chainwheel(Stella?) , Simplex, dural bars stem and pillar, £12 Wandsworth.
- 6 April; Paris TdF 23 inch 531 73-71 27 Conloys, HP covers, Airlite Solite, Durax Super Course, Chater pedals, AVA bars and stem, B37 alloy front aLytaloy Bluemels £21 Glasgow.
- Same date; 1949 Paris Professional 26 pressures Atom hubs, Brooks, GB bars and stem brakes, alloy guards, Cyclo 4, pump, lamps, cape and bottle. Manor Park.

- Same date; Rensch –Chater DG tandem 23/22½ Hardens Sprites, Pelissiers, B17N cantilevers, Cyclo, Grey lustre, Chingford £40.
- 13 April ; Paris TdF 74-72 27 HPs Hardens B17 GBs alloy bar stem etc £27 . Lower Tooting.
- Same date; Paris TdF 23 inch Blue Dunlop alloys HPs alloy Maes and extension GBs, guards, Brooks Flyer, Stella, Philites, saddlebag, lamps nylon cape leggings £20, Greenford Mdsx.
- Same date; 1950 Paris 531 73-71 Blue/white 27 airlites Osgear Professional Brampton 3pin Allez Mistral, Maes Brooks, Offers Catford.
- 20 April; Paris 23 in 73-71 Red 27 HPs B17N, Maes, Durax, simplex 4 £36 W3.
- 27 April; Paris TdF Hardens in conlys Simplex all alloy accessories, saddle bag cape £19 SE24.
- Same date; Paris Tour de France 20inch Derailleur 3 speed,lamps etc £22 N22.
- Same date: Paris Tour de France 22½ 73-71 26 Dunlops on LF Hardens gear/fixed rear GB wing nuts, John Bull Safety Speeds GB brakes SoF bars ob GB extension, Cl fluted cranks, Cl pedals, Brampton 3/32 chain £16 10s without chainset or £20 with. Valentine W3.
- Same date; Rensch 22½ 73-71 27 pressures KPs Simplex 5 Stella, Gbs, Ormond Maes CL pedals, lilac and white, cages £23 10s Leyton.
- Same date; Paris *Galibier*, 22½ Simplex etc £22 or p/e 23 or 24 in TdF.
- 4 May; Paris 22½ 73-71 Blue 27HPs B17N Maes Durax Simplex 4 GBs Ultralite hubs £25 N16.
- Same date; 23 Rensch 73-71 27 in alloys Osgear, £20 Southall.
- Same date; Rensch USWB tandem Cyclo 4 cantilevers, Sprites, Offers, Brixton.
- 18 May; 1950 Paris 23in 27 Alloys Gnutti hubs Simplex 3 alloy fittings £25 SW7.
- Same date; 1949 Paris PRR 24 in Green 27 in Dunlops BW unit rear simplex 3 GBs Durax £25 or offer Birmingham.
- Paris TdF 24inch 74-72 27HP hardens B37 GBs alloy bars and stem £20 Lower Tooting. Same bike as offered on 13 April but £7 less asked!
- 25 May; Paris 23in 27 HPs 8 speeds Swallow, spare chainset £25 West Drayton.
- Same date; Paris USWB DG tandem 22½/22 SA3 Cantilevers, Dunlop Sprites £45 Luton.

- Same date; Rensch –Chater DG tandem 23/22½ Pelissiers, Brooks, Hardens, Sprites, Cyclo £35 Walthamstow.
- Same date; Paris 22½ black and chrome frame only 73-71 £6 Hayes.
- 1 June; 24in Paris Simplex 4 Savilles £22
- Same date; Paris TdF 23 74-72 Red forks and head cream frame 700c wheels Star hubs, BSA chainset GBs Maes B17N Constrictor gear, £20
- Same date, Rensch CdM 531 22inch £16 Homerton
- 8 June; Paris tdF 23in Vianzoni rims on SF Fbs, Gbs,all alloy fittings cost £30 accept £18 Sidcup.
- Same date; Paris DG tandem 22½/21½ Silver Simplex 3 alloy cantilevers Sprites, finest alloy fittings New £48.
- 15 June; Paris TdF 23 inch 74-73 French woods on Gnuttis, Tubs 4,5,6, Durax, Major Taylor, Ormon Offers £25 Warwickshire.
- Same date; 22 inch Paris *Galibier* touring lustre finish 4 speed Bargain at £18 10s SE15.
- Same date; Paris original Brighton-Glasgow model (PRR?) Brroks BSA Osgear 4 Bluemels £15 E17.
- Same date; Paris ladies Lighweight whilte lined 22inch all alloy fittings Cyclo £18 Preston.
- Same date, 19inch Rensch frame 72/72 blue with white panels £7 10s W12.
- 22 June; Paris *Galibier* 23 Benelux 5 speed handlebar control 27HPs FB hubs Maes Gbs B37, Italian chainset, lights, guards alloy throughout Cost £45 accept £35 Mitcham.
- Same date; Rensch 73-71 27Conlyoy HPs Durax alloy fittings £17 Edmonton.
- Same date; Rensch DG tandem Derailleur 3 Cantilevers Alloy fittings £30 Maidstone.
- 7 July; 1949 paris TdF 23in 26 alloys Gb brakes, Durax, simplex alloy fittings as new £25 Balham.
- Same date; Rensch Superlight USWB tandem Trivelox Sprites, dynamo £30 ono Pinner.
- Same date; Paris PRR 23inch frame 72-70 £6 Ilford.
- 20 July; Paris Path No 6728 Green lustre £15 .
- Same date; Paris TdF 23in 73-71 27 Conloys Simplex 8 Maes on Titan stem, B17N, Gbs Offers Trowbridge.
- Same date; Paris *Galibier* racing cycle 2 months old as new £25 Bexley Heath.
- Same date; 1950 Rensch USWB 23/23 in 73-71-71 alloy Resilions Cyclo 4 Airlites conloys, brooks, Strata bars Blumels the lot! £45 Lewisham.

- 27 July; Rensch Dg USWB 22½x21½, SA Resilions 1948 £30 Slough.
- 3 August;
- Paris TdF Chrome ends 27 wheels as new £18 Hillingdon.
- 24 August; Paris, Simplex 8 nearest £28 W4.
- Same date; Paris specially made for Paris Team member double chainrings 3 tubs £32 Gleblands Av Ilford.
- 31 August; 24inch Paris 73-73 27in alloys GB front cantilever rear 7in cranks nearly new £19 19s Brixton.
- Same date; Paris TdF 23inch 1949½ 27in Weinmans FBs SoF bars Double chainset Simplex 5 B17N £28 South Croydon.
- Same date; !949 Gold Rensch road race tandem 21/22 DG Endricks Sprites Alloy fittings Brooks, dynamo, panniers, Williams transmission GB brakes £35 Tottenham.
- 28 September; Paris TdF 23inch 27 Asps on Airlites Durax Simplex, £25, Victoria SW1.
- 9 November, Paris PRR 24 in 73-71 GBs, Hps sprites Bwunit hub Simplex 4 Gnutti B37 TdF bars Blue metallic £30 (cost £38) W5.
-

1951

- 1 February; H Rensch Continental, alloy bars, brakes, B17N 26 in Endricks , Solite, Osgear, good condition complete £10.
- 22 March; Paris 1949,complete MS machine, genuine MAES on Titan, GBs, B17N, KPs, Dunlops on Gnutti, Simplex 8,.
- 23½ Paris TdF, 74/72, red, chrome ends 27in Asps, DBs, Hardens, Osgear –Huret 8, Durax, Chaters, Doherty, B17 Sprinter,, perfect, £27 10s. Lowestoft
- Paris 22½ 531, Conloys, Hardens, Chater pedals, all alloy fittings, perfect condition, £18 West Hampstead.
- 1950 Paris 22½ 73/71, SS, HPs, Solites, Allez chainset, showroom condition, £20 ono Chiswick
- 27 April; Paris 22½ inch, 73/71, welded, Brooks, Bluemels, BW hubs, 26x1¼ Endricks, Phillips pedals £10 10s Janes, Harlow.
- RENSCH (blue) 21½ in, 75/73, 40½in WB, 26in pressures, Sprites, Simplex 3, GBs' B15, C1000, , lightweights dynamo, pump, £23. Catford.

1952

This record shows only a selection (chosen for the best descriptions of kit) of the 62 advertisements

- 3 January; Paris 23 Black, D'Alessandro tubs, 26sprints, gear, Durax, B8s, B17, South of France, £24, N16.
- 10 January; PARIS Tour de France 1950 Chrome ends Gnutti, San Georgio, ,GBs, Reynolds Simplex 3, Maes, Stored after less than 1000 miles £27 cost £32 Middlesex
- 14 February; Paris Professional frame only 74-72 24in re enamelled gold Continental finish £7 Yorkshire.
- Paris Tour de France 23 in , 27in Conloys, Simplex 4 double chainwheel, B17S £22.10s Waxlow.
- Rensch double gents, 22in 21 in 26 x1¼, Trivelox 3, blackcurrant continental box lines, B17s, Brooks saddle bag, panniers alloy carrier, Chater fittings, Williams chainsets £30 Seven Sisters
- 13 March; Rensch 24 in, 27 steels, LF hubs, GBs B17, Simplex 4 3-32 fluted crankshaft (sic!) showroom condition £24 SE4
- Paris Tour de France, 23 in , all alloy latest fittings, 27 wheels with hardened (sic!) hubs £24 ono Sydenham.
- Rensch double gents, 22 X 22 26 by 1¼, Simplex, cantilevers as new bargain £35 Mitcham.
- 20 March; Paris 24 in 531 welded, red enamelled, 27 in alloy pressures, Simplex 4, Maes, B17, Gbs good condition £15 SE9
- Paris TdF 23 , 73-71, £6 Coulsdon
- Paris Professional road racing sprints, 4 speed Benelux, Simplex twin chainwheels, B17N, cellulose mudguards, £25 Birmingham.
- 27 March; Paris Professional road, 27 Boa alloys, Duralight LF hubs, gear, B17, alloy bars etc perfect £22 ono Birmingham.
- 1951 Paris double gents, double torsion frame, 531 tubing, 22 by 21 cantilevers dynamo, Cyclo 3, Dunlops, Brooks touring bag, hardly used, cost £54 Offers Mill Hill.
- 5 April; Rensch 23in royal blue, 27 in Samirs on BW Continentals , B17N, GBs, Gnutti, Ambrosia, Chater Lea, bag, lamps, showroom condition, £28 *Cycling* Box
- 1949/50 Rensch double gents short wheel base 22 in, four gear perfecy £60 ono Cheam.
- 8 May; Rensch 24 in 73-71 Gold flam Continental finish, brand new 27 HPs on Airlite Coninentals, rear BW unit, DB rustless, Simplex, Durax, Dunlop Sprints immaculate showroom condition, £27 Greenford.
- 15 May; Paris Tour de France 23 in chrome forksB17, GBs Ardens(sic) HP Allez pedals 200 miles only £25 Birmingham.

- Paris professional 24 in eight speed, new condition 27 in HPs Dagenham.
- 29 May ; Paris TdFFlam green, Sprites, SA FMWilliams B17 GB, Baileys, £20 Wembley.
- Paris Double gents 22/19, 531 tubes, late model as new, very light strutted tubes model six gears 26 x1¼ sprites, Sturmey Cyclo, alloy carrier, cantilevers, dynamo £26 Finsbury Park.
- 10 July; Paris 23in , gear and fixed. Immaculate condition £18 Ilford.
- Paris *Galibier*,23in, red and chrome ends, in showroom condition, 27 Dunlpo HPs on FB hubs, Alps B17 Gnutti chainset, Cobra pedals, Simplex four gear, £27 ono Romford.
- 17 July; Paris Galibia (sic) Green flam, chrome ends, 27 in alloys, Harden hubs, Olympic 3 , Alp brakes, alloy bars, stem, chainset guards, pedals, B57 large hide bag, all as new £25 ono Hackney.
- Paris 21½ Modified type 26 x1¼ Weinmans, Atom hubs, alloy bends,stem and brakes etc, complete with pump, pannier carrier, lamps , in excellent condition, £15 Arlesey.
- 24 July Paris *Galibier* 24in white lined with red FB wide flange hubs, Wilby 17 , Stratas, Simplex gear almost new £25 ono Ewell.
- 21 August; Paris TdF 23 in 73/71, alloy wheels, simplex, 10speed, Juy 51, cost £40, £22 ono Middlesex.
- Paris TdF alloy wheels Simplex Maes Brooks £10 ono Mitcham.
- Rensch Simplex 4 double chainset, sprints quick release also extra wheels and tyres, £35 ono *Cycling* Box.
- Paris TdF 23 in French woods, used road-track, good condition £14 Warwick.
- 4 September; 1951½ Rensch DG Tandem 22½/21½ USWB 26 x1¼ Sprites FW4 B17s, panniers, cantilevers, superb lugged(sic) frame costing £34 10 itself. £35 no offers Cambridge.
- 27 November; Paris 22in Copper lustre, 26 in endricksSimplex Maes, excellent condition £15, Maidstone.

1953

- 15 January; Rensch tandem23/22in DG curved tube six speed, Cyclo 3 SA AW three brakes coupled cantilevers Maes tandem Sprites, panniers 3000 miles only £35 Middlesex.
- 5 February; Wrench USWB tandem red and chrome alloy Watsonian sidecar and Power Pak engine all as new £53 or separate £30, £10, £15 E8.
- 19 March ; Really good tandem for sale Rensch short wheel base23/22in 73/71 27in stainless HPs Airlite tandem Continen-

tals, fixed or free, Simplex 4, Cantilevers, green lustre, showroom condition under 2000 miles nearest £45, SW12.

- 26 March; Paris *Galibier* 27 in alloys all alloy fittings, B17 etc £13 10s Bacup

- Paris 23in 27in HPs, BW Continentals, C-1000, Alps £12 Guildford.

- 2 April; 1951 Paris Triplet. Front and rear cantilevers and rear hub brakes four speed cycle gears frame 23-21-19 immaculate nearest £45 Coventry.

- 9 April; Rensch USWB, Weinmanns Airlites, Williams, Simplex, Lucifer,, Bluemels, Major Taylor, Brooks, panniers £35 ono York.

- 16 April; 1952 Rensch DG 23/21 26 in on solites, cantilevers Simplex 3, Ormondes, excellent with spares and tools £40.

- 23 in Rensch track Weinman Scherens, Leones, Chater Lea B17 front brake £17 10s Kew.

- Rensch long WB DG twin tubes Cyclo 4 , first class accessories panniers, £40

- 23 April; 22½Rensch Orange lustre71/72 Hardens Alumlite KPs, HPs B17N, GBs, Maes, £20 ono Abbey.

- 14 May; 22½ Paris TdF Mephisto HPs Ambra Superga brakes, Simplex 5 B17 nearest £20 Barnett.

- 22 in Paris Copper lustre, Maes Simplex 3 26in endricks £12 Maidstone.

- 21 May ; Rensch USWB DG 22½/22 , Osgear 4, wheels and fittings alloy, showroom condition £40 Leeds.

- 23 in Paris TdF black with white double box lining 27in HPs BWLF ,B17, GBs , Bluemels, immaculate £20 Maidstone.

- H Rensch road tandem 23/22½ Fiamme sprints and HPs, 5 tubs, 8 speed Osgear –Simplex (Nivex) 3/32 chain recently enamelled immaculate £25 SE25.

- Paris lightweight racing cycle handbuilt special Tour de France frame as new with pumps lamps, feeding bottles etc £25 ono W10.

- 4 June; All-chrome Paris TdF GBs, 27s, B37 alloy fittings unmarked perfect condition £18 SE4.

- Brand new 23in Rensch racing special 27 HP alloys, lavish specification, selling through illness cost £75 ask £ 47 10s (In tandem sales)

- 6 August; Rensch 23/23 DG, USWB Chater fittings 26x1¼ Airlites LF hubs, Cyclo 4, Cantilevers cost £81 1952 ask £50 Birmingham.

- 27 August; Rensch tandem conversion unit C/W chainwheels to fir 22in solo £6 Scunthorpe.

- 29 October; Paris TdF White lugs flashed red, hardens, HPs, Bluemel red guards, GB superhoods,, Reynolds stem, Chater, Allez, immaculate £23 ono Worthing.

* 3 December; Paris 23in Road/Track complete sprints tubs, winter wheels £25 ono N8

Some stated characteristics of late post war (1948-53) Rensch and PARIS bicycles

Category	Example
Frame	73/71, 75/72, 74/72welded, 22-24in
Colour	Blue lustre, green flam, copper lustre, yellow, Gold, Maroon&cream, Amber flam, Black chrome ends, lilac and white
Saddle	Flyer, B17, B17N, Wilby, Swallow, B37,
Wheels	Sprints, 27 HPs, Steels, Conloys, Samirs, Stainless HPs, Alumlites, Scherens, French woods, Fiammes, Mephistos, Airlite Continentals, Harden, Blumfield, FBs, Atom, Vianzoni
Gears	Simplex4 & Juy 51, Osgear 4, SA3 &4, Cyclo 3 and Olympic and Ace Trivelox 3, Constrictor
Brakes	GBs & Superhoods, Doherty, Weinmann, Alps, Stratas, Resilions, Ambra Superga, San Georgio, alloy Resilions
Chainset	Durax Supercourse, Chater Lea, Simplex double Williams, Stella, Belgian, Italian
Mudguards	Alloys, Bluemels Noweight,
Handlebars/Stems	Highgates, Maes, South of France, Ambrosias, Tour de France
Saddle bag/pumps	Brooks bag,
Tyres	Dunlops, Sprites, John Bull Speeds, D'Allessandro tubs, Leones,
Pedals	Boa, Allez B8s, Pelissiers, Philites, Chater Lea

APPENDIX 4:
Details of the Firms' Advertising & Publicity

This is the full account of the advertisements placed by the two Rensch owned firms in *Cycling, The Bicycle, The Cyclist* and the *CTC Gazette* most editions of which have been examined for 1935 to 1954. A summary of this information was given in Chapter 4. This appendix lists all the known firms' advertising starting with the pre war **H Rensch** and then the much more elaborate post war **PARIS** campaign.

It is interesting to note that by the 1930 and 1940's *Cycling* had a system of large page or half page advertisements and also an arrangement for small advertisements which were always in the Advertising supplement at the end of each edition[1]. The Supplement was separately page numbered from the main text but was bound in with each magazine. The small advertisements were split into sections for *Gents* and then *Ladies Secondhand* bikes, a section for *New Bicycles* followed by a section for *Tandems* and if needed sections for *Tricycles, Racing Machines* and finally and very rarely *Veteran machines*. Following this were larger sections normally wholly for traders such as, *Various, Clothing, Frames, Enamellers* and *Repairers* though on occasion the odd private advertiser would use the *Frames* and *Wheels* categories. Finally there were the other trade categories such as *Situations* (Vacant and Wanted) and then the personal *Wanted* section before the *Club Notices* ended the Supplement. In 1936 a new journal *The Bicycle* appeared and its advertising followed a similar but less stratified system.

Some of the largest cycle makers such as Claud Butler, Raleigh, New Hudson, Royal Enfield, Sun and Holdsworth tended to take half or whole page advertisements in the main journals whilst moderate size traders such as Hetchins, Grose, Hobbs, Excel, Pride and Clark usually advertised in the Classified in *New Bicycles* and then for components in *Various, Clothing* and *Wheels*. Certain companies such as PARIS, Ephgrave, Cusworth nearly always seemed to use *Frames* – although one supposes that most of these admittedly smaller concerns would of course always sell the customer a completed bicycle if requested to do so.

H Rensch advertisements

The first known H Rensch publicity was a simple and bald one line advertisement placed in a new, then one month old, cycle magazine, *The Bicycle*, for 31 March 1936. This weekly magazine came out with a blaze of publicity offering a more international and "newspaper" approach to cycling in all its ramifications than that offered by the long established *Cycling*.

The advertisement was in the New Bicycles section and was follows:-

---

1   All advertisements placed in *Cycling* from 1935 to 1954 have been examined for this history.

HH Rensch. Builder of Continental design cycles and tandems. 245 Balls Pond Road, Dalston.

We do not know how soon this advertisement was after his firm's start up, but it cannot have been long. Also it is interesting that he should have stated that he made tandems so soon in his career, and this presumably indicates that he may have had a business plan for a rounded cycle marque for his firm. By the early spring of 1937[1] he was regularly advertising and had dropped the initials H. H from in front of his surname. The message was a little punchier but had the same message :

Rensch for that super CONTINENTAL DESIGN lightweight cycle or tandem, Path or road. 245 Balls Pond Road Dalston London N1

Then in May 1937 came news of a change[2] in address. In *Cycling* there was a text entry in the short article occasionally printed entitled "Trade Notes and News".

OWING to an increase of business H. Rensch, lightweight cycle and tandem manufacturer, has found it necessary to move to larger premises. The new address is 132, Balls Pond Road, London, N.1. This firm specializes in cycles of a Continental design and finish.

Figure A4.1 The first intimation that Cycling editorial staff knew about the marque.

It is clear from this statement that Rensch had now got his firm nicely underway, and had sent into *Cycling* some sort of mission statement with regards to his sales aims. In Bicycle of the same week the firm took out a small advertisement in the Classified Section:-

---

1   *The Bicycle* 12 January 1937 to 23 February 1937
2   *Cycling* 5 May 1937 Page 24, Trade Notes and News

*Rensch The Continental Cycle Specialist will continue business at new premises. All
enquiries should now be addressed to 132 Balls pond Road, London N1.*

We know that Rensch had needed to expand his may be two years old firm
and doubtless the new shop which was a mile or so along Balls Pond Road was
larger, though the move may have temporarily slowed up production somewhat. As it happens there were no further advertisements by the firm until
August 1937 when the following[1] appeared :-

*Rensch for that Continental style, cycles welded or brazed. 132 Balls Pond Road,
Islington London.*

This then is the first time that we have in print any coupling together of
Rensch and welded frames. It seems probable that the move to 132 Balls
Pond Road and the expansion that it had allowed was made to allow the introduction of the new technology of bronze welding Later that same month
(August 1937) was also the very first known advertisement for a second hand
Rensch bicycle- a *Continental Road Racer.*[2] All the early secondhand bicycle advertisements in *Cycling* and *The Bicycle* have been listed in Appendix A.3, where
additionally the reader can see in the prepared tables the ranges of components listed with the bicycles in three periods, pre war, immediately post war,
and later post war (1948 to 1953).

On 11 January 1938 there was another advertisement in Bicycle by the
firm:-

*RENSCH for real welded cycles, same type as used in the "Tour de France". On
cash or terms. 132 Balls Pond Road, Islington, NI*

This advertisement seems to be the first actually printed explanation by
Rensch of their welded machines by stating that this technique was a continental practice. Placing the firm's small advertisements was clearly followed
by the firm sending their new 1938 catalogue to *The Bicycle*. Then sometime
later on 18 January 1938 the magazine reviewed the catalogue and introduced
Rensch products to its readers, listing the bikes as *Continental Road Racer, Tour de
France*, the *Club* and the *Touring*, the *Path* and the *Grand Tourist*. This latter model shared with the *Tour de France* model a welded construction of the frame.
The writer of *The Bicycle* review did not attempt to explain the significance of
a welded construction or draw the readers' attention to it other than repeating
the catalogue's statement that the Tour de France is a "special welded model"
—one wonders if the magazine's own staff writer himself understood?

1   *The Bicycle* 10 August 1937
2   *The Bicycle* 17 August 1937

Of course there may well have been earlier brochures or catalogues available from the shop which have not survived but which told potential owners about the new techniques, but it would not have escaped many readers in the period that just exactly at this time Holdsworth were advertising their *La Quelda* models which have already been mentioned as welded, though these appear to have been steel welded machines.

In June 1938 we have another example of Harry Rensch's love of continental cycling with the first advertisement for the sale of imported French newspapers :-

RENSCH for French Sports Papers during the Tour de France: indispensable for massed start riders. Full particulars from Rensch 132 Balls Pond Road London N1

There were other repeat advertisements from the firm in 1938 but we can assume it was a busy period. Then, early in 1939[1] the firm placed its very first box type advertisement. This step up in publicity costs was probably due to the need to announce the third change of address within a four year period and of course coincided with the issuing of a new Rensch catalogue. Possibly the firm had yet again outgrown its premises or the firm had new backers, but of course this move, as has already been discussed came at a time when the world in general was becoming a very insecure place and Rensch's own private

THE WORLD'S BEST RACING CYCLES

H. RENSCH for HAND-BUILT, CONTINENTAL DESIGN LIGHTWEIGHTS, WELDED OR BRAZED
Send for our New List.
NEW ADDRESS :—362, OLD ST., LONDON, E.C.1 (Near Shoreditch Town Hall

Figure A4.2 The H RENSCH name in Germanic script seen in *The Bicycle*.

1   *The Bicycle* May 1939

life was in flux.

As mentioned earlier there must be some reservations over what actually happened in 1939 and 1940 as the shop new premises in 362 Old Street were recorded by the ratings authorities as being empty until June of that latter year. The Old Street bomb damage may not have directly affected 362, but Rensch's name was not on the Shoreditch rates record book for 362 for any part of 1940 and just after the bombing on 7 October 1940 a new tenant started to pay the rates from 16 October 1940 onwards. Whether the firm had never in fact moved or perhaps had withdrawn use of the premises.

After this advertisement no more advertisements by the firm or second-hand bicycle advertisements by the public appeared before the war. However Rensch or someone else in the firm must have been busy thinking about bikes during the move and probably wanting to ginger up customers, because the firm sent to *The Bicycle* a publicity brochure for a novel attachment devised to turn a solo into a tandem[1].

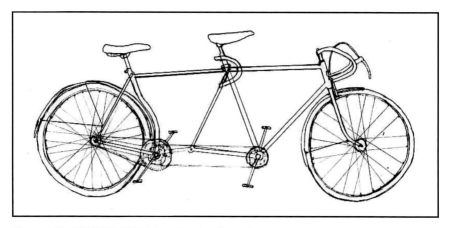

Figure A4.3 RENSCH 1939 Solo to tandem illustration

The article mentioned that Rensch had patented and was marketing this attachment. The article referred interested parties to the firm (at the old 132 Balls Pond Road address!) and informed them that the prices started from £4 19s 6d which also included the new tandem chainset that would be needed. No other mention was made by the firm in its literature of this model in the intervening years until 1953 when one was advertised and a Cardiff agent took advantage of the firm's closing down to advertise this kit at £5 each reduced from their previous price of 12 gns! Unfortunately none of these machines are known to have survived to be on the V-CC Register.

---

1   Single into Tandem *The Bicycle* 26 July 1939.

PARIS advertisements in the commercial press

The first known advertisement for PARIS bicycles, and therefore the first published evidence of PARIS as a marque, was not an advertisement placed by the firm but was a private advertisement placed in *Cycling* in January 1943 :

22½ Paris frame by Rensch. BSA chainwheel, Bindas, Bulla brakes, Dunlops, Mansfield Ormond saddle, excellent condition, £12 or nearest offer, owner is in Navy. 50 Devonshire Road, Harrow, Middlesex.

This is an interesting advertisement for a number of reasons. It could be inferred from that wording that "Paris" was only the name of one model of a range of frames produced by Rensch. The advertiser is not the owner, who is on active service – but we do not know how long he has been away – and the vender may have known little about what he was selling –see later comment! The owner may as far as we are informed have bought the frame at any time in the past -even before the war – yet we know that the surviving pre-war **Rensch** catalogues do not show or list a "Paris" model. As the advertiser was not the owner, in order that the advert could have described the machine as "Paris frame by Rensch", this information must surely have been on the frame – probably written in its transfers. Other early **PARIS** machines have been found with PARIS on the head tube and the standard **Rensch** diamond transfer on the seat tube. One other reason for the advertisement being interesting is that the name "Paris" is in lower case apart for the initial letter P; in the other advertisements the advertisers had all put the maker's name in capitals. Could this be an indication that "Paris" was not commonly known to be a bicycle marque? Or, perhaps just another indication that the advertiser was not the owner of the bike and did not know the normal vendor's convention in bicycle small ads – and as subsequently inferred by this writer – did not know the true value of the machine?

This last suggestion is because this first advertisement in the 6 January 1943 edition of *Cycling* was to be followed three weeks later by another advertisement[1], which read as follows:-

*22½ **PARIS** cycle, built by Rensch, as used in Tour de France, upright Continental, feathered lugs, Ava bars and stem, Bulla brakes, new Brooks B17 alloy saddle, Noweight guards, B.S.A.chainwheel set, B.W.hubs in Endricks, enamel and maker's name as new, perfect condition £20 or nearest offer. Can be seen any evening. Cpl Hall, care of 37 Bell Street, Sawbridgeworth, Herts.*

It is interesting to compare these two advertisements. Although there are

---

1   *Cycling* 27 January 1943 page 5 (Supplement i)

distinct differences in details of the fittings, there is considerable similarity between the wording of the two – perhaps enough to suggest the writer of the second advertisement used the first as a crib? Additionally of course one wonders whether this great similarity in the advertisements also extended to the machine itself – could this be the same machine now being moved on at a more realistic price for a top notch bicycle? After all, this first advertisement is the first known advertisement for a **PARIS** and the second is the last one to appear for a number of years (at least 3 years in terms of advertisements in *Cycling*) and as far as can be determined any **PARIS** frame or bicycle at this time must have been as rare, if not rarer, than hen's teeth. Bearing in mind that these advertisements were placed some three years before the first known advertisements for the **PARIS** marque by the new firm, it seems most likely that this is one and the same bicycle. Clearly though the writer of the second advertisement also knew some good selling points – including use of the capitals for **PARIS** - for a machine emanating from the Renschian loving massed start fraternity. I wonder too whether the almost doubling of the asking price suggests that the good corporal might have had slicked backed hair and a pencil moustache?

At present the first known advertisement that **PARIS Cycles** placed using their own name did not appear until *Cycling* in November 1945[1] when the advertisement was placed in the *Frames* section. This section had been seldom used during the war, doubtless as few companies had sufficient stock to keep in regular production, with at this time the other advertisers being Pomeroys and Braham's –both these being long established London shops similar to Centric of Birmingham or Cusworth of Manchester with small scale frame building facilities. This first **PARIS** advertisement was :-

> **Racing** *cyclists. Do not order your new cycle frame until you have seen our Continental range. Reasonable prices; prompt delivery. Paris Cycles, 133 Stoke Newington Church Street, London N16.*

This advertisement was not repeated the following week but did appear every so often until, in mid February 1946[2] a new wording and advertisement appeared and lasted for about 6 weeks. This advertisement was also in the *Frames* section. The advertisement was quite long and ran as follows:-

> **PARIS** *Continental style cycle frames. Professional road racing model 531 tubing £8.17s. 6d; Tour de France model 531 tubing £12.12s.6d: finished in real continental style. Delivery 5 to 6 weeks. Paris Cycles, 133, Stoke Newington Church Street, London N16.*

Note the use of *'Continental and Continental style'* – a hangover from the pre-war Rensch selling point, though still of course a powerful seller to massed start enthusiasts in these early post war days. What we don't know is what prompted the change in name from *Continental Road Racing* to *Professional Road Racing* model, had there been a new issue raised amongst clubmen about professionalism during the war? At this stage the firm's name was "Paris Cycles" ie the Paris was not capitalised. Note also the use of 133 only in the address – as this was early in 1946 the shop was perhaps still only in one building with future expansions yet to come. In fact we do not know quite what accommodation 133 provided at this time, though it was possibly still in part residential. The stated delivery period of 5 to 6 weeks also probably tells its own story – no stock items then, and perhaps no employees to get on with orders –Rensch was probably working on the frames in his evenings or was he even farming them out?

The second advertisement placed by the firm ran for about six weeks, then there was gap before in July 1946[1] a slightly different wording :

PARIS CYCLE CO. *High class Continental cycle frames, Tour de France model £12.12s.6d; Professional road racing £9.9s. Your frame cleaned off and enamelled with superior quality enamel, £1; lining extra. 133 Stoke Newington Church Street, London N 16.*

The firm's name has the PARIS name in capitals at last but notice that price for enamelling. It was low even for the times – it must have been a real loss leader to help build up some custom amongst the clubmen. Note that there had been an increase in the price of the newly named *Professional* model, but not that of the *Tour de France*. Important however that the TdF had now been named first – suggesting the intention was to emphasise this as the top of the range machine?

The advertisements placed by the firm are at this point influenced not by the firm but by events - though these may have been triggered intentionally by Rensch's efforts at publicity. Of course it might just have been serendipity. Which ever it was, it was the shapely new PARIS *Galibier* strut frame model which suddenly caught people's eye and imaginations. At this time we should remember that England and English cyclists were starved of innovation and spangle-ly bright new things so that the new *Galibier* model must have really stood out and grabbed their attention in a way that only a fast supercar is likely to do in modern times. Although not strictly an advertisement, the photograph[2] is reproduced here as Figure A4.4

1   *Cycling* 10 July 1946 Page 10 (Supplement)
2   *Cycling* 28 August 1946 page 173

Naturally enough this brilliant free advertisement was soon followed up by PARIS:- two weeks later in an article in **News of the Trade**, one of *Cycling's* regular features, a short mention[1] of the firm and its new model appeared. Although the name *Galibier* was not as yet in use, the article stated that it, the illustrated model, was now being built in limited numbers at 16 gns for the frame, and that the weight of the frame set and chain set was "about 9 lb". It is interesting to contemplate the fact that to many clubmen in UK mentioning PARIS brought up – and still does for many - only the mental image of the *Galibier* design –although the firm made a so much wider range of models which were well known in the London area. Is this just because it was the *Galibier* which people had first seen illustrated[2] and which had been given prominence in the contemporary literature?

An unusual lightweight shown in London recently. The unorthodox design includes a stout central tube member and a twin top tube. The weight was reported as 12 lb. These models are not on sale in Britain.

Figure A4.4 Perhaps the first signs of new life in cycling design late 1946?

1   *Cycling* 11 September 1946 Page 230.
2   As judged by articles in *Cycling* as for example Ref 14 op cit.

After this major coup the firm responded with two advertisements in *Cycling* for the next few months. Even so, they were not overly extravagant – perhaps because *Cycling* was the bastion of NCU activities, particularly time trialling for which the *Galibier* was not designed, and was strongly against BLRC and its supporters of Massed Start racing. As has been mentioned PARIS never – or hardly ever - advertised in the *New Bicycles* section where the likes of *Hetchins, Bates, Hobbs, Higgins, Pollard,* and *Thanet* were regulars.

PARIS

A New All-welded Frame of Novel Design

THE Paris Cycle Co. is manufacturing a limited number of bicycle frames, as shown on page 173 of the August 28 issue of " Cycling." These frames are of novel design and include a stout central frame tube that meets the seat-tube at its middle and dispenses with an orthodox down-tube. The frame is made of Reynolds 531 tubing, and all joints are welded. The weight of the frame, complete with chainwheel and cranks, is about 9 lb., while the finish is of the metallic Continental type. Complete frames only can be supplied at present, at a cost of £16 16s.

(Paris Cycle Co., 133, Stoke Newington Church Street, London, N.16.)

Figure A4.5 An advertisement in *Cycling* following the earlier photographic dénouement

So the advertising continued in the Frames section. This next advertisement in the Frames section in September 1946 was hardly written by an inspired publicist trying to capture a public that might have been licking its lips for cycling innovations though:

PARIS high-class Continental-style lightweights in 531. Write for particulars. 133 Stoke Newington Church Street, London N16.

From September 1946 onwards the firm did also have a separate entry in a new *Enamellers* section along with other specialists such as Andy's of Beckenham, and Hendry Bros. The advertisement in the *Enamellers* section was equally rather terse though it was somewhat longer than that in *Frames*:

PARIS CYCLE CO. Your cycle frame cleaned off and re enamelled in best quality enamel. Any colour 25s: metallics 32s6d. Lining extra. 133 Stoke Newington Church Street London N16.

One wonders whether it is reasonable to conclude from the first of these September 1946 advertisements that no advertising policy was yet in place - for example no name was given to their splendid new top model and there was no brochure on offer at this time. This fits in with comments recorded by one owner[1] who bought his bicycle from the shop in 1947/8 and who said that the shop only had their old 1939 (Rensch) catalogues available to show customers. Note that the price for re-enamelling had gone up from the £1 rate, to more like their competitors' charges which were then 30s or 35s for single colour finishes.

In December 1946 the firm started running a more expansive advertisement in *Cycling* –though still only in the *Frames* section.

PARIS *Continental-style cycle frames are the finest available.*

These frames are the outcome of the best British and continental materials under the supervision of expert workmanship.
We pride ourselves in keeping up to date with all the latest improvements in frame design and fittings.
List available. 133 Stoke Newington Church Street, London N16.

Then in March 1947[2] PARIS CYCLES had another write up in *Cycling's* **'News from the Trade'**. It is clear from the text that this was prompted by a new PARIS catalogue having been sent to *Cycling*. This must have been the small A5 size page catalogue (probably only a series of single page sheets) or perhaps it was a very early draft of the A3 folded version - one that has not survived. The *Cycling* review article in fact concentrated almost entirely upon the new model, and now it could be fully identified as the **Galibier**. At last! but wouldn't it be good to know just how that name was chosen? The article even included a good full side view photograph of the new machine. So some crumbs for the firm…..but although *Cycling* mentioned "the rest of the PARIS range", this was in a dismissive reference by referring to the *Galibier* as "Among the range of machines in the catalogue issued by the Paris Cycle Co is the *Galibier* model." Whilst this article was doubtless highly desirable publicity and infinitely better than none, (it certainly explained the design intentions of the new model) there was probably some grinding of teeth back at the ranch over the ignoring of the rest of the range of beautiful and well made bikes – models which had already and indeed would continue to contribute

1   Frame 1382 Was owned at one time by Don Stephens, though it is not currently on the register
2   *Cycling* 26 March 1947 News from the Trade page 222

much more to the firm's coffers than did the elegant but specialist *Galibier.*
The same edition of *Cycling* carried –again only in the *Frames* section - a newly
worded small advertisement.

*PARIS Continental lightweight cycle-frames built to your own individual specification
under the personal special supervision of Spanner Rensch. If you require a genuine
Continental-style cycle frame, place your order early to avoid disappointment. We have
a number of show frames for immediate delivery. Completion time for special specification frames is five to six weeks at present. List available from 133 Stoke Newington
Church Street London N16*

One wonders which Show these show frames had been made for? Perhaps
though they were in reality just stock examples built for the firm's own show
room. Nevertheless in April 1947[1] PARIS had to advertise for frame filers –
perhaps some additional orders were coming through?

During the summer the firm repeated its regular advertisements in the
Enamelling and Frames sections. Then in late August 1947 came a change in
the Frames[2] entry :-

*The Paris team wins the Brighton to Glasgow 6-day marathon. All five members of
our team were supplied with standard Paris frames and equipment.*
*We wish to thank all clubmen for the valuable help and good organisation all along the
route.*
*All five members of the Paris team completed the route. G Kessock 1ˢᵗ T Saunders
2ⁿᵈ. Stoppa Clark 13ᵗʰ. R Moreby(sic) and H Burvell. Good luck boys and we
wish you many more successes.*
*The Will Mather Trophy, BLRC Winners jersey and the original cycle ridden by G
Kessock are on show at 131 Church Street Stoke Newington.*

Note that this advertisement says the bikes are on show at 131 Stoke Newington Church Street – this is the first time in these advertisements that 131
(not 133) has been mentioned so may be the "show room" was a real new
venture as both 131 and 133 had been in use about a year by this time. It is
interesting that in *Cycling* the firm had had to be its own publicist for the success in the Brighton to Glasgow 6 Days - there was no reference to, mention
of, or report on this event, or most other BLRC events, in *Cycling*. Though
the magazine stated that it was scrupulously fair between the warring factions,
the magazine seldom at this time reported any BLRC activities and doubtless
was much less open to firms like Rensch/PARIS which drew their supporters
from road racing.

1   *Cycling* Situations Vacant 9 April 1947, page 10
2   *Cycling* Frames 20 August 1947 page 14

The Valedictory advertisement was continued in successive *Cycling's* until 16 September 1947, then after a gap the following shorter advertisement was issued for the *Frames* section[1] :-

Paris Super Continental lightweight cycle frames in Reynolds special section 531 carbon steel tubes. Order your frame now to avoid disappointment.
PROFESSIONAL Road Racing model £11 18s 6d.
Tour de France model and Path £13 18s 6d
GALIBIER £16 18s 6d.
Finished in superior Continental style, unequalled.
133 Church Street, Stoke Newington, N16.

This October advertisement by the firm of the whole range of models was an expansion to include the **Galibier** with the other models. It incidentally showed an increase in the price of this top machine. The writer won him or herself no favours by describing Reynolds 531 as a carbon steel but perhaps no one minded this understatement. This advertisement was used every week until November, after which an additional line was added saying[2] :-

Winners of Brighton to Glasgow 1947 six day Marathon
2nd and 3rd national Hill-climb Championships and many other successes.

On 19 November 1947 the same advertisement was used except that the name *Professional* was dropped and this basic model was described as Special Road-racing Model. Interestingly a typo had crept in and the spelling for the top model was wrong - the *Galixier* – a similar but different mistake had also been seen on the special A5 sized one page brochure/advertise issued about this time: in this case the name was given as the *Galabier*. Significantly the address of the firm was now given as *129-133 Stoke Newington Church Street, N16*. This seems to be the first time that the published address had included all 3 buildings i.e. 129,131, and133 in Stoke Newington Church Street, though the Council rates books do not refer to the Paris Welding Company as the tenant –perhaps they were subtenants to the previous official tenant who paid the rates - until November 1948[3].

By 5 May 1948 the firm's advertisement in the *Frames* section had been re jigged to modernise and extend the range somewhat[4], viz :-

1   *Cycling* Frames section 22 October 1947 page 8
2   *Cycling* Frames section 5 November 1947 page 8
3   Analysis of rate payers in Ref 10 of Chapter 2 op cit
4   Cycling - Frames section 5 May 1948 page 9

The world's finest racing cycles – Paris
All frames finished in full Continental style, in any colour, metallic or enamel.
Frame prices:-
531, Special design **Galibier** *model,   £16 18s. 6d.*
531, Famous **Tour de France** *model, £13 18s. 6d.*
531, **Professional** *Road Racing model, £11 18s. 6d.*
A Type **Homme** *£9 18s. 6d.*
A Type **Dame**   *£10 10s*
531, Rensch special **Tour de France** *model £15 15s.*
531, Rensch short wheeled tandem with curved seat tube, complete with chainwheel and
cranks £28 10s.
Paris Cycle Co., 129-133 Stoke Newington Church Street, London N16

Note that the Rensch version of the *Tour de France*, the Rensch special Tour de France model, was now being emphasised in this advertisement, though not the *Champion du Monde* despite its presence in the catalogue. Had this model's time not yet come?[1] In that same May 1948 edition of *Cycling* there was also an advertisement by the firm in the **Various** category :-

Paris improved all steel home trainer in any colour £8. 8s.
Paris continental pannier carriers, in any colour 18s 6d.
Continental type flint catchers, few only 4s 6d. pair.

It is interesting that the two least expensive PARIS models (*Homme and Dame*), the more expensive *Rensch Tour de France* and tandem and these minor items, were now, May 1948, being promoted by the firm. This almost full collection of models had first been listed for sale in the firm's A3 size catalogues and the additional items mentioned in these May 1948 *Cycling* advertisements amount to good evidence that by this time at least the first green coloured edition of the large A3 catalogue had been circulated. Doubtless the additional items in the range –almost a return to the wide variety of items available from Rensch before the war - were made possible by the greater space provided by the additional premises. Equally however there were greater costs -those additional premises would be needing to be paid for and presumably Rensch had also taken on more staff to operate additional machinery and jigs- so that more products to sell in the shop would be essential. This leads on to the next development –agents to widen the market area!

   A small advertisement was also placed by H Skidmore of Oldham in the same May 1948 edition, this listed Paris *Course Piste, Galibier* and *Sport Dame* models. It is somewhat noteworthy that PARIS themselves never used the

---

1   Surviving machines with the model features which currently identify them as Champion du Monde
    do not appear until 1949.

Course/Piste name, but this frame was presumably the track frame, what had been the *Continental Path.* Was this evidence that Rensch was now arranging agencies for his products as part of a country wide sales plan?

In August 1948[1] PARIS CYCLE's were advertising in the *Enamelling* category an advertisement which was identical to their 1946 enamelling advertisement except that two additional items were listed, viz:

> *A Full Continental enamel finish £1 17s 6d*
> *A Full Continental metallic £2 12s.*

Note the other items were still at their September 1946 prices –fantastic price stability by 21st century standards!

During autumn 1948 *Cycling* ran a number of articles on new features of frames and components that would appear in the 1948 Cycle Show at Earl's Court – the first post war London show. As *Cycling* crowed afterwards, Britons had had the spectacle of Paris and Geneva shows ever since the war – but it was the 1948 London Show which had really shown them how to do it! One wonders what our continental friends thought of that claim! However Paris Cycles had stand No 44 in the main hall –not a large stand but there anyway. *Cycling* described the Paris Cycles entry in their Show Guide – an enlarged version of the magazine –this Show Number had of course been an annual feature of *Cycling* from pre war days and now resumed.

CONTINENTAL MODELS
Paris Cycles.   **Stand No. 44**

RENSCH and Paris models based on Continental designs make an interesting display on this stand. The models include the Rensch "Tour de France" machine, which carries with it some exceptional cut-out lugwork. Also there is the well-known Paris "Galibier" welded model, which has frame tubes of varying gauge, and the "broken" seat tube, which was the cause of considerable interest at its initial appearance. Of more orthodox pattern are the Paris "Path" and "Professional Road Racing" models, and the Paris "Type Homme," which is designed again on the Continental principle for the tourist and clubman. For the ladies, there is the Paris "Type Dame," which follows very closely the patterns for this type of machine on the Continent.

Figure A4.6 Advertisement in Cycling for 24 November 1948

No surprises that the Continental theme came out to the fore!

Then in December 1948 came a special advertisement in the firm's usual place in the Frames section of *Cycling* :-

THE PARIS CYCLE CO
If you could not obtain our latest catalogue owing to the large interested crowd on our stand at Earl's Court, we shall be pleased to supply you with our latest list of Continental lightweights upon request. THE PARIS CYCLE CO 131-3 Stoke Newington Church Street, LONDON N16

Presumably the firm had underestimated interest in their products and run out of their somewhat expensive A3 size catalogue during the Show.
There was little to speak of in terms of a change in advertising in 1949 but in September 1949[1] the firm placed their first advertisement in *Cycling's New Bicycles* category for sales. Note that the address 131-3 was consistently used for the advertisements in the *Enamelling* category of advertisements.

PARIS CYCLE CO
131-3 Stoke Newington Church Street, N16.
See a selection of the world's finest continental lightweight cycles, tandems and triplets on Stand 164 at the Earls Court Cycle Show.
PARIS and Rensch models of unequalled design and finish.

Then the following article (Figure A4.7appeared in *Cycling's* 1949 Show Number.
Just a few weeks later *Cycling* carried a short entry about PARIS CYCLES in their major Show review article that listed most of the major stands in the 1949 Earls Court Show on October 21 to 29.[2]
On 9 March 1950 there was an advertisement appeared in *Cycling's* Situations Vacant :-

Wanted. Frame filers or keen clubmen to learn trade, piece work, 5 day week. PC 131/3 Stoke Newington Church Street, London N16.

In *Cycling* for 18 May 1950 the firm decided to use another piece of artwork that has also figured widely as a model transfer; this was the map of France with a rider in the Tour de France race which has already been illustrated as Figure 22 in Chapter 5.
This PARIS *Tour De France* box advertisement appeared in *Cycling* altogether about 5 times, the last occasion being in early August 1950.
Two other advertisements that used the PARIS marque appeared in 1950. These were the now wel known A& P advertisements that have already been used in this history In the first advertisement a Rensch tandem was used as one example of a fine Kromo built bicycle, and in the other a PARIS *Tour de*

1   *Cycling –New Bicycles* section 22 September page 14
2   *Cycling –Guide to the Stands* 20 October 1949 page 447

CONTINENTAL BREEDING

Paris Cycle Co.   Stand No. 164

THE Paris exhibit will be very comprehensive, including three complete tandems, one triplet, ten racing models, four touring machines, a selection of frames and two home trainer sets. Included in the racing machines on show will be the " Rensch Tour de France " model, the unique Paris " Galibier " model, the Path model with upright angles and the " Professional " road racing model. For the ladies there is the smart Paris " Type Dame " touring machine which is built in conformity with current Continental standards. The " Rensch " tandem exhibited has a curved rear seat tube and double narrow gauge cross tubes giving a rigid lively short-wheelbase machine

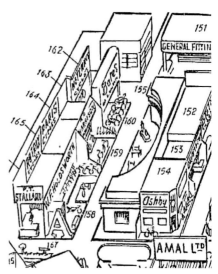

Figure A4.7 *Cycling's* London Show time article for the 1949 Show.

Figure A4.8 the 1949 London Cycle Show stand 164

France, in both cases the machine specification was also given.

Later in 1950[1] there is the first of an increasing number of trade advertisements by large retailers, evidence perhaps that agents sales were working and PARIS as a marque no longer had to struggle by itself to advertise its wares –others were prepared to take on that role – doubtless of course taking some of the profit margin in order to do so.

This Read Bros Cycles advertisement, which is for frame only prices, allows current day readers to compare contemporary retail prices of competitor machines with their Paris possessions. It is the first mention in any published document other than the firm's fold out catalogues of the *Rensch Champion du Monde* model, though being a trade house it erroneously calls this machine a PARIS Champion du Monde[2].

By 1951 the changes in the firm due to Harry Rensch's illness and marital infidelities had begun to affect the firm and there had been other changes which were perhaps unrelated –certainly not wholly predictable! The main catalogues issued by the firm were not dated but there are changes in the later versions (which are identifiable as such because of minor price increases in these versions) such as the increased range of tandems offered as time goes on. Whether this was a result of a increased demand for tandems at this time or whether it reflects the talents and predilections of the staff then present

---

1   *Cycling* 13 April 1950   Frames section of classified advertisements
2   Recently a machine badged as a PARIS but apparently a Champion du Monde due to its bilaminations has appeared but as it is not on the Register has not been examined.

Figure A4.9 A standard marathon tandem shows the way in 1950

is difficult to know, but certainly more of the surviving tandems come from the last few years of the firm. Whilst Harry Rensch was said initially to be the main tandem builder, by the early 1950s Dusty Miller, the last works foreman was known to have taken over this role in these years. Apart from his lower management role he did become a specialist tandem specialist builder at this time, when in fact and indeed metaphorically Rensch had passed on his brazing torch to younger hands.

For example, for the first time we have a **PARIS** advertisement in the New Bicycles category of *Cycling's* classified advertisements[1].

Figure A4.10 Read Brothers Cycles 1950 advertisement for lightweight bicycles

1   *Cycling* 22 March 1951 p14 (Supplement)

You have not achieved your best ride until you have ridden a "Paris."
Full 1951 range of racing and touring tandems and solos.
Your old frame re –enamelled as new, 25s; lines extra.
Catalogues on request.
PARIS CYCLE CO 129-131 Stoke Newington Church Street, London, N.16
Clissold 2031

Note that though solos are included it is tandems that are mentioned first in this new advertisement.

As if to reinforce these changes in advertising practice and perhaps capitalise on buoyant tandem sales the only detailed 1951 advertisements that have come to light show a change in pattern in advertising. The detailed PARIS product listings were no longer issued by the firm but were instead provided by agents' advertisements. For example, in the Diamond Jubilee edition of *Cycling*[1] the following advertisement was placed – in the usual Frames section.

This advertisement is very interesting for a number of reasons. The first is the name of the organisation – George Cycle Works, which had not previously advertised in *Cycling* in any of its many categories and which did not appear to survive very long. Could this have been a venture by George Worrall, who is suspected as being one of the firm's main financial supporters and who was in this way assisting the firm's marketing? The second change is that in this mail order advertisement all the models are priced only as "Never –Never" or sales agreement prices –no cash sales here! The third feature of the advertisement is that there is a significant

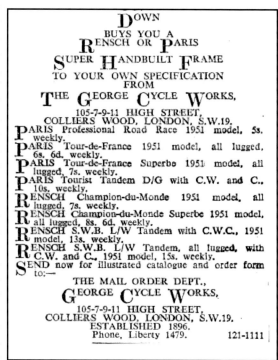

Figure A4.11 Advertisement for George Cycle Works

enlargement in the range of models offered. PARIS were apparently now offering two versions, the standard and the *Superbe*, of the old faithful, the *Tour de France*, as well as the *Rensch Champion du Monde* models. In addition the Rensch tandem now had the option of a *Superbe* variant. It is interesting that this model variant was never named in the firm's catalogues although for the catalogued Rensch tandems the catalogue offered an option to order machines with more bilaminated joints than the standard product. For example in the last known catalogue, which is thought to be 1952, a Rensch tandem variant (The Rensch model was itself a more expensive variant on the basic PARIS model) was offered :- *with superbly cut out lugs at all joints* at some £4.10 more than the catalogue Rensch. It is this model which I consider to be worthy of the model name *Superbe*. Finally the George Cycles advertisement refers to all the models, with the exception of the lugless *Professional Road Race*, as being lugged. Is this because the copywriter was not a dyed in the wool PARIS man who would have known about lugs or bilaminations eg the brazed or welded frame divide? Or does it represent a sea change in the attitude of the whole firm to frame construction now that Harry Rensch was on his way out? Or again it could be an agent's lazy misinterpretation and the standard bike was just a bilaminated model with the *Superbe* name being used for the lugged alternative?

Later in the year more suggestions of a change in the firm's production of models are offered by the advertisement than appeared in *Cycling*[1] in the usual Frames section ;_

Paris and Rensch Super Continental lightweight tandems
Paris Tourist tandem, straight seat tube, less lugs £24.10s.
Paris ladyback tandem £24.10s.
Rensch tandem, short wheelbase, curved seat tube, £29.10s.
Rensch tandem, curved seat tube, lugs at all joints£33.15s
PARIS CYCLE CO, 129/133 Stoke Newington
Church Street, London N16 Clissold 2031.

This advertisement was repeated in December 1951 and on 3 and 17 January 1952. Note that the firm quoted only cash prices and that there was now no mention of solo bicycle models at all. What was that all about?

In December 1951, for the first time since advertisements in *Cycling* started in 1947 the firm took out a Christmas Greetings box . Nearly all regular shops which advertised in *Cycling* during the year took out these boxes. This PARIS box simply said[2] :-

1   *Cycling* 25 October 1951
2   *Cycling* 20 December 1951

Paris Cycle Co., Ltd., 129/133 Stoke Newington Church Street, N16
Send old friends and new
Best wishes for Christmas
and the New Year.

Despite this front at friendship, after this time PARIS never again advertised their solo machines; promotion of sales for solo machines was only through the various agents throughout UK who stocked and sold them.

On 14 February 1952 the first of a series of weekly advertisements were placed in the Frames Section by Read Bros of Leytonstone and West Ham – PARIS machines were included in the advertisement but PARIS was just one of the marques listed in a range which consisted of ten specialised lightweight marques[1]. If this pattern of advertising was intentionally chosen it might well suggest that selling off existing stock of solo machines through the trade was now a priority. That was certainly WB Hurlow's strategy when he took over management of the dying firm in April 1952, as reported in conversations in 2006.

The lack of new advertising for these models suggests that the firm had no real interest in making further stock or frames- perhaps no longer had the skilled staff to do so? One is reminded here of the experience of Neville Ireland who as a young man pestered the firm in November 1951 for a *TdF;* Neville even believed he had spoken to Harry Rensch himself. Whilst meeting the latter at this time would not have been impossible, it does seem unlikely that Rensch would have been in the shop, where Mrs Rensch was now the owner and key player, and certainly could have been reluctant to make himself available to young shoppers. In the end Neville's bike, #8208, was only supplied some four months later. Most disappointingly for this young idealist aficionado of the *TdF,* his bike as supplied was not lugless or bilaminated as he requested but was lugged using Nervex Professional lugs. Neville said that apart from the badges and transfers the frame was hardly recognisable as a PARIS. Arguably, and as Neville himself came to think of it –it was not a PARIS –except in the narrow legal trading sense that it was a bike supplied by the PARIS firm in exchange for money.

After this time there are no more advertisements by Paris Cycle Co in the Frames section of *Cycling.*

Amongst the last PARIS advertisements was the other Accles and Pollock single pager, this time using the *Tour de France* as an example of a fine bicycle – no arguments there then!

---

1   This list was Bates,Claud Butler, Granby, Hill Bros, Hobbs, Holdsworth, Harrison, Maclean, Paris, Stuart Purves, and Skeates

MR. RENSCH OF PARIS CYCLES, STOKE NEWINGTON, SAYS—

"There's tubes and tubes".

We think Paris cycles are the finest machines available to the Club Cyclist. But they don't just happen that way. We start with what we think is the best idea, we use only the best material, and apply the best methods in the best workshop in the trade. In pursuit of that policy we produced the first bronze welded lightweight in this country. That was in 1936, and we pride ourselves that we have held that lead by keeping up-to-date with all the very latest improvements concerning frame designs and fittings. That is why we use on our best machines what we believe to be the finest tube steel available today—KROMO (chrome molybdenum). We use it for frames, forks, handlebars, seat and chain stays, knowing that nothing can do the job better—and we reckon to know quite a bit about tubes, both British and Continental. Here is our latest TOUR DE FRANCE model.

H Rensch.

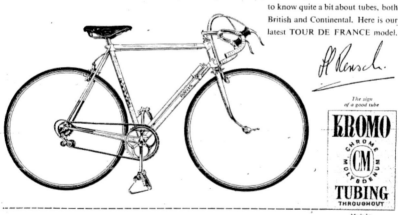

The sign of a good tube

KROMO

CM

TUBING
THROUGHOUT

Made by
Accles & Pollock Ltd.
Oldbury, Birmingham.

A ⓣ COMPANY

SPECIFICATION

Built throughout with Accles & Pollock's Kromo tubing, made specially to "Paris" specification to gauges to suit the size of frame and weight of rider. Special small section seat stays neatly shaped and finished at top ends, giving a real super finish to the machine. All lugs superbly cut out, filed and polished. This frame can be had in any dimensions to suit the rider's own special requirements, or in the "Continental" design as follows:

SIZE. 22½ in. wheelbase 41 ins. Head angle 73° and seat angle 71°. Bracket height 11" for 27" wheels.

BRAZE ON PARTS. All the usual braze on parts including—brake eyes, cable clips, chain hook, pump pegs, gear pieces etc.

FORKS. Oval to round Continental pattern made specially for us by Accles & Pollock.

FINISH. The famous "PARIS" Continental finish in any colour. Chromium plating extra.

Chainwheel set—Continental chromium plated. Wheels 27" x 1¼" H.P. D.B. Spokes—F.B. Hubs, Simplex 4-speed gear with ³/₃₂ chain. Pedals, Tour de France Rat-trap. Saddle, Brooks B.17. Brakes, G.B. front and rear. Chain, Brampton.

A cycle is as good as its frame

Figure A4.12 Accles & Pollock repeat their ploy though Rensch himself had now left the firm.

Index

Glossary

This glossary is provided as background to this particular history and to explain the meaning of some of the terms used in the text. There will be readers who might wish to define some of these terms differently but these explanations take into account the particular needs to explain the usage within this story. They should not be taken as necessarily directly applicable to all other situations.

Alloy steels.

Steels in use in bicycles were originally mild steels and as duties became more onerous and strong lightweight tubing became a prime need so the use of higher carbon tougher steels became more common place. Mixing rarer elements in the steel was found to give improved strength and lighter weight and aircraft use in WW1 hastened such alloy steels with the British companies Reynolds and Accles &Pollock leaders in this field. These alloys are however rendered weaker if overheated and when marketed in the 1920s (manganese steels such as HM) and 1930s (manganese or chromium -molybdenum steels such as R531 and A&P Kromo) new fastening techniques had to be introduced. Suffolk Iron Foundry developed SIF bronze in 1925 as braze with specialist flux that gave low temperature but strong brazed joints and preserved the 1000 MPa tensile strength of the new lightweight steel tubes –compared to that of the 500 MPa of the older medium carbon steels of the 1920s and earlier.

Brake bridge

Tear drop reinforcements. These were a uniquely PARIS speciality and stiffened up the upper seat stay triangle whilst providing improved anchorage of the brake bridge, other builders often used diamond shape reinforcements and Paris Lightweights combined the two approaches.

Brazing and fillet brazing

This is the technique of using brass based solders with appropriate fluxes on steel tubes allowing them to be joined using iron lugs with the brass providing a metallic bond with strength provided by the lugs and fit of the tubes. Skilled welders using hand held gas welding torches found that working with the low temperature brazes on the stronger alloy steels tube allowed them to build up fillets of braze around joints which avoided the need for lugs and as tubing strengths increased so the strength of these brazed-only frames could match the strength of orthodox lugged frames.

Bilaminations.

It appears Rensch could have seen this technique in use on the Schulz main strut frame and introduced it at the end of the 1930s as an ornamental strengthening on his bronze welded (fillet brazed) frames. Clearly other frame builders would have been aware of the technique and its current name bi-lamination appears to have been coined in Claud Butler's workshop perhaps in 1947 when they were experimenting with a frame for a new model marketed in 1949. The spelling without the hyphen has been adopted in this text as more typical of modern usage.

Chainstays

Rensch made much of rigidity in the rear drive triangle and at this time (1930s) Reynolds had developed - possibly with the driving force of Hobbs or at least that's how Hobbs claimed it- specially rigid front fork blades with the use of oval section blades. At this time chainstay rigidity was provided by special rapid tapering but retaining a true cylindrical structure. The elliptical chainstay that Rensch made his trademark can be seen to be essentially a front fork tube that has not been bent –making use of the technology developed for the front forks. Mountain bike frame builders adopted the same strategy in the 1980s recognising the advantages the elliptical tubes gave when increased tyre width made space in the rear triangle a premium.

Chainstay protector

This is an elegant Rensch solution to the problem of chain slap damaging the chainstays –particularly important because of the use of Osgears on massed start machines.

Chamfer and top eyes.

This refers to the simple chamfer or smoothed profile given to the tops of seat stays where these joined the seat tube top; originally a step was used then the smoother profile offered by the chamfer adopted.. In lugged frames an eye had to be made in the seat stay to anchor onto the pin of the seat tube top lug, so this area of the seat stay became known as the top eye. Once the lug is no longer provided on fillet brazed frames the frame builder can end the seat stay in more pleasing shapes than the step or indeed the chamfer, and so the narrow curving taper and long concave ends came into use.

Epaulette fork top

The descriptive term to describe the traditional fork top with the top of the forks flat and covered, perhaps with a triangular rib reaching the edge of the top and having decorations which descend the vertical arms of the fork blade looking like a soldier's shoulder tab or epaulette decoration. These have been cut out of the original tubular part of an uncut lug. These decorations can consist of horizontal slots, open or closed circles or dagger shapes.

New Welded

The name given in the PARIS catalogues to a bilamination pattern introduced in the version of the PARIS *Tour de France* produced for the 1948 London Show, and later used on some tandems and even some *Galibiers* at the close of the firm. The shape of this bilamination pattern appears to have been lifted from the Oscar Egg Super Champion frame of 1939.

Oiler

A gravity fed oil drip directed onto the top of the chainwheel from a pipe leading from an internal oil reservoir in the seat tube of the bicycle –plainly a competition device as it requires removal of the saddle to top up the reservoir. Originally a Claud Butler speciality, however, CB referred to it as a "continental" fitting in their 1939 catalogue so may be a proprietary unit.

Oil bath

Part of the name of the Bayliss Wiley company's patent sleeved bottom bracket developed to fit in a simple tubular housing in the bicycle frame. This system meant the frame's pedal axle axis did not require the awkward heavy thread cutting machines needed to ensure alignment of the bottom bracket casting (or sometimes of the whole built up frame) prior to machining, and allowed easy repair of damaged threads by filing them away and introducing a complete prior threaded sleeve.

Sprints

The terms used in the 1930s to 1950s to describe a wheel fitted with tubular tires. The term could be applied to both the rim or the tubular tire itself. Rims could be alloy or wooden (sometimes called cane rims).

Steels

The term in the same period for wheels with steel rims for wire- on type tires.

Twin plate crown

A type of fork crown consisting of a roof provided by an upper plate across the top of the two fork blades and brazed to the fork steerer. The roof plate was above the other plate which was pierced to carry the blades and located some half to 1 inch below the "roof". The lower plate was brazed to the bottom of the fork steerer tube. The type was extensively using in the Victorian period and remains known as the Bastide pattern fork in lightweight bicycle usage. In PARIS applications the edges of the top plate overhung the top of the fork blade in the manner of sloping roof tiles and this upper roof edge was variously straight or scalloped from the front and rear edges to meet a slight dome or middle ridge to the "roof."

Twin top tube

This was a design introduction for the *Galibier* model where two half inch diameter tubes replaced the orthodox one inch or one and an eighth inch single top tube which connects the seat tube top to the top of the head tube. The twin tube can also be seen as part of a family of approaches to frame design where twin tubes were also used in the twin laterals of the mixte frame design or in the twin laterals and also for some the twin drainpipes of high quality tandem frame design. Twin tubes are a concomitant feature of the "Open frame" design seen by Rensch in France in the mid 1930s and for which he became enamoured.

Upright angles

Safety bicycles started with the frame angles (first the angle between head tube and top tube and secondly between seat and top tubes) being about 60 degrees. These angles began to steepen in competition applications and had generally approached 70 degrees by the late 1920s with a tendency for the first, head angle to steepen slightly by 1 or 2 degrees over the seat tube. After this time an appreciation of the head angle being defined by steering head design with fork rake also taken into account. Angles at the head as high as 75 degrees are suitable for track and sprint bicycles with 73 ranging to 71 degrees favoured for accurate steering for massed start road racing to those wanting a relaxed for touring machines which may carry luggage loads and heavier riders. Seat tube angles may commonly be the same as at the head but tend to be lower than steeper head angles and perhaps up to 2 degrees greater in the case of lower head angles depending on frame size. In Britain in the mid 1930s angles started to follow continental practice and steeper angles such as 74/71 became the sprinter's ideal being referred to as "Upright angles"; the less extreme "semi-upright" being nominally 70/71. Over the years this clubman's standard itself steepened and reached 73/71 on post war machines, a shape adopted by PARIS though frames with other angles could be supplied. This pattern was enormously popular across the lightweight world and a commonly found variant became 72/72 or square.

JPMPF Publication List:-

- *Lightweight Cycle Catalogue Volume 1*: (2005)
- *An Encyclopaedia of Cycle Manufacturers* - compiled by Ray Miller: (2006)
- *Frederick H Pratt and Sons* - Complete Cycle Engineers - Alvin J E Smith: (2006)
- *The Electric-Powered Bicycle Lamp 1888-1948* - Peter W Card: (2006)
- *The Pedersen Hub Gear* - Cyril J Hancock: (2007)
- *It wasn't that Easy. The Tommy Godwin Story* - Tommy Godwin: (2007)
- *The End to End & 1000 Miles Records* - Willie Welsh: (2007)
- *Lightweight Cycle Catalogue Vol II*: (2007)
- *Origins of Bicycle Racing in England* - Andrew Ritchie: (2007)
- *Here Are Wings* - Maurice Leblanc (Translation by Scotford Lawrence): (2008)
- *The Origins of the Bicycle* - Andrew Ritchie: (2009)
- *Lightweight Cycle Catalogue Vol III*: (2009)
- *East Anglian Rides* - Charles Staniland, Edited by Gerry Moore; (2009)
- *The Stanley Show, Review* 1878 to 1889 & Catalogue 1890: (2009)
- *Flying Yankee* - The International Career of Arthur Augustus Zimmerman - Andrew Ritchie: (2009)
- *An Encyclopaedia of Cycle Manufacturers* - 2nd Edition- compiled by Ray Miller: (2009)
- *Cycle History 19*- Proceedings of the 19th ICHC, Saint-Etienne, France, 2008: (2010)
- *Cycle History 20* - Proceedings of the 20th ICHC, Freehold, New Jersey, USA 2009: (2010)
- *Boneshaker Reprints Vol 5, Issues 41-50:* (2010)
- *The Veteran-Cycle Club 1955-2005* - compiled by Cyril Hancock: (2010)
- *A History of the Tricycle* - Roger Alma, Cyril J Hancock and Derek Roberts (2011)
- *Marque Album No. 1 Centaur* - Alvin Smith & Lionel Ferris (2011)
- *Cycling History No. 1, Malvern Cycling Club 1883-1912* - Roger Alma (2011)
- *Marque Album No. 2, Ivel* - Ray Miller & Lee Irvine (2011)
- *Dan Albone, Cyclist, Inventor & Manufacturer.* - Ray Miller & Lee Irvine (2011)
- *Cycling History No. 2 - Rough Stuff, Charly Chadwick Story.* David Warner (2012)
- *Marque Album No. 3, Rensch - PARIS* - Alvin Smith at al (2012)
- *Cycling History No 3 - Vernon Blake 1875 - 1930* - Steve Griffith (2012)
- *Cycling History No. 4 Charlie Davey* - Christine Watts (2012)

All publications are available through the Veteran-Cycle Club Sale Officer.
www.v-cc.org.uk